ARCHITECTURAL
GUIDES FOR TRAVELERS

ANCIENT
EGYPT

To the people of Egypt,
builders and custodians of a noble tradition,
in token of their kindness to a stranger

ARCHITECTURAL
GUIDES FOR TRAVELERS

ANCIENT EGYPT

DELIA PEMBERTON

CHRONICLE BOOKS • SAN FRANCISCO

First published in the United States in 1992 by Chronicle Books.

Series conceived by Georgina Harding
Editor: Bridget Harney
Series design: Clare Finlaison
Design: Wendy Bann
Maps and plans: David Woodroffe
Picture research: Nicholas Shaddick
Index: Hilary Bird

Printed in England by Jolly & Barber Ltd., Rugby, Warks.

Library of Congress Cataloging-in-Publication Data:
Pemberton, Delia.
    Ancient Egypt / Delia Pemberton.
        p.   cm. – (Architectural guides for travelers)
    Includes bibliographical references (p. 146) and index.
    ISBN 0–87701–847–2 (pb)
    1. Architecture, Ancient–Egypt.   2. Temples–Egypt.   3. Tombs–Egypt.
    I. Title.   II. Series.
    NA215.P36   1992
    722'.2–dc20   91–31635
                                                                        CIP

10 9 8 7 6 5 4 3 2 1

Chronicle Books
275 Fifth St.
San Francisco, California 94103

CONTENTS

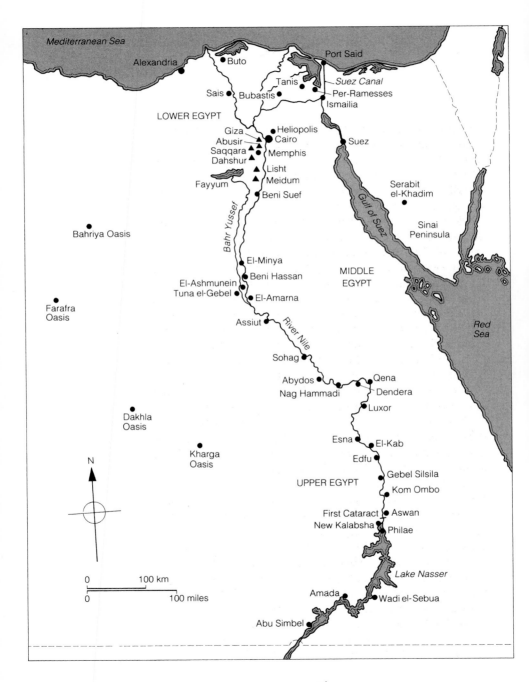

Mediterranean Sea

Alexandria • Buto

Port Said

Suez Canal

Tanis •

Sais • Bubastis • Per-Ramesses

Ismailia

LOWER EGYPT

Giza ▲ Heliopolis
Abusir ▲ Cairo • Suez
Saqqara ▲ Memphis
Dahshur ▲ Serabit
Lisht ▲ el-Khadim
Fayyum Meidum ▲
Beni Suef • Sinai
Peninsula

Bahriya Oasis

Gulf of Suez

Bahr Yussef

El-Minya •
Beni Hassan • MIDDLE
El-Ashmunein • EGYPT
Tuna el-Gebel • El-Amarna •

Farafra
Oasis

Assiut • Red
Sea
River Nile

Sohag •

Abydos • Qena
Nag Hammadi • Dendera

Dakhla
Oasis Luxor •

Kharga Esna • El-Kab
Oasis Edfu •
Gebel Silsila •
UPPER EGYPT Kom Ombo •

N First Cataract • Aswan
New Kalabsha • Philae

0   100 km

0   100 miles Lake Nasser

Amada •
Wadi el-Sebua •

Abu Simbel •

vi

PREFACE

Awed by its antiquity, the visitor gazed around the little painted tomb chapel, admiring its colourful paintings. He especially liked the group of pretty female musicians. Moved by an urge to record his visit, he leaned forward to inscribe his name above the scene, adding as an afterthought the comment 'very beautiful!' Paser, arguably the world's first art critic, had no fear of recrimination for his action—he was, after all, the most powerful man in the land; chief minister to the divine king Ramesses II.

For over thirty centuries, the tombs and temples of Egypt have continued to charm, baffle and inspire visitors from every corner of the earth. Egyptian officials, Sudanese nomads, Greek mercenaries, Roman emperors, Arab conquerors, Napoleonic engineers and British soldiers—all have stopped here, marvelled, and left their mark. While nobody today would condone such defacing of archaeological monuments, the graffiti of our predecessors serve as a reminder of the awesome heritage which has passed into the care of the present generation.

This work is intended as a guide and companion to these ancient monuments, spanning the period from the Old Kingdom up to, and including, the Egyptianizing architecture of the Graeco-Roman era. Concentrating on sites accessible from the centres of Cairo, El-Minya, Luxor and Aswan, where hotels and other facilities for visitors are available, the book is divided into chapters arranged geographically from north to south, which broadly fits the chronological order of the major archaeological sites. This arrangement is loosely adhered to within each chapter, except where another arrangement makes more sense for chronological or other reasons. A final chapter deals briefly with outlying sites—the Delta, Sinai, the Oases and Nubia.

The greatest attention has been devoted to the major monuments which every itinerary should include, while

(Opposite) Map of Egypt.

vii

additional descriptions are given for interesting but less famous sites which, time permitting, can be visited from the major centres without too much difficulty. Remote and inaccessible sites are mentioned only where their monuments are of the first importance, otherwise they have been omitted for reasons of space; readers intending to visit them are advised to check beforehand with the local Inspectorate of Antiquities, as special permits may be required. The sites are generally open from around 6 a.m to 6 p.m. in the summer and 6 a.m. to 4 p.m. in the winter, with some local variations. Conditions described here applied at the end of 1990, but it should be borne in mind that monuments may close without notice or explanation; conversely, it is hoped that some presently closed to the public may become accessible.

In terms of itineraries, the modern visitor to Egypt is spoilt for choice. A variety of ready-made packages—Nile cruises, overland tours or a combination of both—are available to those requiring the maximum cultural exposure in the minimum time, while the increasingly popular one- and two-centre stays based around Cairo, Luxor and Aswan offer greater scope for leisurely sightseeing. Independent travellers flying into Cairo or Luxor will find regular flights and comfortable overnight sleeper trains linking Cairo, Luxor and Aswan; long-distance buses and regular rail services between these centres also serve El-Minya.

In Cairo, a full day should be allowed to visit the monuments of Memphis and Saqqara, while half a day will suffice for Giza. The Egyptian Museum takes a full day, but half a day is adequate to see the highlights; if entering and leaving Egypt via Cairo, the ideal plan is to visit at both the beginning and the end of the tour. Meidum and the Fayyum can be visited as an excursion from Cairo, or en route between the capital and El-Minya. Two days are ample for visiting the sites of Middle Egypt, though the visitor may be tempted to linger longer among its beautiful landscapes! The temples of Abydos and Dendera are an easy day trip from Luxor, or can be taken in between El-Minya and Luxor; they are also included in many cruise itineraries. If time is limited at Luxor, the east bank monuments can be seen in a single day—a long morning for the Karnak complex, the late afternoon for Luxor Temple and the early evening for Luxor Museum. To visit all the west bank monuments takes at least three full days, but the highlights can be seen in two. The possible permutations of itinerary are endless, but a good plan is to allocate the morning hours to the mortuary temples and private tombs, leaving the afternoons, when the tour groups have gone, for the leisurely enjoyment of the Valley of the Kings.

All the sites between Luxor and Aswan can be visited by road from either centre, or en route between the two; the temples of Esna and Kom Ombo only require relatively short stops, but that of Edfu merits a longer visit, as does the site of El-Kab. The very popular three- and four-night Nile cruises also call at the major temples along this stretch of the river. The Aswan monuments can easily be seen in two days—one day for the granite quarries, Elephantine and the Qubbet el-Hawwa tombs, and a half day each for Philae and New Kalabsha.

Abu Simbel is accessible by road or air from Aswan, and there are also regular flights from Cairo and Luxor. Alexandria is an easy day trip by road or rail from Cairo, and the other Delta sites can be reached by car from the capital. Arrangements for visits to the monuments of Sinai and the Oases are more complicated, as four wheel drive vehicles are required for many sites, and in some areas permits must be obtained from the military authorities; readers are advised to consult a specialist travel agent.

Today, the tombs and temples of ancient Egypt are under unprecedented environmental stress from the constantly rising water table and the increasing volume of visitors. Readers are entreated to shun the examples of our predecessors and avoid further damage by remembering not to touch or clamber on ancient buildings and by observing photographic restrictions. The monuments of Egypt are an irreplaceable part of our common human heritage, and we are all responsible for their care.

INTRODUCTION

Origins

Writing in the fifth century BC, the Greek historian Herodotus described Egypt as 'the gift of the river', neatly summing up the fact that without the Nile, the unique Egyptian culture could never have evolved.

The longest river in the world, the Nile has two main sources—the White Nile, which flows from Lake Victoria, providing a constant flow of water throughout the year, and the Blue Nile and Atbara which carries run-off waters from the winter rains on the Ethiopian Plateau, creating annual flooding. Unique to the Nile, it was this inundation which brought the river's 'gifts'—the fertile black silt which became Egypt's cultivable land and the flood waters which enabled her inhabitants to develop their characteristic style of basin agriculture. In recognition of this fact, the ancient Egyptians called their country *Kemet*, the 'Black Land', in contrast to *Deshret*, the neighbouring 'Red Land', or desert.

Approximately 20 km (12 miles) north of modern Cairo, the ancient Nile divided into seven branches as it began its final journey to the sea, creating a vast triangular delta 15,000 km^2 (5,792 miles^2) in area. Until a shift in the land occurred between forty and fifty million years ago, this northern part of the country had been submerged beneath the sea, resulting in the surface strata of sedimentary limestone visible today. The underlying Nubian sandstone does not emerge until south of Luxor, and only at Aswan do the first outcrops of the basal strata—the hard metamorphic and igneous rocks which form the Nile cataracts—begin to appear.

Predynastic Egypt

Until about 20,000 years ago, the entire region enjoyed savanna-type conditions, enabling hunter-gatherer peo-

(Opposite) The land and the river: Qubbet el-Hawwa tombs on the Nile's west bank at Aswan. (Old Kingdom – Roman Period).

1

ples to roam freely in pursuit of the abundant game. However, the climate gradually became drier, and as vegetation dwindled there was a shift to a pastoral economy as nomadic tribes—the ancestors of the modern bedouin—wandered the plains in search of grazing for their flocks. As this change continued, the Nile became increasingly attractive to settlers, and concentrations of peoples with origins as diverse as the modern Levant and Sudan began to establish centres along its banks and in the Delta. These predynastic communities, whose cultural diversity strongly influenced the subsequent development of Egyptian civilization, soon learned to exploit the rich black earth, and as time passed urban life and simple industries such as pottery-making and copper-smelting began to evolve. Irrigation, essential to agriculture, required a degree of coordination to ensure the efficient use of water, and this in turn hastened the development of local government and the appearance of small states. At the same time, there arose the greater concept of the Two Lands of Upper and Lower Egypt—the Nile Valley and the Delta.

The Two Lands

The idea of the Two Lands played a crucial role in ancient Egyptian history and is central to any understanding of Egyptian thought. The early Egyptians saw their country as standing in isolation, bordered to the north by the sea, and to the south by the Nile cataracts and the desert. Set apart by the gods, it was doubly blessed by two great life-giving sources—the sun above, crossing the sky from east to west, and the Nile below, flowing from south to north. This gave rise to a dualistic view of the cosmos, in which opposing forces—day and night, life and death, good and evil—balanced and succeeded each other, moving in cycles: the rising and setting of the sun, the flooding and recession of the Nile, the sowing and harvesting of the grain. It was consequently natural to perceive the coexistence of the open, moist and marshy Delta with the confined, arid Valley as yet another expression of this duality. It was therefore a momentous event when the Two Lands were united around 3150 BC, through the conquest of the Delta by a powerful southern dynasty. The most famous of their rulers, a legendary figure called **Narmer**, was regarded in antiquity as the first king of Egypt, and the model for all future monarchs. Henceforward every king was crowned separately with the Red Crown of Lower Egypt and the White Crown of Upper Egypt before receiving the Double Crown of the Two Lands and the titles 'King of Upper and Lower Egypt' and 'Lord of the Two Lands'. In royal monuments much was made of symbols expressing the union, such as the *sema-tawy* emblem, representing fertility gods binding together the lotus of Upper Egypt and the papyrus of Lower Egypt.

The archetypal image of kingship: on the reverse of the Narmer Palette, Narmer, wearing the White Crown of the south, unites the Two Lands by subduing the personification of the Nile Delta. (Early Dynastic Period). Egyptian Museum, Cairo.

The time of unification, perceived as a golden age, was held in great esteem by the later Egyptians, who regarded anything old as especially venerable. In consequence, ancient beliefs and practices were maintained long after their original relevance had been lost, a practice known as archaization. One of the most distinctive characteristics of the ancient Egyptian culture—particularly its architecture—archaization contributed greatly to national stability throughout Egypt's troubled history by providing a measure of continuity which speeded recovery after periods of disruption.

Historical Outline

Although the broad outlines of Egyptian history are well understood, the absence of accurate records for many crucial periods means that precise dating, particularly in early times, is impossible. One reason for this is that the Egyptians had no absolute chronology, taking their dates from the regnal years of the current king. The system used today, and outlined in the chronology on page 140, derives from that evolved by **Manetho**, an Egyptian priest of the third century BC. Drawing on mythology and earlier king-lists, Manetho was the first to divide Egyptian history into thirty Dynasties, or ruling houses, tracing the descent of **Menes**, the first king—now identified with Narmer—from the gods. Later historians have grouped these Dynasties into Kingdoms, when unity and stable government prevailed, separated by Intermediate Periods of fragmentation and disorder; further headings to cover the periods before Narmer and after Manetho have also been added and are modified from time to time.

Now known as the **Early Dynastic period**, the time of the **First** and **Second Dynasties** saw the unification of the Two Lands; the establishment of the first national capital at Memphis created the need for an administrative system, which in turn hastened the development of writing. By the **Old Kingdom**, which spanned the **Third to Sixth Dynasties**, the classic form of the state had been established. Expansion into Nubia provided wealth in the form of gold, and the might of Egypt's divine kings, expressed in the colossal pyramid building projects of the **Fourth Dynasty**, reached its zenith.

Following the collapse of the **Sixth Dynasty**, the country entered a period of chaos and civil unrest known as the **First Intermediate Period**. This ended two centuries later with the victorious emergence of the **Twelfth Dynasty** of

The *sema-tawy* symbol: fertility figures bind together lotus and papyrus plants, symbolizing the union of Upper and Lower Egypt. Luxor Temple. (New Kingdom, Nineteenth Dynasty).

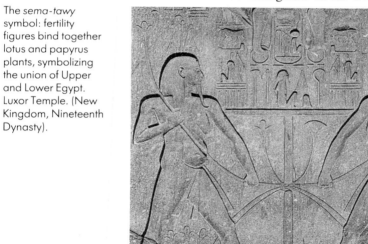

4

Thebes, whose accession marked the beginning of the **Middle Kingdom**. A period of restoration and consolidation, emphasis was on the recovery of lost territories and the rebuilding of defences; the atmosphere of the time is vividly conveyed by the paintings of military scenes in the tombs of Beni Hassan.

The collapse of the **Thirteenth Dynasty** heralded the end of the Middle Kingdom and the beginning of the **Second Intermediate Period**, distinguished by the Hyksos occupation. The expulsion of these Middle Eastern settlers by the Theban **Eighteenth Dynasty** marked the beginning of the **New Kingdom** and the relocation of the capital to Thebes. Despite a series of crises which would have destroyed a weaker family, Egypt enjoyed its golden age of art and architecture during this period. The first of these crises followed the death of **Thutmose II**, when his queen, **Hatshepsut**, assumed the throne in place of his legitimate heir **Thutmose III**. Later, there was a major religious upheaval under **Akhenaten**, who abandoned Thebes and the state god **Amun** to worship his own god, **Aten**, in his new capital at Akhetaten. Although both cult and capital were restored under Tutankhamun, the empire was crumbling, and rule soon passed to the Ramesside rulers of the **Nineteenth** and **Twentieth Dynasties**, who between wars with their Middle Eastern neighbours constructed some of Egypt's most magnificent monuments.

The end of the New Kingdom ushered in the **Third Intermediate Period**, another era of chaos and decline, characterised by intermittent invasions and occupations by a variety of foreign powers including Libyans, Assyrians and Persians. Although there were short-lived artistic revivals under the **Twenty-fifth** and **Twenty-sixth Dynasties** and the **Late Period Thirtieth Dynasty**, comparatively little remarkable architecture survives from this era. However, a revival was at hand with the arrival of **Alexander the Great** in 332 BC; the **Greeks**, and later the **Romans**, aiming to control the indigenous population by adopting the traditional roles of kingship, constructed numerous monuments incorporating all the established Egyptian conventions.

The Delta goddess Wadjet (left) and her southern counterpart Nekhbet, wearing the Red Crown of Lower Egypt and the White Crown of Upper Egypt, present the 'pharoah' Ptolemy VIII with the Double Crown of the Two Lands. Temple of Horus, Edfu. (Ptolemaic Period).

Egyptian Religion

Divine Kingship

Whether Egyptian or Libyan, Persian, Greek or Roman, the central figure in ancient Egyptian society was the king, known as 'Pharaoh' (*per-aa*), literally 'the Great House'. In many ways this society resembled the feudal order of medieval Europe, with power devolving downwards from the throne via a pyramidal hierarchy of hereditary nobles and local administrators. At the base lived the mass of impoverished peasantry, who provided the intensive labour demanded by Egypt's agricultural economy and by her rulers' grandiose building projects.

Since the time of Narmer, whose union of the Two Lands was seen as establishing earthly and cosmic order, the king was viewed as an incarnate god whose chief function was to guarantee the divine balance, or **Maat**, by repelling the forces of chaos. Maat, personified by a goddess, expressed the state of rightness when opposing forces are held in a state of equilibrium, encompassing such related concepts as truth, justice and harmony. The royal responsibilities, therefore, did not end at the ordering of the state, but extended to the regulation of the inundation and the rising and setting of the sun. Even the royal names were regarded as sacred, and enclosed for protection within the symbols of eternity known as *cartouches*. Thus although the state government was loosely divided between civil, military and religious affairs, religion permeated throughout, with a priestly rank and duties attached to most official posts. Similarly, the temples, presided over by a high priest acting as the king's proxy, also served as local administrative centres, providing educational, judicial and medical services to the community.

Cults

A major reason for the complexity of Egyptian religion is its origin in the innumerable local cults which arose during the predynastic period, when each settlement worshipped its own deity. Many of these gods took the shape of birds or animals, for example, the falcon **Horus** and his bovine spouse **Hathor**; personifications of cosmic forces also sometimes aquired zoomorphic features, as in the case of the hawk-headed solar deity **Re of Heliopolis**. These divinities were typically represented as bird- or animal-headed humans, but there were also wholly anthropomorphic gods like **Ptah** and **Osiris**, who personified such mysterious abstract forces as creation and regeneration. While each cult had its own mythology, these were often variants of a common theme, usually connected with the natural cycles of the sun and the river. One such example is the creation myth in which the first god emerged from a mound which arose from the primeval **Waters of Chaos**, a beautiful image clearly derived from the appearance of vegetation on small islands left by the receding waters of the inundation. At Memphis it was Ptah who came forth from the **Primeval Mound**, while the inhabitants of Hermopolis Magna believed in eight creator deities, one of whom, **Amun**, later became the chief state god under the Theban rulers of the New Kingdom. At Heliopolis it was **Atum**, the aged form of Re, who emerged to produce **Shu** and **Tefnut**, the personifications of air and moisture. Setting the divine precedent for royal marriages, the brother and sister espoused one another and, in her turn, Tefnut gave birth to **Geb** the earth god and **Nut** the sky goddess. This pair produced two couples—**Isis** and **Osiris** and **Seth** and **Nephthys**—completing the group of nine gods known as the **Great Ennead**, the closest Egyptian approximation to a national pantheon.

With the passage of time the local cults were brought together under the umbrella of state religion, whose purpose was to enlist the support of the gods in the struggle against chaos by means of propitiation with prayers and offerings. Despite this, each cult retained its identity within its own region, where the principal temple was generally dedicated to the local deities—often a triad comprising a male god, his consort and their child. For this reason the religious capital shifted as dynasties from different provinces came to power, although the great national shrines of Memphis, Heliopolis and Thebes retained their status, together with that of Osiris at Abydos.

Relief in the Temple of Seti I at Abydos: Seti I offers Maat to Osiris, Isis and Horus. (New Kingdom, Nineteenth Dynasty).

One of the key mythological cycles of ancient Egypt, the **Osiris legend** was closely related to the institution of divine kingship, and may have derived from actual political occurrences at the beginning of the Early Dynastic period. In the best-known version of the myth, related by the first-century Greek philosopher Plutarch, the brothers Seth and Osiris were entrusted with the care of Egypt. However, while the part of the land given to Osiris prospered, Seth's half wasted. Enraged, Seth tricked his brother into climbing into a casket which was then sealed and thrown into the Nile. After a long search, Isis eventually located her husband's body and took it back to the Delta, where, assuming the form of a kite, she magically conceived her son Horus. Later, the corpse was discovered by Seth, who hacked it into sections which he scattered throughout Egypt. Leaving her child in the care of Nephthys, Isis once again travelled the country, collecting the pieces and erecting a shrine where each was found; Abydos was one of these, Biga Island adjoining Philae another. Beyond restoration to earthly life, Osiris was appointed Lord of the Underworld and judge of the dead; represented mummiform, with green or black skin, he symbolized the regenerative forces of the earth. Horus assumed the throne, and with it the responsibility of avenging his father, in an ongoing struggle symbolic of the eternal conflict between order and chaos. Thus the king came to be seen as the incarnation of Horus in life, and Osiris in death.

Death and the Afterlife

It is often claimed that the Egyptians were obsessed with death. In fact, quite the opposite is true—they were obsessed with life to the point where their chief concern was its infinite prolongation. This was no simple task, as a person was deemed to be composed of seven parts—most importantly the body, the name, the spirit double (*ka*) and the soul (*ba*)—all of which had to be preserved to ensure survival after death. Derived from the natural desiccation which occured in early pit burials, the process of mummification was intended to preserve the body. After cleaning and evisceration, it was dried with natron, a naturally-occuring

Book of the Dead of Ani: Opening of the Mouth Ceremony. The tomb is a typical Theban tomb of the New Kingdom. (New Kingdom, Nineteenth Dynasty). British Museum, London.

form of sodium carbonate; the internal organs were treated separately and preserved in special vessels known as canopic jars. The process, attended by complex rituals, lasted for seventy days, culminating in the elaborate funeral ceremony. Just prior to burial, in a special rite called the Opening of the Mouth, ritual implements were touched to the mummy's head to restore the senses. Outside the tomb, a funerary stele preserved the deceased's name and titles, while within were mounds of food, drink, clothing and other essentials for his sustenance in the next life; in case these should be destroyed, they were duplicated by models or wall paintings, which could magically substitute for the original.

By the New Kingdom, this type of burial had become the norm for royalty and nobles, though remaining well beyond the reach of commoners. In the Old Kingdom, however, the afterlife had been the virtual prerogative of the king, whose destiny, according to the solar religion predominant at the time, was to ascend to the sky to join the 'everlasting' circumpolar stars and to sail with the sun across the heavens. It was believed that as the sun set in the world of the living, it rose in the underworld, thus the west became the location of the royal cemeteries, where the tombs of nobles and courtiers clustered around those of the masters whose entourages they hoped to join in the next world.

From the end of the Old Kingdom the growing popularity of the cult of Osiris brought a shift in funerary belief. Now the afterlife became accessible to any pure soul—any pure soul, that is, who could afford the proper funerary equipment and rituals necessary to negotiate the perils of the underworld, which included lakes of fire and hideous monsters. Assuming the deceased survived the judgement of Osiris, in which the heart was weighed against the feather of Maat to verify its purity, he could look forward to a peaceful afterlife in the Fields of Iaru, the Egyptian equivalent of the Elysian Fields, where he could enjoy the provisions of his tomb in a perfected version of his former home.

Egyptian Architecture

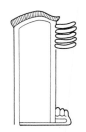

Predynastic Shrine of Upper Egypt

Predynastic Shrine of Lower Egypt

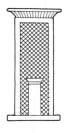

In predynastic Egypt, as in modern times, the people of the Nile built their homes from readily-available natural materials—reeds, mud and the trunks of the palm trees which even then flourished along the river banks; in Upper Egypt, these supplied poles to support tented pavilions hung with matting. Due to the tendency to archaize, these forms were translated first into mudbrick, and then, for monumental architecture, into stone. For obvious reasons, few traces of these early structures have survived, but some idea of their form can be derived from models and depictions. The earliest representations of mud huts date from the predynastic period, and show small, single-roomed structures with battered (inward-sloping) walls and flat roofs, presumably of palm logs; ventilation and light were provided by tiny windows near the ceiling and access was through a single door. Other types of buildings are shown in the hieroglyphs for the predynastic shrines of Upper and Lower Egypt. The Upper Egyptian shrine is depicted as a kind of tent with a shallow convex roof, while the shrine of Lower Egypt shows a tall hut of matting, its eaves and corners reinforced with bundles of plant stems tied together; at the top their free ends fall forward, forming a concave cornice. Thus the basic repertoire of later Egyptian architecture—the battered wall and flat roof, the shallow

10

vault, the torus moulding and cavetto cornice, and the kiosk was already present in its earliest buildings.

In the earliest stone structures such as those of the Step Pyramid complex at Saqqara, these elements were faithfully translated into the new material in all their detail, providing much valuable information about their origins. Such transitional buildings preserve the proportions of their organic prototypes, the width of their rooms being determined by the span and carrying capacity of the original palm-log roofs. In the mudbrick palaces of the Old Kingdom, themselves derived from tent prototypes, these ceilings rested on architraves supported by wooden posts; an arrangement recalled in the hypostyle halls of later temples.

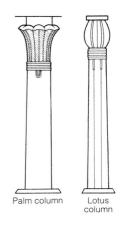

Palm column   Lotus column

Columns and Pillars

Among the earliest types of structural support were the columns of bundled reeds or plant stems reproduced in the entrance hall of the Step Pyramid complex. From the Old Kingdom onward these were supplemented by the many different types of plant columns which began to appear. One type common in the Old Kingdom and thereafter abandoned until revived by the Ptolemies was the palm column, which does not represent the palm tree itself, but rather eight palm fronds lashed to a pole by several bands of stylized bindings. The same feature can be seen on two other early forms, the lotus column and the papyrus-bundle column. The palm column and papyrus-bundle column, having religious associations with Upper and Lower Egypt respectively, were often employed in temples, while the lotus column is more commonly found in a domestic context.

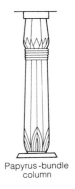

Papyrus-bundle column

During the New Kingdom, two simpler types of papyrus columns were introduced—the open papyrus column—with a full, bell-shaped capital and the papyrus bud column—a simplification of the papyrus-bundle column with a closed bud capital. In common with the papyrus-bundle column, their shafts taper upward from a characteristic swollen base carved with stylized stem sheaths; symbolizing the plants of the primeval marshes, these types often appear in the hypostyle halls and colonnaded

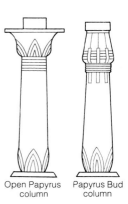

Open Papyrus column   Papyrus Bud column

11

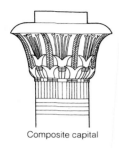

Composite capital

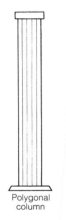

Polygonal
column

Hathor capital

courts of the period. From the Late Period, shafts were simplified into cylindrical columns, but, as if in compensation, wonderful and complex varieties of capital began to appear, especially during the Graeco-Roman period. Known as composite capitals, they are composed of various combinations of plants and flowers bunched together by traditional bindings, and probably represent ceremonial bouquets.

In the earliest stone temples, the very simple covered halls were roofed with slabs supported by great square piers without any base or bearing slab. Probably derived from quarry supports, during the Middle Kingdom these pillars were refined into eight- or sixteen-sided polygonal columns by shaving down the corners; at the same time they aquired the flat circular base and square abacus common to all Egyptian columns. Later versions of these columns are fluted, a tradition referring back to wooden prototypes trimmed with the curved blade of the Egyptian adze; copies of such fluted masts are found on chapel façades in the Step Pyramid complex. Among other forms which emerged in the Middle Kingdom were the Osiride pillar, a square pillar with an engaged statue of the king in the form of the god Osiris, and the Hathor capital, a four-sided capital bearing the features of the cow-eared goddess, which is found both on pillars and round columns.

The flat roofs of the temple buildings were supported on simple architraves, often crowned with a torus moulding and concave cornice; in later temples, a high parapet screened rooftop rituals from the public gaze. A slight pitch allowed the drainage of rainwater through spouts, which, to avert evil influences, were shaped like the foreparts of lions. The pylon, whose huge twin towers were elaborated from earlier ceremonial gateways, was carved with scenes of the king subduing enemies which fulfilled a similar apotropaic function.

Materials and Techniques

Mudbrick Architecture

Leaving aside the organic prototypes, Egyptian

architecture can be divided into three groups—mudbrick buildings, monumental stone structures and rock-cut monuments. Among the oldest of building materials, sundried bricks of Nile mud were fashioned from very early times, although the invention of the wooden brick mould during the Early Dynastic period greatly speeded their production. Versatile and readily available, mudbrick was (and is) the ideal building material for the Egyptian climate, providing welcome insulation from extremes of temperature. It is also surprisingly durable; those buildings which have escaped the depredations of the *sebakhin* (plunderers of the nitrogen-rich earth from ancient sites for use as fertilizer) are often in quite good condition. However, because such examples are few, ancient mudbrick architecture tends to be overlooked. In fact, throughout Egyptian history, mudbrick was the most favoured material for domestic building, and was often employed in funerary architecture; both the Early Dynastic period mastabas and late Middle Kingdom pyramids were built of mudbrick, and later tombs often had brick additions such as pylons or pyramidions. The fortresses which protected Egypt's borders were also of mudbrick, as were the massive walls which enclosed temple compounds and city precincts. Mudbrick technology has evolved very little since ancient times; the dome and arch were already known early in the Old Kingdom, and some fine vaulting can be seen, for example in the storage magazines of the Ramesseum. The characteristic battered walls of Egyptian mudbrick buildings—thick at the base and thin at the top—were developed as a strengthening

Making mudbricks using a wooden mould. Painting in the tomb of Rekhmire, Luxor. (New Kingdom, Eighteenth Dynasty).

measure against the movement of the underlying silt during the annual inundation. Similarly, the pan-bedded enclosure walls were built in short separate sections which could survive the flood by rising and settling independently.

Stone Architecture

From the Third Dynasty onward, a desire for more permanent religious monuments led to the adoption of stone construction for tombs and temples. Where possible, stone was quarried locally—hence the preponderance of limestone buildings in the north and sandstone in the south—although at all periods opulent Aswan granites were transported around the country. Since no site was situated very far from the river, transportation of stone was seldom a problem, since even the heaviest pieces, such as obelisks, could be floated to their destination on barges during the inundation. It is likely that much of the work on major building projects was undertaken during the flood season, when large numbers of manual workers, temporarily relieved of their usual agricultural duties, became available. In addition to this mass of unskilled labour, such undertakings also called for teams of skilled masons. Stoneworking techniques remained simple, but required great precision, as the finely-dressed inner surfaces of the blocks were fitted together with a minimum of mortar, whose function seems to have been more as a lubricant than a bonding agent. As the principles of the arch and vault were known, the refusal of the Egyptian architects to make the transition from trabeate to arcuate construction in religious architecture must be attributed to deliberate archaization. From the Old Kingdom, however, corbel vaulting was employed in the interior chambers of pyramid tombs, and another type of false vaulting, achieved by hollowing out the roof slabs, appears in later temples.

Before work could commence on a religious monument, the site had to be levelled and the building's orientation determined by astronomical alignments; only then could the foundations be cut. These tended to be scanty, usually consisting simply of a shallow trench partly filled with sand, although the builders of the Graeco-Roman period introduced more substantial foundations of reused masonry. As the walls of the building rose, access ramps of earth or rubble were constructed, being raised and extended with each succeeding course. Once the structure had attained its full height, the ramps were dismantled, the rough exterior surface of the stone being dressed on the way down. Decoration may have been executed at the same time, or by means of scaffolding at a later date.

Whether this technique, which was certainly used in the temples (part of a builders' ramp survives at Karnak) could have been employed in the construction of enormous monuments such as the Great Pyramid is open to question, due to the size of the ramps that would have been required. Various alternatives have been proposed, including systems of levers or rockers, but the debate is far from settled.

Rock-Cut Architecture

The simpler techniques of rock-cut architecture, derived from quarrying practices, are far better understood, thanks to the large number of unfinished monuments. As elsewhere, the work was carried out by a number of specialist teams succeeding each other in turn, rather than completing one stage at a time. Thus it is not uncommon to find a tomb whose outer rooms are completely carved and painted while its inner chambers have been only partially excavated.

The working party was divided into two gangs, allocated to the left and right sides of the monument. First came the stone-cutters, whose job was to roughly maul out the chambers and corridors; these were followed by the masons who completed the cutting and finished the surfaces, working by reflected sunlight or the glimmer of oil lamps. The chambers were excavated from the ceiling down to the floor, leaving supports to be shaped into pillars or columns. Vaulted ceilings, niches and statuary were cut in a similar fashion. Behind the masons came the teams of draughtsmen, sculptors and painters who prepared the colourful relief decoration.

Luxor, West Bank: a modern workman cuts a polygonal column for restoration work on the Temple of Hatshepsut at Deir-el-Bahri.

Egyptian Art

Carved reliefs were an essential part of Egyptian religious monuments, sometimes to the extent that the architecture was subordinate to them, serving only to provide convenient areas for their accommodation. They were, of course, regarded as functional rather than decorative; every image, every hieroglyph, was imbued with its own magical power. Even the cheerful painted designs found on the walls and ceilings of homes and palaces have symbolic undertones, incorporating, for example, small images of deities or repeating patterns of protective amulets. In a temple, the purpose of the reliefs was to maintain the state of Maat by repelling evil forces from its precincts and by ensuring the continued enactment of its rituals; since in Egyptian belief the depiction of an act could substitute for the deed itself, this was achieved by carving them in eternal stone. In the royal tombs, the same principle was applied to aid the deceased king on his journey through the Underworld; magic spells and images

Slab stele of Rahotep from his mastaba at Meidum. (Old Kingdom, Fourth Dynasty). British Museum, London.

16

of protective deities were installed to guard his path, and symbolic enemies were rendered harmless by being shown bound, headless or mutilated.

In private tombs, reliefs and wall-paintings ensured that the tomb owner would have everything necessary for a contented afterlife. At the beginning of the Old Kingdom, these needs were considered to be met by the inclusion of grave goods and—for those who could afford the services of a priest—by daily offering at the tomb. However, as both these sources were prone to failure, small offering stelae began to be incorporated into the offering chapels of the tombs of the nobility. Such stelae included a figure of the deceased (which could act as a substitute body should anything untoward befall the original), his name (also necessary for survival in the Underworld), his titles (ensuring his continued high status) and stylized representations of food, drink and other necessities in the form of a list: 1,000 loaves of bread, 1,000 jugs of beer, oxen, geese, alabaster vessels, bolts of linen, and so on.

Artistic Conventions

In essence, all later tomb art is simply a development of the offering stele, from which all the major conventions of the form can be traced. Immediately noticeable is the link between size and importance; the tomb owner (and sometimes his wife) is shown full scale, while doll-sized children cling to his ankles. The same principle applied in later royal sculpture, and is vividly illustrated in battle reliefs, where the king and his chariot are shown many times the size of the opposing forces' city.

The offerings represented on such stelae are more like diagrams than lifelike depictions of their subjects. The first principle of Egyptian art was that an object should be portrayed as unambiguously as possible, therefore it was drawn as an assembly of its most characteristic aspects. In a painting of a pool surrounded by trees, for example, the pool is shown as if from above, as a blue rectangle, but the trees are shown from the side, the resulting combination conveying the curious impression that they are lying down by the poolside.

When the artist wanted to depict something normally

Part of a draughtsman's drawing board with an unfinished royal figure; the proportional grid is clearly visible. (New Kingdom, Eighteenth Dynasty). British Museum, London.

hidden from view, he would either move it to make it visible or draw its container as if transparent, since failure to depict the contents would imply emptiness. Where the context is religious, idealization is the rule: there is no place for age, sickness or deformity in tomb or temple reliefs—people are always represented young and beautiful, fowl and animals are sleek and well fed, glistening fruit at the peak of its ripeness. Just as the scenes in the reliefs stand apart from ordinary time, the neutral background removes them from ordinary space, depriving them of depth and context; instead, they are organized into horizontal bands, known as registers. It is greatly to the credit of the Egyptian artists that despite these restrictions so much of their production appears natural and harmonious. In part, this is due to the fact that a rigid canon of proportion, based on a square grid, ensured a constant relationship between the elements of a composition, in accordance with the principle of Maat which required balance and symmetry. The grid was used not only for composition, but for transferring drawings to the surfaces to be cut, and as a guide during execution.

Relief Decoration and Wall Painting

Two broad categories of relief were employed in ancient Egypt—sunk relief, where the figures are cut beneath the surface of the stone, and raised relief, where the background is removed, leaving the figures standing proud. Sunk relief was quicker, cheaper and more effective in sunlight, and thus was commonly used in open situations where large areas of carving were required, such as temple exteriors; since it is also less laborious, it was also the method of choice when working hard stones such as alabaster and granite. Raised relief, more expensive and time-consuming, but better suited to softer stone, was normally reserved for tombs and temple interiors. Prior to cutting reliefs, the stone surfaces were smoothed and patched where necessary with plaster. Good quality stone could be carved directly, but sometimes a coat of plaster was necessary; very poor stone could not be cut at all, and was simply plastered and painted. All surfaces received a thin skim of plaster before painting; as this was allowed to dry before work commenced, Egyptian wall paintings should not be confused with frescoes, which are executed on wet plaster.

All buildings were originally intended to be painted in bright colours, although very often the painting was left unfinished or even unstarted. The basic palette, comprising red, yellow, green, blue, black and white was derived mainly from mineral colours, though the bright blues and greens were artificial frits. The pigments were suspended in a gum solution, and applied in flat washes with brushes made from chewed wood or palm fibre; outlines and details were added later with a fine reed brush. The first stage in relief carving or wall painting was the laying down of the grid. The figures were then sketched in red paint and corrected in black by the master draughtsman before work began. In both disciplines, the basic work was carried out by specialist teams of artisans, the final touches being added by the master craftsmen. Any mistakes were simply plastered over and recut or repainted; much of this plaster has since fallen away, leaving the corrections visible. The different stages in the production of painted reliefs are very well illustrated in the unfinished decoration of the tomb of Horemheb in the Valley of the Kings.

Domestic Architecture

Town Planning

Although few examples are now visible, archaeological work has yielded much useful information concerning Egyptian domestic architecture. Early settlements consisted of groups of simple huts constructed of reeds or wattle and daub, but by the Old Kingdom, regular town planning had appeared, with buildings laid out on a grid of intersecting streets. For security, towns and cities were generally enclosed on the landward side by massive mudbrick walls, such as those which still survive at El-Kab, but open on the side adjoining the river or canal, where a harbour served their transportation needs. The enclosed area was subdivided into various districts; the temple complex, with its own workshops, administrative buildings and priests' houses, formed what amounted to a town-within-a-town inside its own enclosure walls, and there were separate areas for commerce and industry. Residential districts were segregated by wealth and status, and covered the whole spectrum from the close-packed cramped dwellings of the labouring classes to the opulent villas of the nobility in their elite suburbs.

Residential Buildings

The basic layout of the Egyptian house conforms to the tripartite plan found throughout the contemporary Near East, comprising three rooms of increasing privacy and a corridor leading to an open area for cooking at the rear; houses of this type can be seen in the village of the royal necropolis workers at Deir el-Medina on the Theban west bank. With their battered mudbrick walls, palm-log ceilings and small windows with wood or stone grilles, they must have differed very little from the rural dwellings of today.

Excavations of nobles' villas at El-Amarna and elsewhere have revealed some very grand residences, with shady gardens, pools and courtyards, and sophisticated suites of inner chambers, including reception halls, family rooms, bedrooms, bathrooms and latrines, storerooms and servants' quarters. Whitewashed on the outside, the plastered interiors had a painted dado, and sometimes wall decoration as well. Wind catches on the roof

Book of the Dead of Nakht: the deceased and his wife in their garden, worshipping Osiris and Maat. Note the rendition of the pool and the house, which has wind catches on the roof. (New Kingdom, Eighteenth/ Nineteenth Dynasty).

delivered a cooling breeze to the inner apartments. The country villa was even more extensive, incorporating workshops and granaries, kitchen gardens, vineyards and stabling for animals.

This was doubly true for the royal palace complex, which was effectively a town-in-miniature, with its own temple, workshops, offices, service areas and residential districts. Beside these were the royal residences themselves, along with the state apartments such as banqueting halls and audience pavilions, whose splendour, if we are to believe contemporary accounts, far outstripped all other buildings of the ancient world. Destroyed almost beyond recognition, these magnificent structures now exist only in the imaginations of archaeologists, and in the reconstructions they assemble from fragments of their brilliant wall paintings, polychrome tiles and gilded columns.

Funerary Architecture

Because of the different conditions prevailing in Upper and Lower Egypt, separate burial practices arose in the two regions. Since precious arable land could be not be spared for cemeteries, southern interments were made in the desert, beyond the Nile floodplain, while in the Delta the dead were buried beneath the floor of the home, enabling their spirits to remain among the family.

Predynastic Upper Egyptian inhumations consisted of simple oval or rectangular pits in the desert, in which the deceased was buried in a contracted position, accompanied by a few simple grave goods, such as pots of food and flint knives for hunting. For the impoverished bulk of the population, this type of burial remained standard throughout history. More affluent burials, however, became increasingly elaborate; the pits were lined with matting, wood or mudbrick, and extra chambers were added to accommodate the increasing number of grave goods. At the same time, the simple mound which had served to mark the grave was enlarged and elaborated into a low, rectangular superstructure called in modern times a *mastaba*, the Arabic name for an earthen bench. At Abydos, the royal cemetery of Thinis, the southern capital, such tombs were usually surrounded by the small pit-graves of retainers, and separate dummy palaces provided for the ruler's use in the afterlife.

Early Mastabas

When the Archaic period kings moved their capital from Thinis to Memphis, they also brought their tomb-building traditions, founding the royal desert necropolis at Saqqara. By the First Dynasty, their mastabas had already acquired elaborate niched façades imitating the exteriors of their palace buildings. This development could have been influenced by the Lower Egyptian idea of house burial, or may represent an amalgamation of the Upper Egyptian mastabas and dummy palace. Whatever the truth of the matter, from this time onward the notion of the tomb as a 'house of eternity' dominated Egyptian tomb-building until the advent of Christianity, when grave goods and extravagant burials were forbidden.

Over time, the southernmost recess of the eastern wall of the mastaba was developed into a small chapel for offerings, where a false door stele, often depicting various

False Door stele.

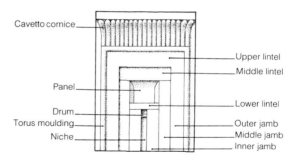

types of offerings, allowed the passage of the deceased's *ka*, or spirit, between the tomb and the world of the living.

Pyramids

During the Third Dynasty, the idea of providing the king with an eternal residence was further advanced by the construction of the Step Pyramid complex at Saqqara. Enclosed by a niched palace façade, the complex contained a dummy palace and Jubilee court as well as the royal tomb, all built in stone for added permanence. The tomb was of a new design, comprising a series of mastabas built one on top of another, creating a stairway by which the deceased king could ascend to heaven. Since his spirit would be guided by the pole star, the entrance to the pyramid was on the northern face, where the offering temple was also located.

For the remainder of the Old Kingdom, the pyramid complex was to become the norm for royal burials. The first true pyramid was built at Meidum, probably for Huni, the last king of the Third Dynasty; like the later pyramids, it was built as a stepped pyramid and then faced with polished stone. Beside the pyramid itself, the Meidum complex comprised a small offering temple with twin stelae, linked by a causeway to a valley temple beside the Nile. This combination of pyramid tomb, mortuary temple, causeway and valley temple became standard for later pyramid complexes, which reached their zenith in the Giza group constructed by the powerful Fourth Dynasty monarchs. Reflecting a shift in the balance of

Djoser's step pyramid enclosure showing the niched wall derived from the façade of the royal palace.

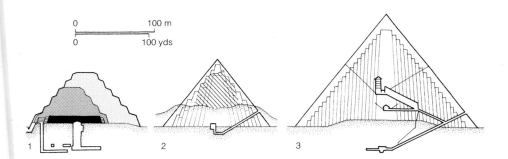

power between the nobility and the throne, the pyramids of the late Old Kingdom show a marked decline in size and quality. Constructed of polished stone casing blocks over an inner rubble core, the inferiority of these later building techniques is eloquently demonstrated by the pyramids' poor state of preservation. In compensation, their subterranean chambers boast magnificent high gabled ceilings and elaborate carved hieroglyphic texts—a

Development of the Pyramid
1. Step Pyramid. Third Dynasty, c. 2650 BC.
2. Meidum Pyramid. Third-Fourth Dynasty, c. 2610 BC. 3. Great Pyramid. Fourth Dynasty, c. 2560 BC.

23

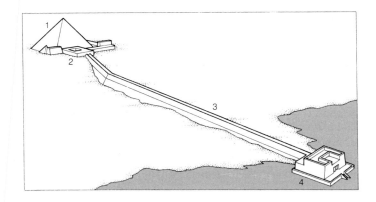

striking contrast to the simple undecorated rooms of the earlier royal monuments. With the collapse of the Sixth Dynasty, and the decline of centralised power, pyramid building was abandoned until the practice was revived by the rulers of the Middle Kingdom.

Late Mastabas

Nobles and courtiers, however, were being interred in opulent stone-faced mastabas with internal offering chapels evolved from the earlier outside offering niches. In addition to the false door stelae, these now included *ka-statues*, images of the deceased which could act as substitute bodies, and reliefs depicting offerings and activities meant to enable the tomb owner to maintain his lifestyle and status in the next life. By the Fifth Dynasty such tombs had developed elaborate superstructures with chapels and courtyards, and were embellished with fine painted bas-reliefs, a process which continued into the following dynasty and culminated in mastabas like that of Mereruka, which comprises over 30 rooms and incorporates separate funerary suites for his wife and son.

Rock-Cut Tombs

Meanwhile, in the Nile Valley to the south, away from the broad plateaux of Giza and Saqqara, a new type of tomb architecture was evolving at sites like Aswan, Beni Hassan and the Theban west bank. As the influence of the capital at Memphis waned, the power of the provincial governors—the *nomarchs*—grew, and with it their desire for tombs worthy of their new status. As there was little space for building mastabas or pyramids, they cut their tombs directly into the limestone or sandstone cliffs of the narrow valley.

With local variations, the basic plan of these tombs consists of an open court, a rock-cut façade and an enclosed offering chapel with a false door or statue niche; this is normally decorated with painted scenes of offerings, everyday activities and funeral rites. A shaft from

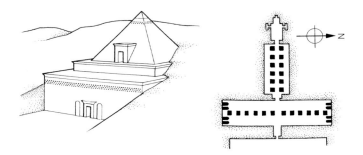

A nobleman's rock-cut tomb. Typical Theban tomb of the Eighteenth Dynasty, c. 1570–1293 BC.

the court or chapel leads down to the undecorated burial chamber, and some tombs have dramatic rock-cut causeways up which the sarcophagus was dragged to its final resting place. At Thebes, the chapels were often surmounted by small brick pyramids. Such rock-cut tombs were to become the Upper Egyptian norm throughout the Middle and New Kingdoms, and survived in a somewhat altered form into the Third Intermediate Period. Few tombs were cut after this date, but there was extensive reuse of existing monuments, at first by the original owners' families and then by usurpers, until by the Graeco-Roman era they were being used as repositories for mass burials; a recent excavation of three small Theban tombs produced the remains of over 200 bodies!

Royal Monuments

The first rock-cut royal tombs at Thebes were the so-called *saff* ('row') tombs of the early Eleventh Dynasty at El-Tarif on the west bank. These, however, were overshadowed by the magnificence of **Montuhotep I**'s extraordinary funerary complex at nearby Deir el-Bahri. Comprising a combined tomb and temple linked by a causeway to a valley temple, it made clear reference to the monuments of the Old Kingdom, anticipating the Twelfth Dynasty revival of pyramid building at Dahshur, Lisht, Lahun and Hawara.

During the troubled times of the Second Intermediate Period, the Theban Seventeenth Dynasty resumed the custom of rock-cut burials—this time in small tombs at Dra Abu el-Naga close to Deir el-Bahri—but again little of these monuments survives. It was not until the advent of the Eighteenth Dynasty at the beginning of the New Kingdom that the great royal tombs of the Valley of the Kings were conceived. It would seem that the original motive behind this development was the quest for tomb security, since no previous royal burials had survived intact: even the labyrinthine inner passages of the Middle Kingdom pyramids had not been proof against the ingenuity of the tomb robbers.

Therefore **Thutmose I** instructed his architect **Ineni** to construct a secret tomb, cut deep into the rock of a remote wadi on the west bank of the Nile. Unlike all the earlier royal monuments, which vied to outdo each other in splendour, this tomb was to be concealed; once the king had been buried, it was to be sealed and its entrance disguised. It would never be visited; henceforward, offerings to the deceased monarch's spirit would be made at a separate mortuary temple, which replaced the tomb as the chief royal memorial. This separation of tomb and mortuary temple represented as radical a departure from tradition as had the development of the pyramid some 1,000 years before.

Comprising a series of corridors and chambers plunging deep into the earth, the tomb represented the deceased king's journey between earthly and eternal godhood, and its walls were covered with religious texts and images intended to assist him both in his passage to the Underworld and in his future divine role. Although efforts to maintain secrecy were quickly abandoned as futile, and

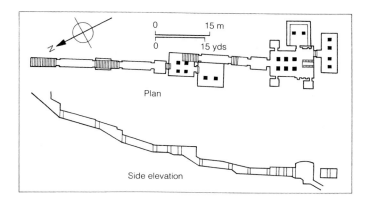

A royal rock-cut tomb. The tomb of Seti I in the Valley of the Kings, c. 1270 BC

tombs were once again given impressive façades, the basic elements of these monuments remained essentially unchanged until the last royal burials were made in the Valley at the end of the Twentieth Dynasty. By this date, all the elaborate security measures had been proved useless—several of the royal tombs had already been plundered.

Chapel Tombs

Undeterred, the Tanite kings of the Twenty-first and Twenty-second Dynasties adopted a new approach: instead of choosing a remote location for their burials, they built their tombs within temple compounds, right under the watchful eyes of the ever-present priests. This ruse achieved a measure of success, as in 1939 six substantially intact tombs were discovered by the French archaeologist Pierre Montet. Their superstructures had not survived, but probably took the form of decorated chapels. Dating to the Twenty-fifth and Twenty-sixth Dynasties, the chapel-tombs of the Divine Votaresses of Amun built within the courtyard of Ramesses III's mortuary temple at Medinet Habu are later examples of this type.

Shaft Tombs

Another successful Twenty-sixth Dynasty solution to the tomb security problem was finally evolved in the form of the shaft tomb, found only in the Memphite necropolis. This ingenious design involved the construction of a burial

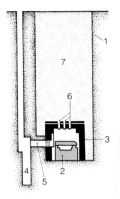

Shaft Tomb
1. Bedrock
2. Sarcophagus
3. Burial chamber
4. Access shaft
5. Access passage
6. Pottery jars
7. Sand-filled shaft

chamber at the bottom of a huge, deep pit. Pottery jars, open end uppermost, were set into the ceiling of the chamber, which when complete was inaccessible from the pit, access for the burial being via a short passage connecting with a narrow parallel shaft. The pit was then filled with sand. Once the body was installed in the sarcophagus which had been built into the tomb, the last man to leave broke the jars, allowing the sand from above to fill the room. The burial party then retired up the parallel shaft, which was filled in afterwards. Any subsequent attempts to enter the tomb by this route would have been met by an endless cascade of sand from the burial chamber; the only way to reach the burial was to clear all the sand from the pit, a task well beyond the capabilities of the average band of tomb-robbers.

Late Tombs

From the Late Period onward, a great variety of tombs were constructed in various parts of the country. During the Greek period, the idea of the 'house of eternity' was still current, as can be seen in funerary towns like that of Tuna el-Gebel, while at Alexandria, the decorations of the Roman catacombs, hardly an Egyptian concept, nonetheless drew on Pharaonic prototypes for artistic inspiration.

On the whole, however, tomb-building was already in decline. By the Graeco-Roman period the poor were generally interred in communal tombs, and coffins were simply placed in brick compartments or shallow graves, sometimes within the superstructure of earlier tombs. Egyptian funerary architecture was almost back at the point where it had started.

Temple Architecture

Egyptian temples were normally located at sites of great antiquity, occupied in predynastic times by small shrines dedicated to the local deity. Early representations suggest that these may have consisted of a simple reed or wooden structure, perhaps enclosed by a picket fence: shrines of this type were reproduced in stone in the Jubilee court at the

Step Pyramid complex at Saqqara. With the passage of time, such buildings became increasingly larger and more elaborate: because of this process of constant renewal, very little extant temple architecture predates the New Kingdom. However, due to the tendency to archaize, even the temples of the Graeco-Roman period consist mainly of stone copies of archaic organic structures. The royal mortuary temples were an important exception to this rule, since the fact that they were always new foundations allowed their builders complete freedom of design.

The Temple Plan

By the time of the New Kingdom, the standard temple ground plan had assumed a conventional pattern based on a single axis, reflecting the processional nature of temple ritual. This plan comprised a pylon, peristyle court, one or more hypostyle halls, vestibules and a sanctuary surrounded by small chapels and storage magazines. Intended to stand for eternity, the temple was sited just beyond the edge of the cultivation in order to preserve it from the inundation, and supported by steeply battered walls which would protect it from earthquakes and flooding. The orientation was determined by Egypt's two divine life-giving sources, with the pylon generally facing the Nile, and the axis aligned east-west on the sun's daily path: the perfect symmetry of the structure served to underline the temple's role in the maintenance of Maat in the state and cosmos.

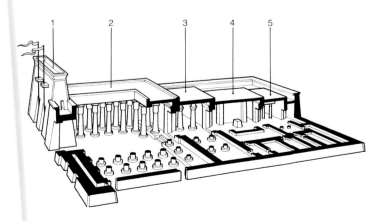

Section through a typical New Kingdom temple
1. Pylon
2. Peristyle court
3. Hypostyle Hall
4. Sanctuary
5. Chapels and storage

Representing a model of creation, the temple was always built on rising ground, with the sanctuary sited at the highest point, symbolizing the primeval mound. Surrounding it, the halls and courtyards represented the primordial marshes, while outside, the wavelike pattern of the pan-bedded mudbrick enclosure walls was reminiscent of the waters of chaos. The resulting effect, as one travels along the axis, is of moving from bright, open, sunlit space through increasingly darker and more restricted areas to the pitch dark, womb-like intimacy of the sanctuary itself.

The commonest Egyptian term for a temple translates as 'God's House', and the local god was in fact regarded by the community as a living entity actually resident in the temple. It is interesting in this context to note that in temple reliefs and sculpture the god is normally shown facing outward from the sanctuary. Reflecting the segregation of areas in a private house, every part of the temple was clearly demarcated, and access to each was governed by status; the sanctuary, for example, was the exclusive preserve of the king and the high priest who acted as his proxy, while the lay public were almost exclusively confined to the outer precincts. In keeping with this, the themes of the relief carvings change, as one travels through the temple, from the public acts of the king represented on the pylon and outer walls to his intimate relationship with the god, as shown in the sanctuary area.

The approach to the temple was normally by a paved processional route, sometimes flanked by an avenue of sphinxes. This terminated in a paved forecourt, usually embellished with obelisks and statuary, directly in front of the pylon. Most temples were connected by canals to the river, and quays were incorporated to facilitate the arrival and departure of waterborne processions.

Providing an impressive entrance to the temple, the pylon comprises twin rectangular towers, with battered walls and flat roofs crowned by concave cornices, flanking a central gateway. As this form bears some similarity to the hieroglyph for the horizon, it may have represented the twin mountains between which the sun was believed to rise. Niches in the façade once held wooden flagpoles from which hung long coloured pennants symbolizing guardian goddesses. As additional protection the pylon was carved with massive reliefs of the king as defender of Egypt against its foes. Sometimes these represent battle scenes, as in Ramesses II's reliefs of the Battle of Kadesh on the Luxor Temple pylon, but by far the most common scene shows the ruler in the traditional attitude of the Narmer Palette, seizing foreign enemies by the hair and threatening them with a mace, while the local deity offers him the sword of victory. Widely visible from the surrounding countryside, temple pylons also served a second purpose as hoardings for the dissemination of state propaganda; a use which appealed particularly to Ptolemaic and Roman 'pharaohs' hoping to convince a sceptical population of their legitimacy as rulers.

Main Axis

In the centre of the pylon was the first of several great doors barring the main temple axis. Such doors were no doubt made of wood, sheathed in precious metals and adorned with gems, adding to the impressive aspect of the entrance. Representing points of transition or transformation, doors and gates had a very special religious significance for the Egyptians, as is amply illustrated by their prevalence in funerary art and literature. In the context of the temple, these doorways served to demarcate areas of restricted access; they could only be unsealed by authorized persons at specified times and with the appropriate ritual. To avoid any disruption this might have caused in the daily running of the temple, there was normally an ambulatory which gave access, via service doors, to the inner apartments without the necessity of opening the main doors, thus allowing the temple servants to go about their duties unhindered.

No examples of temple doors survive, but the visitor can gauge their size and weight from the size and placing of their sockets, and from the grooves sometimes visible in the ancient paving. On the jambs, a special motif known as the 'Shadow of the Door', and composed of the hieroglyphs for life and power, marks where the door leaves rested when open.

'Shadow of the Door Motif'

31

Peristyle Court

The peristyle court comprises a central open courtyard enclosed by a colonnade supporting an architrave and roofed with stone slabs. The type of column employed varies greatly according to the date of the temple; simple papyrus columns, or square pillars, were popular during the New Kingdom, while in Graeco-Roman temples columns with elaborate composite capitals are common. As the assembly point for processions, the peristyle court was regarded as a semi-public area, and it is possible that on certain occasions privileged lay persons may have been admitted. In keeping with this, the reliefs around the court resume the theme of divine kingship, but on a slightly more intimate scale: typical scenes include the purification of the king by the gods Thoth and Horus, and his coronation by the goddesses of Upper and Lower Egypt.

Hypostyle Hall

In New Kingdom temples, a raised portico was generally employed to separate the hypostyle hall from the peristyle court, but in Graeco-Roman temples this was replaced by a screen wall. Access is normally via a shallow ramp or staircase, since it is from this point that the floor level begins to rise towards the sanctuary. Hypostyle halls vary greatly in size and complexity, though the number of columns is normally a multiple of three or four, numbers of magical significance. Since this part of the temple was intended to symbolize the marshes about the primeval mound, plant columns and capitals are almost universally employed. Roofed with stone slabs and lit by clerestory windows or slits in the ceiling, the hall creates the effect of standing within a vast petrified forest, as shafts of light from a remote sky play among the massive columns.

Since the ceiling actually was intended to represent the sky, it is usually decorated with carvings of celestial themes: vultures, winged discs or scarabs, or stars. During the Graeco-Roman period, these developed into complex astronomical calendars, which charted the movement of the constellations throughout the year. On the walls, bas-reliefs show scenes of increasing intimacy between the king and the god of the temple; he may be shown, for example, assisting the deity in his processions, or participating in the temple's foundation rituals.

Inner Chambers

Until the late New Kingdom, most temples had only one hypostyle hall, but from this date, perhaps as a result of the practice of extending temples, it became increasingly common to include another, so that by the Graeco-Roman period a second hall became the norm. From this smaller hall, side doors gave access to the ambulatory, and to small chambers for the storage and preparation of materials used in the temple rituals. Further doorways along the main axis lead into the Hall of Offerings, a small columned hall where the daily offerings were assembled before their presentation to the god. Appropriately, the reliefs in this room depict the presentation of various types of offering, underlining the importance of propitiation in Egyptian worship. The Hall of Offerings leads directly into the vestibule, which marked the boundary of the most sacred part of the temple. From here, narrow corridors run to the suite of chapels, magazines and treasuries behind the sanctuary, to staircases leading to the roof and to various other areas including, in the Graeco-Roman era, the New Year Chapel and crypts.

Sanctuary

Standing at the highest point of the temple, the sanctuary is a small, free-standing, unlit chapel containing only a stone naos, or shrine, to hold the god's image, and a pedestal for the sacred bark, the portable boat in which it was carried in procession. The reliefs on the walls illustrate the king performing the twice-daily offering ceremony enacted in temples throughout Egypt. The most detailed sequence of such scenes is found in Seti I's temple at Abydos, where every stage of the ritual is shown, from the initial opening of the shrine through the washing, anointing and dressing of the image and the presentation of offerings, to the final sweeping clean of the sanctuary before the celebrant's withdrawal.

Dendera, Temple of Hathor: Hypostyle Hall. (Graeco-Roman Period).

34

MEMPHIS AND ITS CEMETERIES

For the modern visitor arriving in Cairo, it can be difficult to believe that this bustling centre, the 'Mother of Cities' to the medieval Arabs, has not always been the capital of Egypt. However, while it was not until the Roman era that settlements were established on the site of the present capital, two of Egypt's largest and most important ancient cities were located in its immediate vicinity. The scanty remains of Heliopolis, cult centre of the solar deity Re, have long since disappeared under Cairo's northeastern suburbs; as the sole reminder of its former greatness a solitary obelisk stands incongruously on a traffic island outside Cairo International Airport.

Memphis, the Old Kingdom capital, located some 43 km (27 miles) southwest of central Cairo, has fared little better. Established around 3150 BC as the capital of the newly-united kingdom of Upper and Lower Egypt, it was deliberately sited close to the junction of the Nile Valley and the Delta; even during the Middle Kingdom, after the capital had been moved elsewhere, Memphis' symbolic location was underlined in its title of *Ankh-Tawy*—'Life of the Two Lands'. Its advantageous position ensured that the city retained its importance as a commercial and administrative centre well into the Christian era, and it was usual for the ruler to maintain a sizeable residence there. One reason for this was Memphis' religious significance as the cult centre of the creator god Ptah, patron of craftsmen and one of the principal gods of the national pantheon. In addition, from the New Kingdom onwards, the associated cult of the Apis bull achieved increasing popularity and was heavily patronised by the rulers of the Late and Graeco-Roman periods. Both cults were closely related to funerary belief and practice, and although the ancient city has now largely disappeared, its size and significance can be gauged from the extent of the Memphite necropolis. Stretching over 30 km (19 miles)

(*Opposite*) Saqqara, Step Pyramid Complex: Chapels in the Jubilee court. (Old Kingdom, Third Dynasty).

35

from Abu Roash in the north to Dahshur in the south, it includes the important cemeteries of Saqqara and Giza which contain some of the most famous Old Kingdom monuments.

The Egyptian Museum, located in central Cairo, is open daily, and offers an excellent opportunity not only to take an overview of Egyptian history, but also to see fragments of long-vanished buildings together with the statuary, painting and artefacts which once graced homes and palaces, temples and tombs.

MEMPHIS

Ancient Memphis was a magnificent city: writing around 2,000 years ago, the Greek historian Diodorus of Sicily estimated its circuit at 150 stadia or 28 km (17 miles). Due largely to the ancient practice of restricting the use of stone to monumental buildings, it has now all but vanished, buried under the surrounding cultivation. Although the area around the Ptah temple has been excavated, the majority of the remains exposed are unlikely to interest anyone but the specialist. An exception is the eastern corner of the enclosure, which has been turned into an open-air museum displaying sculpture from the site, including a fallen limestone colossus of Ramesses II and an elegant New Kingdom sphinx.

SAQQARA

(Opposite) The North Saqqara Necropolis

Step Pyramid Complex
1. Enclosure Wall
2. Entrance
3. Colonnade
4. Southern Tomb
5. Main court
6. Jubilee court
7. Step Pyramid
8. House of the South
(Cont. p. 37)

Situated two kilometres (one mile) to the west of Memphis, the necropolis of Saqqara was the principal cemetery of the Old Kingdom capital. Over six square kilometres in area, Saqqara is one of the most extensive and important archaeological sites in Egypt, its monuments spanning a period of over 3000 years from the First Dynasty to the Christian era. While large areas of Saqqara remain unexcavated, the earliest tombs uncovered so far have been mudbrick mastabas of the First Dynasty 'palace façade' style and their simpler Second Dynasty successors; located along the northeastern fringe of the necropolis, and now largely sanded over, they are currently off-limits. Instead, most visitors begin with the Third Dynasty Step Pyramid complex, constructed for **Djoser** around 2650 BC.

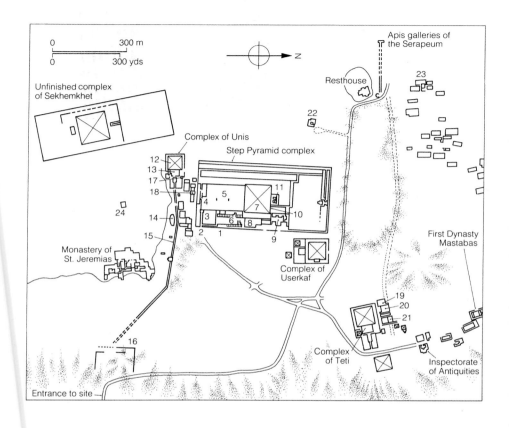

- 0 — 300 m
- 0 — 300 yds

z

Unfinished complex of Sekhemkhet

Complex of Unis

Step Pyramid complex

Resthouse

Apis galleries of the Serapeum

23

22

24

12
13
17
18
14
15

5
4
11
7
3
6 8
2
1
10
9

First Dynasty Mastabas

Monastery of St. Jeremias

Complex of Userkaf

Complex of Teti

19
20
21

Inspectorate of Antiquities

16

Entrance to site

STEP PYRAMID COMPLEX

Representing the transition from the use of traditional, perishable, building materials to the monumental use of stone, the complex was conceived by the royal architect Imhotep to ensure his master's safe transition into the afterlife. Described by Manetho as 'the inventor of the art of building with hewn stone', **Imhotep** was later deified for his genius. A modern-day genius, the French archaeologist Jean-Philippe Lauer, has been responsible for the continuing excavation and reconstruction of the site over the past half-century.

Beside the pyramid itself the complex comprises a mortuary temple together with courts and chapels, all intended to enable the dead monarch to continue to

9. House of the North; 10. Serdab; 11. Mortuary Temple.
Complex of Unis
12. Pyramid; 13. Mortuary Temple; 14. Boat pit; 15. Causeway; 16. Valley Temple.
Private Tombs
17. Amun-Tefnakhte; 18. Idut; 19. Kereruka; 20. Magemni; 21. Ankhmahor; 22. Akhethotep and Ptahhotep; 23. Ti; 24. Horemheb.

perform the rituals of kingship in the next world. Covering an area of 15 ha (37 acres), the whole was enclosed by a massive recessed limestone wall, over 10 m (33 ft) in height, to exclude the gaze of the general populace. Of its fourteen door niches, only one—just north of the southeast corner—was functional, the other being mere dummies: like many other features in the complex, they were intended to fulfil a magical, rather than a practical role. The genuine entrance displays another striking dummy feature in the immovable stone 'doorleaves' which appear to rest in the open position against the vestibule walls.

Throughout the complex earlier architectural forms and elements are replicated in stone, for example in the imitation log ceiling of the entrance passage and the ribbed columns of the adjacent colonnade. Here, the builders' dedication to tradition is again apparent in the use of tongue walls to engage the columns to the side walls, faithfully reproducing the original form. Similarly, only small limestone blocks are employed, possibly reflecting a preference for the familiar scale of mud bricks. The colonnade was originally roofed with stone slabs and lit by slits near the roof; these may have directed light onto statues located in the recesses formed by the engaged columns.

Emerging from the colonnade, the visitor enters a large court with the Step Pyramid located at its northern end. Immediately ahead, in the southwest corner of the enclosure, are the remains of a building in dressed limestone surmounted by a frieze of royal cobras. This may have served as the offering chapel of a large mastaba known as the **Southern Tomb**, whose superstructure is mainly contained within the enclosure wall. The function of this building remains a mystery, for although the deep vertical shaft leads to a granite burial chamber, this is far too small to have accommodated an adult burial. As the reliefs found in the surrounding galleries show the king involved in various rites, it may have served some ritual purpose.

The small courtyard to the east has been identified as a replica of that used for the *Heb-Sed* or Jubilee festival during the king's lifetime. It is unique to the Step Pyramid complex, and imitations of organic elements are again much in evidence as, due to their ephemeral nature, such celebrations were generally conducted in temporary accommodation specially constructed for the occasion. Originating in Egypt's remote antiquity, the festival was a symbolic renewal of the king's strength and virility, on which depended the continued prosperity of the nation. Although normally held about every 30 years, there was no hard and fast rule governing their frequency, and many later kings celebrated several Jubilees during their reigns. It is known that one of the rites involved required the monarch, accompanied by priests, to run a fixed course, and it has been suggested that the curious B-shaped structures outside in the main court may have marked out the track.

The **Jubilee court** itself was the scene of the culmination of the ceremony, when the king was crowned twice as the ruler of the Two Lands: the double dais for this rite survives at its southern end. The twin rows of dummy chapels represent the shrines of Upper Egypt (on the west) and Lower Egypt (on the east). Organic prototypes are clearly recognizable in the façades of the western chapels, which comprise three engaged fluted columns, with pendant leaf capitals, supporting a curved cornice whose ends join two broad pilasters. It is interesting to contrast these graceful forms, evolved from nature, with the stark outline of the Step Pyramid, conceived for stone, which rises up behind them.

To the north of the Jubilee court are two low rectangular buildings of unknown function commonly referred to as the **House of the North** and the **House of the South** because the engaged columns on the east walls of their respective courtyards represent the papyrus of Lower Egypt and the lotus of Upper Egypt. The southern façade of each structure is decorated with four engaged fluted columns flanked by pilasters and supporting a curved cornice. The asymmetrically-placed doorway, surmounted by a *kheker*-frieze representing bundles of reeds tied together, leads by way of a narrow bending corridor with imitation log ceiling to a cruciform sanctuary equipped with statue niches. At one time it was believed that these buildings were tombs for Djoser's daughters, but modern theory favours the idea that they represent the archaic shrines of Upper and Lower Egypt which were located at Hieraconpolis, now Kom el-Ahmar, and at Buto—Tell el-Fara'in—in the Delta.

As the final resting place of the king, the **Step Pyramid** itself is the natural focus of the complex. Egypt's first pyramid, it was also the world's first monumental stone building. The experimental nature of the scheme is highlighted by the fact that there were no fewer than six changes of plan during its construction, while the employment of small stone blocks and wooden supports suggests an attitude of caution among its builders.

It appears that the original plan was to construct a simple stone mastaba, but this was subsequently enlarged in successive stages. Next a step was added, and the design was expanded to form first a four-stepped, and finally a six-stepped pyramid. Measuring 60 m (197 ft) in height, with base measurements of 140 m (459 ft) by 118 m (387 ft), the ground plan, as in a mastaba, remained rectangular. Like a mastaba, the substructure (inaccessible due to the danger of collapse) has a subterranean **burial chamber**—in this case of pink Aswan granite—at the bottom of

Reconstructed panel of blue faience tiles from the subterranean chambers of the Step Pyramid. (Old Kingdom, Third Dynasty). Egyptian Museum, Cairo.

a deep shaft. Less usually, however, it is surrounded by a maze of interconnecting chambers and passages; finds of coffins in these suggest that they served as tombs for other members of the royal family. Large areas of the corridor walls and doorways were decorated with panels of small blue-glazed tiles imitating wall-hangings of reed matting; one of these has been reconstructed in the Egyptian Museum.

Access to the underground levels was via an entrance passage running from the mortuary temple on the northern side of the pyramid. This temple, now very ruined, was the focus of the deceased monarch's mortuary cult, replacing the offering chapel of the earlier mastabas. Nearby is the **serdab**, a sealed chamber of finely dressed limestone containing a statue of the king. Two holes cut in the serdab's face may have been intended to allow the statue, inhabited by Djoser's spirit, to inhale the incense of worship, or perhaps to gaze out at the 'everlasting' circumpolar stars which he was destined to join. Although the statue is a replica, the original having been removed to the Egyptian Museum, it is a curiously moving experience to peer through the holes and into the blankness of those empty sockets which have kept sightless vigil for almost five millennia.

PYRAMID OF UNIS

The pyramid complex of Unis, first king of the Fifth Dynasty, is located close to the southwest corner of the Step Pyramid enclosure. With an original height of only 43 m (141 ft), it is much smaller than its neighbour, and also in a far worse state of preservation, having been constructed of a rubble core with a polished limestone casing. Dilapidation must have set in as early as the New Kingdom, as an inscription on the south face records a restoration carried out under **Khaemwese**, High Priest of Ptah and a son of Ramesses II, whose enthusiasm for such work has earned him the modern nickname of the 'Egyptologist Prince'. However unprepossessing its exterior, an exploration of the pyramid's well-preserved underground chambers is most rewarding. Access to these is via a descending passage located in the pavement on the

41

Saqqara, Pyramid of Unis: Burial chamber. (Old Kingdom, Fifth Dynasty).

north of the pyramid. At the time of burial, this corridor was blocked by a series of three granite portcullis stones, whose sockets are still visible in the roof. The passage terminates in a square vestibule with a rectangular room containing three statue niches on the east, and the **burial chamber** on the west. Constructed in fine white limestone and alabaster, this remarkable room is dominated by a large rectangular sarcophagus occupying its western end. The high gabled ceiling is covered with five-pointed stars, reminders of the king's celestial destiny, incised in the stone and inlaid with blue pigment. The chamber walls are decorated in the same fashion with columns of hieroglyphic inscriptions known as the Pyramid Texts. Comprising a collection of over 200 magical spells concerning the death and rebirth of the divine king, these inscriptions are the first written versions of the ancient ritual chants from which much later funerary literature derived.

Although parts of Unis' valley temple survive, the mortuary temple is largely ruined; however, the **causeway** which linked the two is the best preserved excavated to date, the surviving section extending for over 700 m (765 yds). Comprising a covered corridor approximately 600 m (656 yds) long, the causeway was roofed with thick slabs projecting from either side to leave a central gap where light could penetrate. The interior walls were covered with reliefs, fragments of which survive, depicting a wide range of subjects including the transport of granite palm columns from Aswan for Unis' mortuary temple; these are now displayed in the Egyptian Museum. Just north of the temple lies the enormous **shaft tomb** of the Saite general **Amun-Tefnakhte**, absolutely the last word in tomb security. Readers should spare a thought for its excavators, who—having painstakingly removed all the sand from the shaft—discovered that the general had been buried without any grave goods at all! Nearby is a cluster of Fifth Dynasty mastabas belonging to members of Unis' court, including that of his daughter **Idut**, which has some finely-carved reliefs.

MASTABA TOMBS

The best-known mastabas at Saqqara are those associated with the pyramid of the Sixth Dynasty king Teti. By far the most famous of these belonged to Teti's son-in-law **Mereruka**; built in fine limestone and comprising over thirty rooms, it incorporated separate funerary suites for his wife Seshseshet and son Meri-Teti. At the heart of the mastaba is an impressive pillared **offering chapel** with a false door, from which a *ka*-statue of the tomb owner is shown emerging to receive the offerings placed on the offering-table before him. Typically, this takes the form of the *hetep*-sign—representing a loaf of bread placed on a

Mastaba of
Mereruka
1. Entrance
2. Tomb of Meri-Teti
3. Serdab
4. Shaft
5. Offering chapel
6. False Door with
   Ka-statue
7. Tomb of
Seshseshet

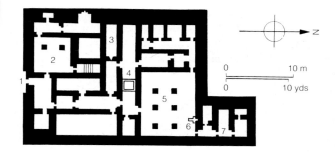

mat—and symbolizes a gift, implying also a wish for contentment or satisfaction. Like most of the rooms in the mastaba, this chamber has delicately-carved raised reliefs depicting funerary scenes and episodes from domestic and working life. That the tomb was completed hurriedly is confirmed in another room where these exquisite carvings are replaced by hastily-executed paintings; an interesting detail here is the use of paint to imitate granite (a more expensive and prestigious stone) on the pillars. Other tombs in the vicinity include those of the vizier **Ankhmahor**, well-known for its unusual reliefs of surgical operations, and **Kagemni**, overseer of Teti's pyramid. Like that of Unis, this is largely destroyed above ground while retaining well-preserved subterranean chambers of polished black granite inscribed with Pyramid Texts.

To the west, beyond the ruined Fifth Dynasty pyramid of Userkaf and close to the resthouse, are two fine Fifth Dynasty mastabas, the first of which belonged to two officials, **Akhethotep** and his son **Ptahhotep**, and the second to the overseer of the pyramids of Ti; both boast magnificent reliefs. The **tomb of Ti** is one of the best preserved and most interesting in the necropolis. Approached by a long ramp, its portico gives onto a spacious pillared court from which a shaft descends, enabling the visitor to investigate the undecorated **burial chamber** with its massive sarcophagus. From the southwest corner of the court a narrow corridor decorated with offering reliefs leads, past the false door of Ti's wife, to the rectangular pillared **offering chapel**. Here one can peer through small openings into the **serdab** to be met by

44

Saqqara, Mastaba of Mereruka: Offering chapel with false door containing a ka-statue of the deceased. (Old Kingdom, Sixth Dynasty).

Saqqara, Mastaba of Kagemni: Detail of relief carving. (Old Kingdom, Sixth Dynasty).

the self-satisfied gaze of Ti himself—or, rather, a replica of his statue, the original having been removed to the Egyptian Museum.

THE SERAPEUM

In antiquity, large areas of north Saqqara were given over to vast, sprawling catacombs where the mummified remains of the sacred animals associated with various religious cults were interred. Excavations have uncovered among others galleries of embalmed cats, jackals, falcons, ibises and baboons. However, the only animal catacombs which can be visited at present belonged to the **Serapeum**, the cult temple of the sacred **Apis bulls** which were revered as manifestations of the god Osiris. Dating from the New Kingdom onward, the accessible galleries belong to the Late and Ptolemaic periods, when the cult was at the height of its popularity. The entrance to the galleries is down a long staircase leading into a hall lined with niches for votive stelae. The **main gallery**, running east to west, has 28 side-chambers, averaging 9.5 m (31 ft) in height, many of which still contain the huge monolithic sarcophagi in which the mummified bulls were interred. The most ornate example can be found at the westernmost end of the gallery, on the right; steps are provided to enable the visitor to examine its elaborate palace-façade decoration in detail.

SOUTH SAQQARA AND DAHS-HUR

On a clear day, the view from the Saqqara plateau is magnificent, taking in almost the whole sweep of the Memphite necropolis from Giza, 25 km (15 miles) to the north, to Dahshur, 12 km (7 miles) further south. Immediately south of the pyramid of Unis is a concentration of New Kingdom stone-built tombs, the most important of which excavated to date belonged to the general (later king) **Horemheb**, last ruler of the Eighteenth Dynasty. Access is restricted at present, as archaeological work continues in the area. Approximately 3 km (2 miles) further south, beyond a group of Fifth and Sixth Dynasty pyramids, looms the unmistakable oblong silhouette of the **Mastabet el-Fara'un** ('Pharaoh's Bench') built by **Shepseskaf** of the Fourth Dynasty, who forsook the pyramid tradition in favour of this massive sarcophagus-shaped limestone tomb. To the east is the small Sixth Dynasty **pyramid of Pepi II**.

The **cemetery of Dahshur** lies in a military zone and special permits are currently required to visit. It is best known for two important Fourth Dynasty monuments, both the work of Sneferu, which together with the pyramid of his predecessor Huni at Meidum, mark the transition from the stepped pyramid to the true pyramid form. The northern pyramid, often referred to as the **Red Pyramid**, was the first to be planned as a true pyramid; the very low angle of incline—43°2′ as opposed to the 52° generally employed in later pyramids—suggest caution on the part of its builders. The distinctive outline of its partner, the '**Bent Pyramid**', caused by a dramatic change in this angle (from 54°27′ to 43°22′) may have been due to a similar crisis of confidence, though it has been convincingly argued that it was simply done to expedite completion of the monument on Sneferu's demise.

About 14 km (9 miles) north of Saqqara, the sites of Abusir and Abu Ghurab are rather difficult to reach and lacking in well-preserved monuments, although the intrepid will find that they have a desolate charm all of their own. Abusir once boasted fourteen pyramids, of which only four Fifth Dynasty examples survive, all in a poor state of preservation. Nearby, however, is the well-preserved Fifth Dynasty mastaba of **Ptahshepses**, which is noteworthy for a fine pair of lotus bud capitals, the earliest examples to survive.

Situated another 2 km (1 mile) on foot across the desert are the sun temples of Abu Ghurab, the work of two Fifth dynasty monarchs, **Niuserre** and **Userkaf**. Although both are mostly ruined, parts of Niuserre's complex survive. Oriented east to west, as befits a solar temple, the heart of the complex was an elevated temple with an open court housing a huge masonry obelisk, connected to a valley temple by means of a covered causeway, rather in the manner of contemporary pyramids.

ABUSIR AND ABU GHURAB

GIZA

Of the seven wonders of the ancient world, only the Pyramids substantially survive in their original location, standing aloof and inscrutable upon the Giza plateau 18 km (11 miles) west of cental Cairo. Built in the middle of the Fourth Dynasty when the power of the divine kings was at its zenith, they testify to the consummate efficiency of the Old Kingdom administrators who were able to organize such vast undertakings so effectively. All three Giza monuments conform to the established pattern of the classic pyramid complex: a pyramid tomb, mortuary temple, causeway and valley temple. Each also has at least one subsidiary pyramid, which probably served as resting places for elevated female members of the royal family.

The Giza necropolis
1. Subsidiary pyramids
2. Boat pits
3. Tomb of Meresankh III

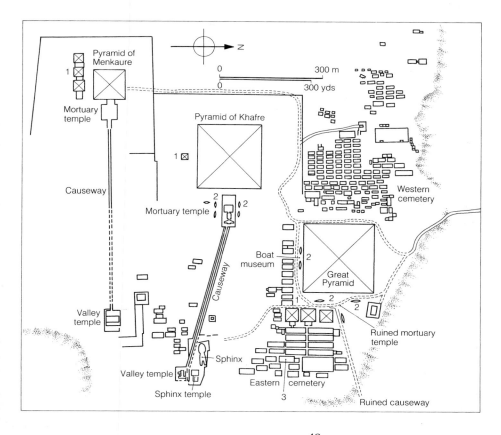

THE GREAT PYRAMID

The earliest, largest and most important of the group is the pyramid of **Khufu**, generally known as the **Great Pyramid**. Originally measuring 146 m (479 ft) in height, with a 230 m² (2,475 ft²) base and an angle of incline of 51°50′, it was built of solid masonry faced with fine white limestone from the royal quarries at Tura, near modern Helwan. Over 2.3 million stone blocks, averaging 2,500 kgs (2.5 tons) in weight, were used in its construction—assuming that the project was completed during Khufu's 23–year reign, a minimum of 100,000 such blocks a year would have had to pass through the hands of quarrymen, transporters, masons and builders. Exactly how this was achieved is unclear; Herodotus, writing some 2,000 years after the event, asserts in his *Histories* that a workforce of 100,000 was employed, but modern studies suggest that it would have been impracticable to accommodate such a number of workers on the site.

Although the exterior of the Great Pyramid seems to have been built according to the original plan, several alterations to its interior arrangements were carried out during construction. Situated roughly 18 m (59 ft) above ground level, the concealed entrance led onto a corridor descending to an unfinished chamber cut into the bedrock and presumably originally intended as the burial chamber; a blind passage leading from this room implies that further chambers were planned. After the abandonment of this subterranean chamber, work began on a new ascending corridor. Following the burial, the entrance to this, cut in the roof of the descending corridor, was closed with a stone slab which completely concealed the opening. This raises the question of whether the underground chamber was constructed purely as an elaborate security precaution, an architectural red herring to throw tomb robbers off the scent. The ascending corridor leads first to another unfinished room, popularly known as the **Queen's Chamber**, and then, via the Grand Gallery, to the burial chamber.

The **Grand Gallery** of the Great Pyramid must rank as one of the outstanding architectural achievements not only of Egypt, but of the world. With a length of 47 m

Aerial view of the Giza necropolis.

(154 ft) and height of 8.5 m (27 ft), its magnificent corbelled roof is unrivalled in scale and in the ingenuity of its construction, which ensures the even distribution of pressure from the weight of masonry above. The purpose of such a spectacularly high chamber buried deep within the pyramid has been the topic of much debate, but at least part of its function must have been to accommodate the huge granite plugs used to block the ascending corridor after the burial; three of these plugs remain *in situ* at its lower end. The narrow passage descending from the bottom of the gallery was probably used as an escape route by the workmen responsible for closing the corridor. The burial chamber, known as the **King's Chamber**, is reached via a low passage at the top of the Grand Gallery, which leads into a small anteroom equipped with slots for

portcullis stones. The undecorated burial chamber, built of red granite, measures 5.2 m (17 ft) by 10.8 m (35 ft) and is 5.8 m (19 ft) high; an empty granite sarcophagus rests close to the west wall. Above the flat ceiling are five relieving chambers, designed to protect it from the pressure of the masonry above.

Apart from the pyramid, the rest of Khufu's complex has fared badly—only faint traces of the mortuary temple can be found in the pavement on the east of the pyramid, and the causeway and valley temple have all but disappeared, the latter buried under the nearby village of Nazlet el-Simman. However, the five **boat pits** around the pyramid have been well preserved, and in 1954 the southeastern pit yielded a complete river vessel; painstakingly restored, it is now displayed in the special museum erected over its pit. A remarkable example of ancient design and craftsmanship, it should on no account be missed.

Numerous subsidiary burials are associated with the Great Pyramid, notably the three queens' pyramids to the east. Khufu also planned extensive cemeteries to the east and west of his pyramid; intended to accommodate the burials of close family members and high officials, the great stone mastabas are laid out in regular streets, giving an orderly impression very different from the haphazard clusters of tombs normally found around royal pyramids. However, many of the Old Kingdom burials in these cemeteries actually date to later reigns, for example the fine **tomb of Meresankh III**, a queen of Khufu's grandson Khafre. One of the most interesting tombs accessible at present, it is notable for an unusually large statue niche accommodating multiple statues of Meresankh, her mother and her daughter. Tombs continued to be built in the Giza necropolis as late as the Saite period, and although few are currently open, a walk around the cemeteries can shed illumination on the development of funerary architecture, especially during the late Old Kingdom. Particularly worthy of note are the early examples of mudbrick vaulting found in the western cemetery and the fine porticoed tomb chapels typical of the Sixth Dynasty.

Giza, Tomb of Meresankh III: Detail of multiple statues of Meresankh and her female relatives. (Old Kingdom, Fourth Dynasty).

THE PYRAMID OF KHAFRE

The second pyramid, constructed for Khafre, is slightly smaller than the Great Pyramid, measuring 136.5 m (447 ft) in height with an inclination of 52°20', and a base measurement of 210.5 m (690 ft). It has two entrances, both on the north side, one in the pyramid face approximately 16 m (52 ft) above ground level and the other in the pavement below; both lead to an undecorated **burial chamber** cut into the bedrock, a duplication which may indicate a change of plan during construction. The chamber itself has a gabled roof of limestone slabs and at the western end a large granite sarcophagus is set into the floor; the broken lid lies nearby, exactly as it was found by the Italian explorer Giovanni Belzoni in 1818. One of the more colourful characters in the history of Egyptology, the erstwhile circus strongman recorded his discovery in the conspicuous graffito on the south wall.

The chief point of interest in Khafre's pyramid, however, is the substantial portion of well-preserved limestone casing which survives at its apex, giving some impression of the monument's original magnificent appearance. At the base, the dazzling white of the polished limestone was set off by a course of red granite blocks probably intended to guard against slippage. The same combination of stone was employed in the **mortuary temple**, which though largely ruined must originally have been an impressive structure. Located on the east side of the pyramid, its central feature was an open court with niches which may have held royal statues, while the carved hieroglyphic inscriptions are among the earliest examples of sunk relief in Egypt.

In contrast, the **valley temple** is in an excellent state of preservation. Constructed of limestone completely faced with red granite, this important building stands as testament to the skill of the Fourth Dynasty masons who—using only stone and copper tools—could work this hard stone to such a high degree of accuracy and finish. The temple layout is uncomplicated: square in plan, with exterior battered walls, its twin entrances lead into a transverse vestibule giving on to a T-shaped pillared hall. Relying on simplicity and mass to create a sense of monumentality, the austerity of its design is softened by the rich contrast between the red granite walls and pillars and the whiteness of the polished alabaster floor. Originally roofed with stone slabs, oblique slits cut into the junction of the wall and ceiling enabled light from above to illuminate royal statues located in the emplacements around the walls. When excavated, a large number of sculptures were found in the temple, including the famous diorite figure of Khafre now in the Egyptian Museum.

A doorway in the northwest corner of the temple leads into the lower end of Khafre's covered causeway, part of which has recently been restored. Beside it looms the colossal form of the **Great Sphinx**, cut from an outcrop of limestone left by the builders of the Great Pyramid. The precise significance of the Sphinx is obscure, but as the features were clearly intended to represent Khafre himself, it may have served as guardian of his funerary complex. The small Fourth Dynasty temple in front of it is largely destroyed, but surviving between its front paws is an altar and votive stele of **Thutmose IV**, recounting the New Kingdom monarch's fulfilment of a vow to the Sphinx to clear away the sand which had engulfed it.

Giza, Valley Temple of Khafre: Interior. (Old Kingdom, Fourth Dynasty).

PYRAMID OF MENKAURE

The third complex of the group belonged to Menkaure, successor to Khafre. At 66 m (216 ft), his pyramid is less than half the height of his predecessor's, graphically reflecting the ongoing decline in centralised power. Menkaure's death was clearly unexpected, as many parts of the complex were either left unfinished or were hastily completed in inferior materials; work on the pyramid's red granite casing, for example, was abandoned after just 16 courses had been completed. Once again, the internal arrangements had undergone revision, and incorporate some innovatory features including a subsidiary chamber possibly intended to accommodate the royal canopic jars. The remainder of the complex is badly ruined, although excavation of the valley temple yielded some fine group sculptures now in the Egyptian Museum.

MIDDLE EGYPT

The route south from Cairo follows the course of the Nile valley, its green cultivated fringes hemmed in on the west by the desert and on the east by high limestone cliffs dotted with rock-cut tombs dating from the Old to the Middle Kingdom. Such landscapes are typical of Middle Egypt, which stretches from ancient Memphis in the north to modern Assiut in the south. The area first assumed importance when, following the collapse of the Memphite throne during the First Intermediate Period, the rulers of the Ninth and Tenth Dynasties established their capital at Heracleopolis, near modern-day Beni Suef. During the Middle Kingdom, the kings of the Theban Twelfth Dynasty chose Middle Egypt for their capital of Ittawy, of which nothing now remains, save two ruined pyramids in its necropolis at Lisht. Bringing order out of chaos, they set about reviving the local economy, particularly in the Fayyum, where ambitious drainage and land reclamation projects were set in motion. Something of a backwater during the early New Kingdom, Middle Egypt entered the limelight once more during the Eighteenth Dynasty when the heretic Pharaoh Akhenaten selected it as the location of his capital Akhetaten. Although the city was abandoned upon his demise, the region continued to prosper, especially in the Fayyum which grew in importance as an autonomous region supporting many flourishing towns.

MEIDUM

Probably begun for **Huni**, the last king of the Third Dynasty, and completed by his succesor **Sneferu**, the Meidum pyramid not only bridged the gap between the stepped and true pyramids, but was also the first to incorporate the elements of mortuary temple, causeway and valley temple which became standard in later complexes. Originally conceived as a seven-stepped pyramid, an eighth step was added before it was finally decided to

(Opposite)
Ashmunein: Colossal figure of Thoth in the form of a baboon. (New Kingdom, Eighteenth Dynasty).

fill in the steps and case the whole structure. The result was a true pyramid with a base measurement of 147 m (482 ft), height of 93.5 m (307 ft) and angle of incline of 51°50′. Unfortunately, the foundations were ill-constructed and this, compounded by the fact that the original stepped faces were too smooth to bond with the later filling, caused the pyramid to collapse in antiquity, creating the huge mound of debris visible around its base. The entrance, located in the north face 18.5 m (60 ft) above ground level, opens onto a straight corridor which plunges 57 m (187 ft) down into the bedrock. Partly cut into the rock, the tiny **burial chamber** has a fine high corbelled roof, now the haunt of bats. Outside, the small, simple **mortuary temple** abuts the pyramid's east face, and the course of the causeway can be traced, although the valley temple has been lost under the surrounding cultivation. To the north of the pyramid, the customary nobles' tombs include a large mudbrick **mastaba** (no. 17) with a fine limestone burial chamber, and the mastabas of **Nefermaat** and **Rahotep** which have provided some of the finest pieces in the Egyptian Museum.

THE FAYYUM

Located approximately 70 km (43 miles) southwest of Cairo, the Fayyum is a large, fertile semi-oasis area watered by an arm of the Nile called the *Bahr Yussef* or 'Joseph's River'. A natural depression, the oasis was once occupied by a vast lake known in classical times as Lake Moeris; today's much reduced remnant, Lake Qarun, occupies the northwestern part of the region. As early as the Twelfth Dynasty, programmes of drainage and land reclamation were directed at increasing the area's agricultural productivity; now, as then, the Fayyum remains an important centre of market gardening, abounding in orchards and olive groves, some of them laid out in the time of the Ptolemies, under whom it enjoyed its second great period of prosperity. It is for this reason that, despite its ancient origins, most of the remains visible today date from the Graeco-Roman period. A typical example is the town of Karanis at Kom Ushim, where the visitor can wander ankle-deep in ancient potsherds among the ruined houses and temples, one of which was dedicated to Pnephenos and Petesuchos, forms of the crocodile god **Sobek**. As the local deity, Sobek naturally had his own cult centre at Crocodilopolis (near Medinet el-Fayyum) where one can visit what remains of the pool which housed the sacred reptiles. Fayyum was already a sightseeing destination in the Graeco-Roman era, and a trip to feed the crocodiles was a 'must' on every tourist itinerary, as was a visit to the 'Labyrinth' described by Herodotus, and by Strabo in his *Geographica*. In reality, this was what survived of the mortuary temple attached to the Middle Kingdom pyramid of **Amenemhat III** at Hawara, comprising a confusing warren of chapels and corridors; today it is almost completely destroyed, like the pyramid of which only the mudbrick core remains.

Situated approximately 20 km (12 miles) south of the provincial capital of El-Minya, the tombs of Beni Hassan are located high in the limestone cliffs on the east bank of the Nile. They are reached by a ferry crossing followed by a stiff climb which is amply repaid by a breathtaking panorama of the river and the surrounding countryside, which can be truly spectacular at sunset. There are 39 rock-cut tombs in all, arranged in terraces along the bluff; traces of the causeways used for the funeral rites can be discerned sloping towards the valley floor. Several of the tombs belonged to rulers and high officials of the Oryx district, four of which are presently open to the public: two from the Eleventh Dynasty (nos. 15 and 17, belonging to **Baqet** and **Khety**) and two from the Twelfth (nos. 2 and 3, belonging to **Amenemhat** and **Khnumhotep II**).

Although all four are similar in plan, the Eleventh Dynasty tombs simply comprise a courtyard and a large columned hall, while the Twelfth Dynasty monuments are more elaborate, incorporating such refinements as entrance porticoes, statue niches and vaulted ceilings. Both types clearly derive from domestic prototypes, underlining the tomb's function as a 'house of eternity'. Both the lotus columns found in the Eleventh Dynasty tombs and the fluted polygonal columns used in those of the Twelfth

BENI HASSAN

Tomb of Khety, Beni Hassan
1. Chapel
2. Shafts
3. False Door stele

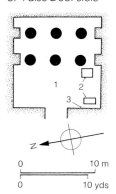

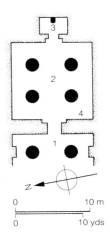

(*Above*) Tomb of
Amenemhat, Beni
Hassan
1. Portico
2. Chapel
3. Statue niche
4. False Door stele

Dynasty are copies of the wooden columns employed in houses, while the painted ceilings of the later tombs imitate the geometrically patterned mats which would be hung in the home. An interesting detail is that, because of the tombs' unusual location on the east bank, the false door stelae which would usually be situated at the far end of the chapel have had to be resited just inside the entrance on the west wall.

The principal attraction of the Beni Hassan tombs,

Beni Hassan, Tomb
of Amenemhat:
Chapel with statue
niche. (Middle
Kingdom, Twelfth
Dynasty).

however, is the variety of lively wall paintings depicting life during the First Intermediate Period and Middle Kingdom. The contemporary political instability is graphically illustrated by the preponderance of martial scenes— battles, a siege—and depictions of military exercises, like wrestling, although gentler pursuits such as industrial and agricultural activities, dancing and children's games are also shown. The best known examples are in the tomb of **Khnumhotep**, where close inspection reveals many charming details, especially in the marvellous hunting scenes where numerous species of birds and animals are depicted in meticulous detail.

The important New Kingdom site of El-Amarna is located approximately 45 km (28 miles) south of Beni Hassan on the east bank of the Nile, again reached by the local ferry. Established by **Akhenaten** to serve as the country's political capital and the cult centre of his solar deity, the **Aten**, the site of **Akhetaten** ('Horizon of the Aten') consists of a crescent-shaped plain roughly 10 km (6 miles) long by 5 km (3 miles) deep, facing the river and enclosed by cliffs which form a natural amphitheatre. Its boundaries, defined by stelae proclaiming the king's vow never to be buried elsewhere, encompassed an area of some 290 km^2 (112 miles^2), including a large area of arable land on the Nile's west bank. Akhetaten's significance to archaeologists lies in the fact that it was built on virgin soil and inhabited for little more than 15 years, sparing it the destruction that would have resulted from continuous habitation. Aside from the huge Aten Temple with its vast open-air court, excavations in the city centre have identified royal palaces, administrative quarters and residential districts as well as workshops; one of these, the studio of the sculptor Thutmose, yielded several masterpieces of Amarnan art, notably the famous head of Akhenaten's queen **Nefertiti** now in the Berlin Museum. The systematic demolition of the city following the collapse of the Atenist revolution was, however, so thorough that few of the surviving remains are likely to be recognizable to the visitor. Nonetheless, the numerous

EL-AMARNA

El-Amarna, South
Palace: Fragment of
painted pavement.
Similar paintings
adorned the North
Palace. Egyptian
Museum, Cairo.
(New Kingdom,
Eighteenth Dynasty).

architectural fragments, painted plaster and glazed
faience tiles recovered from the site and displayed in
museums around the world provide tantalising glimpses of
elegant, airy homes and sumptuous palaces, all decorated
in the graceful, flowing Amarna style.

El-Amarna, North
Palace
1. Entrance
2. Court
3. Altar court
4. Pool
5. Stabling
6. Garden
7. Hypostyle hall
8. Throne room

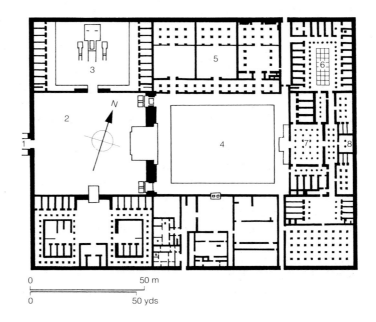

```
0                    50 m

0                    50 yds
```

NORTH PALACE

One such would have been the North Palace, located in
the city's northern suburb. Built of plastered and painted
mudbrick and encrusted with colourful faience tile panels,
its purpose is somewhat unclear; as no living quarters have
been identified, it may have served purely as a res. ouse
or pleasure-palace. The entrance, on the south, led into
an open court with a gateway on the west side leading into
a second court containing open-air altars for the worship
of the Aten. At the heart of the complex was a large pool,
while the northwest corner was occupied by a small
garden, at its centre a small pond, or perhaps a sunken
flower bed, surrounded by a colonnade; the stone column
bases are still visible. The tiny cubicles around it were
decorated with detailed paintings of birds, prompting the
suggestion that they might have served as aviaries.

NORTHERN TOMBS

High in the cliff face nearby, the Northern Tombs are a
group of six rock-cut tombs belonging to court officials.
Comprising a courtyard, one or more pillared halls and a
statue niche, they bear many architectural similarities to
their counterparts in the Theban necropolis. Here,
however, the decoration is dramatically different, with
sunk reliefs in the distinctive Amarna style. The tomb
owners' devotion to Akhenaten is underlined in the
numerous representations of the king and the royal
family, often shown worshipping the Aten in the form of a
sun-disc whose long rays extend into hands offering life
and blessings. Most of these images, along with the names
of Akhenaten, Nefertiti and the Aten, were subsequently
defaced during the organized destruction of Akhetaten
carried out under Horemheb. One of the better preserved
examples is the tomb of **Meryre I**, who served his divine
master as high priest of the Aten and is shown around the
walls worshipping and being rewarded by the king, in
addition to accompanying the royal family on a visit to the
Aten temple. The drawing of the temple, rendered in a
typically Egyptian combination of plan and elevation, is
particularly interesting. Many of the city's other buildings
are also depicted, including the palace (note the standing

(*Above*) El-Amarna, Northern Tombs: Tomb of Meryre I. Outer chapel looking towards the unfinished inner chambers. (New Kingdom, Eighteenth Dynasty).

(*Right*) El-Amarna, Northern Tombs: Tomb of Meryre I. Detail of relief – Blind Musicians. (New Kingdom, Eighteenth Dynasty).

statues of Akhenaten flanking the doorways) and the harbour, together with gardens, storehouses and cattle sheds. On the west wall, just to the south of the doorway, the royal family are shown beneath a unique representation of a rainbow; the carving of **blind musicians** in the sub-register below is exceptionally sensitive.

Like many other Amarnan monuments, the tomb of Meryre was left unfinished when the city was abandoned, allowing the modern visitor an insight into the processes of New Kingdom tomb cutting techniques. Here, the main hall had already been completely carved and painted while the second, planned as a small chapel with four columns, had been only partly cut; a staircase cut by the masons to facilitate their work on the ceiling and capitals remains *in situ*, while what was to be come the statue niche had only just begun to be roughly hacked out.

Less visited, a second group, the **Southern Tombs**, exists to the south, while the tomb planned for Akhenaten is located some 12 km (7½ miles) away in the Royal Wadi.

The ruined city of Ashmunein, ancient Hermopolis Magna, lies approximately 12 km (7½ miles) northwest of the district capital Mellawi, which has a small antiquities museum, open every morning except Wednesday. Known to the ancient Egyptians as *Khmun*—'eight-town'—after eight primeval deities said to have appeared there, it was also the cult centre of the god **Thoth**, patron of learning and medicine. Thoth was generally worshipped either in the form of an ibis or a baboon, and so it is appropriate that visitors to Ashmunein are greeted by a pair of colossal baboon statues which once graced his temple. Part of the temple's mudbrick enclosure wall can still be seen, and carved blocks dating from various reigns are scattered around the site, which is largely overgrown and waterlogged. Extensive reuse of material taken from buildings on site is evident in the number of blocks recarved in the style of another period, and in the foundations of the Christian basilica, which largely consist of column drums taken from earlier structures. The only substantially preserved building on the site, it was built

63

early in the Christian era and is the sole surviving example of its type in Egypt. The blocks for its construction were taken from a Ptolemaic temple of the royal cult whose architrave, carved with a dedicatory inscription in Greek, lies nearby.

TUNA EL-GEBEL

The necropolis of Ashmunein, Tuna el-Gebel, is situated in the desert some 7 km (4 miles) west of the city. Like many towns of the region, Hermopolis Magna enjoyed great prosperity in late antiquity, not least because as the cult centre of Thoth—worshipped by the Greeks as Hermes Trismegistos ('Thrice-great Hermes')—it became an important centre of pilgrimage. This is reflected in the cemetery, where all the monuments so far excavated date to the Late and Graeco-Roman periods. Located in the cliffs just outside, however, is a reminder of an earlier era in the form of one of the 14 boundary stelae of Akhenaten's city Akhetaten. Reached by a scramble up a sandy slope, the stele depicts Akhenaten and Nefertiti worshipping the Aten; beside it are broken statues of the royal family.

Tuna el-Gebel: Tomb of Petosiris. (Ptolemaic period).

The necropolis itself is a well-preserved Greek period city of the dead, with house-like tombs and chapels tidily arranged in streets. Many of the buildings incorporate dummy features imitating contemporary domestic architecture, such as stone lattice windows or plaster stonework. The most remarkable monument, however, is the family tomb of **Petosiris**, high priest of Thoth, built during the reign of **Philip Arrhidaeus**. Appropriately enough, it takes the form of a small temple, comprising a portico, a chapel and underground burial chambers. Now heavily restored, the pretty floral capitals of the pillared portico were originally painted in bright colours; on the screen walls below, Petosiris is represented offering to Thoth in his ibis and baboon forms.

Inside the portico are some interesting raised reliefs of industrial and agricultural scenes, executed in a bizarre mixture of Egyptian and Greek styles; not great art by any stretch of the imagination, they nonetheless possess an unusual charm and vigour. Inside the chapel this innovatory style is confined to the lowest register, representing a procession of offering bearers. The upper registers are decorated with religious themes in a more traditional Egyptian style; in the southeast corner is a scene of the Opening of the Mouth ceremony. The square shaft in the centre of the room leads to a maze of subterranean burial chambers, one of which yielded Petosiris' beautiful inlaid sarcophagus, now displayed in the Egyptian Museum. The texts in the tomb are also of great interest, as, far from being the usual standard formulae, they represent original religious writings, full of poetic imagery, which convey an image of Petosiris as a man of great personal piety.

A short walk from the rest house near the site entrance are the rock-cut catacombs which housed the remains of the sacred ibises and baboons raised nearby in the temple compound. Gloomy and atmospheric, the walls of the winding passages are honeycombed with niches for sarcophagi and votive stelae, and lined with side chambers packed with pots containing the mummified birds.

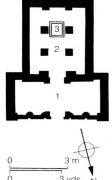

Tomb of Petosiris
1. Portico
2. Chapel
3. Shaft

ABYDOS
AND DENDERA

Continuing southwards, the palm-fringed Nile enters a wide green plain, as the ever-present cliffs recede into the far distance. At Nag Hammadi, 55 km (34 miles) downstream from the provincial capital of Qena, the Nile changes direction; flowing from the east, it forms a great curve extending to just south of Luxor where it resumes its normal course. Abydos is located approximately 40 km (25 miles) northwest of Nag Hammadi, 10 km (6 miles) southeast of the little town of Balliana, while Dendera is just 4 km (2½ miles) west of Qena, close to the furthest extent of the river's bend.

Inhabited from the earliest times, the important pre-dynastic sites of El-Amra and Naqada were located in this region, as was the city of Thinis, Egypt's first capital. Even after the transfer of authority to Memphis during the Second Dynasty, the great antiquity of Abydos, the Thinite necropolis, assured its continued religious significance; its status reinforced by the identification of the tomb of Djer, a First Dynasty king, as that of Osiris, Lord of the Underworld.

As the cult of Osiris grew in popularity from the end of the Old Kingdom, it eclipsed the local funerary cult of the jackal-headed **Khentimentiou**, the 'Foremost of the Westerners', whose title thereafter became an epithet of Osiris. Abydos prospered as a centre of pilgrimage which every pious Egyptian aspired to visit—if not in life, then after death, hence the scenes of the Voyage to Abydos so popular in private tombs from the Middle Kingdom onwards. Because the mythology of divine kingship was so intimately connected with the Osirian cult, it was natural that the Middle Kingdom monarchs, while building their tombs elsewhere, continued to commemorate themselves at Abydos by building cenotaphs, the forerunners of the great commemorative temples of the late New Kingdom. For private citizens, a burial site in the holy cemeteries

(*Opposite*) Dendera, Temple of Hathor: New Year Chapel. (Graeco-Roman period).

67

was of course highly desirable, and many who could not aspire to this instead erected small cenotaphs and commemorative stelae in order that their names at least should be blessed by the divine presence; examples of these are displayed in the Egyptian Museum.

As a national shrine of the first importance, Abydos was exempted from taxes, and care was exercised over the maintenance of its buildings. One of the private stelae recovered from the site recounts how the official Ikhernofret was despatched from the court of **Senusert I** to undertake the restoration of the holy shrines. Having accomplished his task, he went on to supervise the Mysteries of Osiris, the great annual festival of Abydos, during which the god's death and resurrection were re-enacted; celebrated during the inundation season, it culminated in the erection of a fetish known as the **Djed pillar**, a ritual intended to ensure the continued stability of the nation.

Such was the significance of these rites that almost 2000 years later they were depicted in detail in the Graeco-Roman Temple of Hathor at Dendera. The name Dendera is a corruption of the Greek *Tentyra*, in turn derived from the Egyptian *Iunit*. As the ancient cult centre of the love goddess Hathor, identified by the Greeks with Aphrodite, the site dates back to prehistory. However, apart from a limestone chapel of the Middle Kingdom, now in the Egyptian Museum, all the extant buildings date from the Late and Graeco-Roman periods, representing some of the most impressive monuments of that era.

ABYDOS

EARLY MONUMENTS

The site of the ancient **Temple of Osiris** and its surrounding settlement is located at the mound of Kom el-Sultan, just over 1 km (½ mile) northwest of the Temple of Seti I; it can be recognized by its Thirtieth Dynasty mudbrick enclosure walls, but there are few other identifiable remains. Half a kilometre further into the desert is another brick enclosure known as the *Shunet el-Zibib* ('Raisin Store'), which may have been an Early Dynastic funerary complex, perhaps a forerunner of the Step

Pyramid enclosure. The royal tombs of the First and Second Dynasties are located 3 km (2 miles) across the desert, in an area known as *Umm el-Qaab*—'Mother of Pots'—from the enormous quantity of potsherds found there, but apart from these there are few recognizable remains. The same is true of the Middle Kingdom and early New Kingdom monuments, which are located southwest of the Temple of Seti I; like the tombs these are accessible only on foot or by four wheel drive vehicles.

TEMPLE OF SETI I

When **Seti I** ascended the throne of the Two Lands around 1291 BC, he was faced with a diplomatic problem of enormous proportions. Although Seti was technically the second ruler of the Nineteenth Dynasty, his father, **Ramesses I**, had ruled for less than two years, so the family's hold on the monarchy was far from established. The real difficulty, however, was—as so often in Egypt—religious. Their predecessors, the Theban Eighteenth Dynasty, had been devotees of the cult of **Amun-Re**, recently restored to pre-eminence following the religious crisis under Akhenaten. The Ramessides, however, came from the Delta and worshipped the typhonic deity Seth, enemy of Amun and slayer of Osiris. To secure the throne Seti had to convince his subjects not only that a monarch who venerated the agent of chaos might be regarded as

Abydos, Temple of Seti I
1. First court; 2. Ablution tanks; 3. Second court; 4. Portico; 5. First hypostyle hall; 6. Second hypostyle hall; 7. Chapel of Horus; 8. Chapel of Isis; 9. Chapel of Osiris; 10. Osiris suite; 11. Chapel of Amun-Re; 12. Chapel of Re-Harakhte; 13. Chapel of Ptah; 14. Chapel of Seti I; 15. Chapel of Sokar; 16. Chapel of Nefertum; 17. Hall of Ancestors; 18. Butchery; 19. Stores.

Osireion
20. Corridor; 21. First transverse hall; 22. Second transverse hall; 23. Central hall; 24. Canal; 25. Third transverse hall.

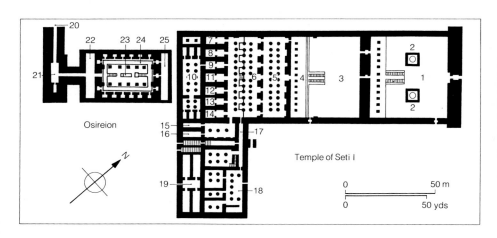

Osireion

Temple of Seti I

the guarantor of national stability, but also that a king bearing the name of Seth could indeed lay rightful claim to the Throne of Horus.

Part of Seti's solution to the delicate religious problem was the establishment of a lavish memorial temple dedicated to Osiris at his cult centre of Abydos. It was to be constructed of the finest white limestone, embellished with delicately-carved bas-reliefs and painted in bright colours. Unfortunately, he died before its completion and the outer part of the monument was finished with rather less subtlety by his favourite son and successor **Ramesses II**.

From the outside, the temple had a conventional appearance, with two pylons fronting courts with pillared porticoes, now ruined; the surviving blocks, with their deeply-carved reliefs, are clearly the work of Ramesses II. Unusually, the first court features a pair of circular **ablution tanks** used for ritual purification, but it is only after passing the second portico that the temple's truly unique features become apparent. Not only are the inner chambers built in an L-shape to accommodate extra cult and service rooms, but instead of a single sanctuary, seven separate sanctuaries were created for the principal gods of Egypt, in addition to separate suites for the cults of Osiris and of the Memphite funerary deities **Sokar** and **Nefertum**. The whole concept is a triumph of diplomacy, for while the Triad of Abydos (Osiris, Isis and Horus) clearly predominate, the prestigious central axis was allocated to the sanctuary of Amun-Re of Thebes; chapels for Ptah and **Re-Harakhte** were also included to appease the old-established and powerful priesthoods of Memphis and Heliopolis. The final masterstroke was the inclusion of a sanctuary to the deified Seti, a clear statement of his parity with the other gods of the national pantheon; located at the opposite end to that of Horus, it provided a kind of symbolic mirror, tactfully yet firmly underlining the legitimacy of the king's status.

The seven **sanctuaries** are approached by separate processional ways leading from the **first hypostyle hall**, which has twelve rows of papyrus bud columns, 7.5 m (25 ft) high, arranged in pairs to form seven aisles. Originally, each aisle had its own entrance from the portico, but all

Abydos, Temple of
Seti I: Seti I offers
incense and libations
to Osiris and Isis.
(New Kingdom,
Eighteenth Dynasty).

save the central doorway were blocked by Ramesses II
during his completion of the temple. His strong, sunk
reliefs contrast dramatically with his father's delicate work
in the **second hypostyle hall**, which serves as a vestibule for
the sanctuaries. Here the carvings—regarded by many as
the crowning achievement of Egyptian art—emphasize
Seti in the role of dutiful son, for example in the scene on
the northern wall where he offers Maat to Osiris and the
other members of the Abydos triad. On the western wall,
outside each sanctuary, is a niche which contained a statue
of the deity worshipped inside: in the relief above, the god
concerned confers blessings on the king.

The construction of the sanctuaries, which emulate
archaic shrines, is most unusual, as the stone roof-slabs
have been hollowed to give the effect of a vaulted ceiling.
With the exception of the shrine of Osiris, which leads
into the Osirian suite behind, all the sanctuaries have a
false door at the western end; their presence is doubtless
connected with the funereal aspects of the monument.

Abydos, Temple of
Seti I: statue niche
outside the chapel of
Amun-Re. (New
Kingdom, Nineteenth
Dynasty).

The reliefs on the sanctuary walls depict the king enacting
the procedures of the daily offering ritual; running in
sequence from the northeast corner of each shrine to the
southeast corner, the final episode shows Seti using a long
broom to remove his footprints from the sanctuary floor
before retiring. Only in Seti's own chapel do the scenes
vary: here the reliefs concentrate on the validation of his
claim to the throne in a series of scenes which include his
depiction as 'Uniter of the Two Lands', and a triumphal
procession in which the royal palanquin is borne by the

royal ancestral souls of Upper and Lower Egypt.

The **Osiris suite**, entered from the southwestern end of the Osiris sanctuary, comprises a spacious columned hall with three small chapels at the northwestern end, and a further three, together with a small vestibule, on the southeast. The latter are in a poor condition, but the northwestern chapels, dedicated to Seti I (identified by implication with Osiris), Isis and Horus, have beautifully preserved painted reliefs. A sealed, inaccessible chamber behind the chapels was probably a crypt for the storage of valuables.

The suite dedicated to the Memphite funerary gods is entered by a door in the southeast corner of the second hypostyle hall, and comprises an outer columned hall with four statue niches, and two chapels dedicated to **Sokar** and **Nefertum**. The chapel of Sokar has some interesting reliefs, including one depicting the conception of Horus.

A second door just northeast of the entrance to this suite leads into the **Hall of Ancestors**, where Seti I is represented with the prince regent Ramesses before the cartouches of 76 previous rulers, beginning with Narmer. Again, Seti's message is clear: he and his descendants are the rightful heirs to the throne. Tellingly, monarchs of questionable legitimacy, such as Hatshepsut, Akhenaten and Tutankhamun, have been omitted from the list. The family succession was clearly as important to Ramesses as it was to Seti, for in his decorations of the corridor to the west of the hall he is depicted participating in symbolic rites with his own son Amenhirkhopshef.

A flight of shallow steps leads from the end of this corridor to the open area behind the temple. Here the visitor can look down on the underground remains of the monument generally referred to as the **Osireion**. The age and function of this puzzling structure was for a long time the subject of contention, but modern consensus favours the opinion that it was constructed as a cenotaph for Seti I. Completed by his grandson **Merneptah**, the plan resembles the early Eighteenth Dynasty royal tombs in the Valley of the Kings. It is approached via a long, sloping entrance corridor partly roofed with a brick vault and decorated with mythological scenes, leading into two

transverse halls, largely ruined. In place of a burial chamber is a huge **hall**, measuring 30.5 m (100 ft) by 20 m (65 ft), whose massive square pillars of red granite, more reminiscent of Fourth Dynasty architecture than anything found in the New Kingdom, contributed to the initial confusion over dating. Its central feature is a rectangular island surrounded by a canal fed by ground water; this may have symbolized the primeval mound, or the tomb of Osiris. Whether the hall was wholly or only partly roofed is still disputed, but whichever was the case, this extraordinary chamber must have possessed a unique gloomy magnificence. Beyond it is a final sarcophagus-shaped transverse hall; now mostly destroyed, its vaulted sandstone roof is decorated with astronomical scenes.

TEMPLE OF RAMESSES II
Some 300 m (328 yds) to the northwest of his father's monument is the Temple of Ramesses II, which was constructed in the early part of his reign. Built of fine white limestone, its sunk reliefs are of extremely high quality, and although the monument itself is very ruined, the short walk through the desert is amply rewarded by these fine painted carvings, which surpass any of his later works. Another striking feature is the extravagant use of coloured stone; even in their present condition, the portals of red and black granite juxtaposed with limestone walls, and the sanctuary lined with sandstone and polished

74

white alabaster, convey an unmistakable impression of luxury. Ramesses' plan, however, was more conventional than his father's, drawing its inspiration from contemporary Theban mortuary temples. As the first pylon and court are destroyed, entrance is from the second court, whose colonnade was supported by Osiride pillars representing the king. Four small chapels opening off the portico at the northwestern and southeastern ends of the court are dedicated to various gods, including the deified Ramesses and his father. The central aisle led through two columned halls to the sanctuary, which houses the remnant of a grey granite statue group representing Ramesses and Seti I

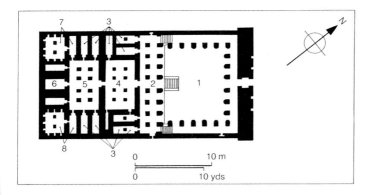

Abydos, Temple of Ramesses II
1. Second court
2. Portico
3. Cult chapels
4. First hypostyle hall
5. Second hypostyle hall
6. Sanctuary
7. Suite of the Theban Triad
8. Suite of the Abydos Triad

with Amun and two goddesses. The suites of chapels leading off the halls are dedicated to various national deities, including the triads of Thebes and Abydos.

DENDERA

From far off, massive mudbrick ramparts announce the location of the **Temple of Hathor**, who was worshipped at Dendera along with her consort Horus of Edfu and their young son, variously identified as **Ihy**, the god of music, and *Hor-sema-tawy*, the Younger Horus, literally 'Horus-uniter-of-the-Two Lands'. The well-preserved walls, measuring 8–10 m (26–32 ft) in height, are a fine example of the technique of pan-bedding. The enclosure is entered by a monumental gateway, or propylon, dating to the reigns of **Domitian** and **Trajan**, which opens onto a

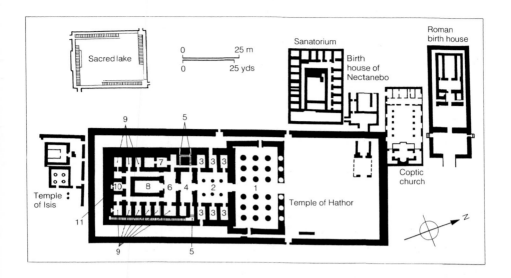

spacious courtyard. On the northwest is a group of buildings comprising, from north to south, a Roman period mammisi, or birth house, an early Christian basilica constructed of reused blocks from the site, a second mammisi dating from the reign of **Nectanebo I**, and a mudbrick sanatorium.

ROMAN BIRTH HOUSE

Of the two birth houses, the first is the better preserved and more interesting, being the latest surviving example of its type. Ostensibly for the celebration of the rites connected with the birth of the goddess' son, such birth houses are related to the birth reliefs of the Eighteenth Dynasty which sought to bolster questionable claims to the throne by promulgating the myth of the monarch's divine parentage. This same convenient fiction was often adopted by Ptolemaic and Roman rulers, in this case Trajan, who is represented in a fine series of reliefs on the southern exterior wall of the ambulatory. The mammisi itself is constructed on a raised stone platform and consists a vestibule leading to three chapels. The central chapel, which served as the sanctuary, is decorated with divine birth scenes; at its western end is a false door below a niche containing a broken statue of Hathor with her son. The building is enclosed by an ambulatory of columns linked by low screen walls; above the fine floral capitals, the abaci are decorated with reliefs of the principal deities of childbirth, the bandy-legged dwarf god **Bes** and the hippopotamus goddess **Taweret**.

TEMPLE OF HATHOR

Although it was never completed, the Temple of Hathor is among the best-preserved of its type, having remained engulfed by sand until its excavation by the French archaeologist Mariette in the mid-nineteenth century. Built of sandstone and facing north, it is the latest of several temples on the site. It is believed that construction commenced around the end of the second century BC, probably during the reign of **Ptolemy XII**, and was abandoned during the first century AD, but exact dating is difficult; due to the political instability of the time, many of the royal cartouches have been left blank, while others simply bear the title 'Pharaoh'.

As the pylon and court were left unbuilt, visitors are confronted by the first hypostyle hall, whose façade, crowned with a cavetto cornice and incorporating the traditional Egyptian batter, dates from the reign of **Tiberius**. Its exterior is lavishly decorated with elaborate reliefs, the

Dendera, Temple of Hathor: Façade of the hypostyle hall. (Graeco-Roman period).

bottom register being occupied by a delightful offering procession of river gods and field goddesses, representing the nomes, or provinces, of Egypt. In the centre of the temple's rear external wall a huge icon of Hathor, flanked by figures of **Cleopatra VII** and her son **Caesarion**, served as the focus of the goddess' public cult, where those not admitted to the temple proper could worship or petition. Originally protected by a wooden canopy and gilded with fine gold, the image was located directly behind the temple sanctuary. Its present damaged condition, caused by the scraping of generations of pilgrims, bears eloquent testimony to the goddess' popularity.

Inside the temple, the 24 columns of the **first hypostyle hall** are carved with mythological texts and scenes, and are crowned with four-sided capitals representing the cow-eared visage of Hathor bearing the sistrum—a kind of sacred rattle—on her head. The ceiling is decorated with elaborate astronomical scenes. The second hypostyle hall, or **Hall of Appearances**, has six Hathor columns and is lined with service rooms and stores; in some, the floor has been lifted to reveal reused material from earlier temple buildings. On the walls, raised reliefs represent episodes from the temple dedication rites. The most sacred part of the temple, the **sanctuary**, or Great Seat, is a free-standing stone chapel with battered walls, located as usual at the temple's highest point. It is approached through two vestibules, the **Hall of Offerings**, where offerings were amassed for presentation, and the **Hall of the Gods**, where the images of the various deities worshipped in the temple were assembled on feast days. Although the stone naos which housed the cult statue of Hathor is missing, it is illustrated in the offering reliefs on the sanctuary walls, along with the sacred bark in which the divine image was carried in procession.

Surrounding the sanctuary is the customary suite of chapels for associated deities. Of particular interest is the **shrine** directly behind the sanctuary which was used to accommodate sacred images of the goddess; a niche high up in the south wall contained an ancient squatting statue of Hathor which was located immediately behind the public cult image on the exterior wall.

Worthy of attention in their own right, the temple walls have three levels of **crypts**—some of them decorated—concealed within their thickness; one of the lower crypts is accessible from the chapel behind the southwest corner of the sanctuary. On the whole, these narrow rooms were used for the storage of temple valuables and cult objects; among the contents of this particular crypt was an image of Hathor used in the **New Year festival**. On the eve of the new year at the end of the inundation season, this statue, accompanied by the images of other gods, was brought from the crypt to the New Year Chapel, which comprises a tiny open court measuring just 5 m (16 ft) by 4.5 m (15 ft), and an elevated kiosk with a representation of the sky goddess on the ceiling. Following an offering ceremony in the court, the divine image was placed in the chapel for ritual robing before the procession proceeded to the roof via the ascending **staircase** in the temple's western wall. The priestly retinue is depicted in the reliefs on the walls of the winding staircase, which is illuminated by slit windows, their lower sills carved with representations of the solar disc radiating beams of heat and light.

On reaching the roof, the statues were installed in a small unroofed kiosk in the southwest corner, to await the sun's rays which would imbue them with power for the coming year. This **Disc Chapel** is simple and elegant in design, comprising twelve small Hathor columns linked by screen walls, and originally covered with a light removable roof of wood or tenting; openings on the north and east allowed the passage of the procession. To shield these rituals from public view, this part of the roof was surrounded by a high parapet; here, at floor level, one can see the openings for the leonine water spouts that project from the exterior walls. At the northern end of the roof are two suites of **chapels** dedicated to the god Osiris, each comprising an open court, a low, covered court and an enclosed room lit only by a slit in the ceiling. The reliefs depict the processions and rituals of the Mysteries of Osiris which were enacted annually during the month of Khoiak in the inundation season. The carvings on the ceilings of the covered courts are exceptionally interesting, especially those in the westernmost chapel, which

Dendera, Temple of Hathor: The Dendera Zodiac. (Graeco-Roman period) Musée du Louvre, Paris.

include a famous representation of the **zodiac**, the original of which is now in the Louvre Museum.

From the lower part of the roof it is possible to climb onto the roof of the hypostyle hall, which offers spectacular views over the temple site and the surrounding countryside. The temple precincts originally extended over a vast area enclosed by a series of three temenos walls, of which only the innermost survives, enclosing an area of just over 8 ha (19 acres). The limestone gateway visible to the southeast marks the entrance to the Precinct of Ihy, while on the west one can obtain a bird's-eye view of the **mudbrick sanatorium**, the only surviving example of its type.

SUBSIDIARY BUILDINGS

In common with many temples, Dendera was renowned as a centre of healing, and pilgrims flocked to spend the night in the chambers visible around the walls, in the hope of receiving a diagnostic or curative dream. The centre of the building housed divine statues whose power was imparted to water poured over them; this was then used for the treatment of the sick. Although such remedies may sound unlikely, the local populace still have a great deal of faith in the temple's power to heal, and it is not at all unusual to encounter a group of black-robed ladies on their way to seek a cure in the crypts of Hathor.

Also visible to the southwest is the rectangular **sacred lake**, which is surrounded by a low wall with a staircase leading down from each corner. Lined with stone, it has a sunken terrace at the southern end from which water-borne rituals could be viewed. Immediately behind the main temple is a small **Temple of Isis** erected by **Augustus**; largely ruined, it is unique in that while the inner chambers are aligned north-south, the outer rooms are on an east-west axis, an arrangement probably enforced by constraints of space. The route back to ground level from the temple roof is via the straight descending staircase hidden within the east wall; again one is accompanied by a procession of the priests of Hathor, the ancient words of their hymns frozen in hieroglyphs before their mouths.

LUXOR–EAST BANK

To the ancient Greeks, present-day Luxor was *Thebai*, famed in Homer's *Iliad* as 'Hundred-gated Thebes'. The ancient Egyptians knew it as *Waset*, while the Arabs, marvelling at its ruined monuments, called it *El-Uqsur*, 'The Palaces'—the derivation of its modern name. According to Diodorus, its boundaries measured 140 stadia or 25.5 km (16 miles) in circuit; this included the inhabited and cultivated areas on both sides of the Nile, but not the extensive cemeteries of the west bank. Today Luxor is a small provincial town, but the ruined pylons and crumbling temples set dramatically among the folds of its pink limestone cliffs still have the power to evoke the city's past splendour, while the excellent Luxor Museum lends new life to the artefacts of its long-vanished inhabitants.

Although there had been early settlements on the site, the city's rise to prominence began at the end of the First Intermediate Period, with the ascendancy of the Theban Eleventh Dynasty. In the first major phase of development the pharaoh **Montuhotep I**, clearly a man of great vision, built himself a massive terraced tomb complex at Deir el-Bahri on the west bank; aligned with his temple and residence at Karnak, 5 km (3 miles) away on the opposite bank, this is the earliest known example of axial city planning on a grand scale.

It was, however, under the New Kingdom Eighteenth Dynasty that Thebes attained the height of its glory. Apart from a brief hiatus during the Amarna period, the city served as the national capital until the advent of the Ramessides, growing in prestige and prosperity as succeeding monarchs sought to outdo one another in the opulence of their monuments.

Long after the Nineteenth Dynasty kings moved the court to their native Delta, Thebes retained its significance as a religious and administrative centre, and

(*Opposite*) Karnak, Temple of Amun. Hall of Annals of Thutmose III: Heraldic lotus and papyrus pillars. (New Kingdom, Eighteenth Dynasty).

83

continued to serve as the royal necropolis until the end of the Twentieth Dynasty. During the weak rule of the Tanite kings of the Twenty-first and Twenty-second Dynasties, the city, under the rule of a series of powerful High Priests of Amun—some of whom went so far as to assume royal titles—effectively became the capital of Upper Egypt. This influence was not entirely lost until the city was devastated by the Assyrian invasions which began in 667 BC, followed just over a century later by the Persian annexation of Egypt. However, Thebes revived under the Ptolemies, and later still prospered as a Roman garrison town. Even in its decline a magnificent city, it was described by contemporary travellers in terms of awe and wonder.

KARNAK

(*Opposite*) Karnak, Precinct of Amun 1. Quay; 2. Sphinx Avenue; 3. First Pylon; 4. First court; 5. Bark shrine of Seti II; 6. Builders' ramp; 7. Kiosk of Taharqa; 8. Open Air Museum; 9. Temple of Ramesses III; 10. Second Pylon; 11. Hypostyle hall; 12. Third Pylon; 13. Obelisk of Thutmose I; 14. Fourth Pylon; 15. Obelisk of Hatshepsut; 16. Fifth Pylon; 17. Sixth Pylon; (*Cont. p. 85*)

Approximately 3 km² (1 mile²) in area, the Karnak temple complex is one of the most extraordinary and impressive religious monuments in the world, comprising an enormous assemblage of gates, courts, temples, chapels and ancillary buildings constructed over a period of more than 2000 years. Known as the 'Most Select of Places', its heart is the Great Temple of the god **Amun**, the 'Hidden One', a local Theban deity whose cult grew in importance from the Middle Kingdom onwards, until finally it was amalgamated with that of **Re of Heliopolis** to become the principal national cult. As succeeding monarchs vied to exceed one another in the generosity of their endowments, the Estate of Amun grew in wealth and prestige; by the late New Kingdom it was second only to the throne in importance, owning roughly 10 per cent of Egypt's arable land, in addition to its mines, quarries and fleets, and the revenue of several foreign cities. With such resources at their disposal, it is little wonder that the High Priests of Amun were so easily able to assume control of Upper Egypt during the following three centuries.

The Karnak monuments are grouped in three areas—the central **Precinct of Amun** is flanked on the north by the **Precinct of Montu**, the hawk-headed Theban war god, and on the south by the **Precinct of Mut**, the female member of the Theban Triad. The latter sites are largely ruined and

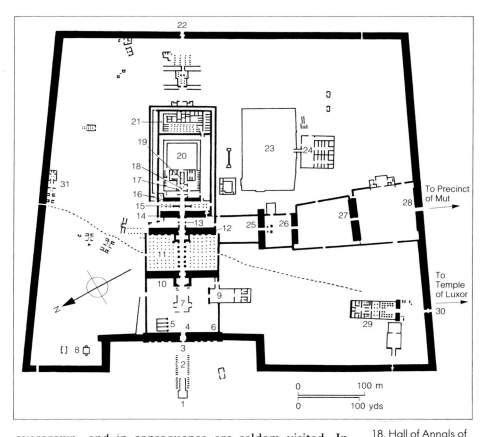

overgrown, and in consequence are seldom visited. In contrast, much of the Precinct of Amun has been cleared, and many of its monuments conserved. Enclosed by a high brick temenos wall, the central feature is the great double-axial Temple of Amun with its sacred lake, which is surrounded by smaller temples and chapels and ancillary buildings.

TEMPLE OF AMUN

In common with most Egyptian temples, the Temple of Amun grew outwards from its original site, although little now remains of the Middle Kingdom structures which lie behind the present sanctuary. As the temple was enlarged, the transverse axis was extended southwards,

18. Hall of Annals of Thutmose III; 19. Sanctuary; 20. Central court; 21. Festival Hall of Thutmose III; 22. Gateway of Nectanebo I; 23. Sacred Lake; 24. Fowlyard; 25. Seventh Pylon; 26. Eighth Pylon; 27. Ninth Pylon; 28. Tenth Pylon; 29. Temple of Khonsu; 30. Gateway of Ptolemy III; 31. Temple of Ptah.

Karnak, Temple of Amun: General view from the Sacred Lake looking towards the main axis.

towards the Precinct of Mut, while the main axis was expanded westwards in the direction of the Nile. Access from the river was by way of a canal (now filled in) which terminated at a landing stage constructed, like the bulk of the temple buildings, in sandstone. Just to the south is a small shrine where the bark of Amun rested on its way in and out of the temple. It is worth pausing to enjoy the stunning view along the main axis before proceeding, via an avenue of ram-headed sphinxes erected by Ramesses II, to the entrance in the **first pylon**. Had it been completed, this massive edifice, probably dating from the Thirtieth Dynasty, would have measured 113 m (370 ft) wide by 40 m (131 ft) high by 10 m (32 ft) thick, but its unfinished state is clear from the undressed blocks projecting from the walls. Immediately behind the southern tower are the partial remains of the mudbrick ramp used in its building; note also the unfinished colonnade in the west corner of the court which illustrates the different stages of construction.

Since the pylon was a late addition, all the buildings in the first court were originally located outside the temple proper; the criosphinxes crammed along the sides of the court, for example, were the continuation of the avenue from the quay when this area was still a part of the temple forecourt. For this reason, the court contains several way-stations, resting places for the divine barks during their processional journeys. In the northwest corner is a small **bark shrine of Seti II**, a simple structure with three chapels for the sacred barks of Amun, Mut and the third member of the Theban triad, the lunar deity **Khonsu**. The small **temple of Ramesses III** in the southwest corner, though fulfilling the same purpose, is an altogether grander monument. It also served as a memorial for the king, who is represented on the pylon, in the colossal statues flanking the entrance, and on the Osiride pillars of the court.

In the centre of the court is the ruined **kiosk of Taharqa**, a Nubian pharaoh of the Twenty-fifth Dynasty. Originally standing 26.5 m (87 ft) high, it consisted of ten huge open papyrus columns linked by screen walls with openings on the east and west. Little more of it survives today than a single reconstructed column and a massive alabaster altar. The colossal royal statue behind the kiosk bears inscriptions of the priest-king **Pinedjem I** of the Third Intermediate Period, but dates to the Ramesside era; it may represent **Ramesses II** with one of his wives or daughters.

Karnak, Temple of Amun: Hypostyle Hall, Transverse axis. (New Kingdom, Nineteenth Dynasty).

The **second pylon** and its portico dates from the reign of **Horemheb** and leads directly into the great **hypostyle hall**, whose gigantic scale and nobility of proportion is often regarded as one of the crowning achievements of Egyptian architecture. Measuring 102 m (334 ft) by 53 m (174 ft), the court was created early in the Nineteenth Dynasty by enclosing the space between the second and third pylons with transverse walls; the joints are visible at the northwest and southwest corners. The central aisle is lined by twelve open papyrus columns, 23 m (75 ft) in height; the remaining 122 papyrus bud columns, 15 m (49 ft) high, are arranged in close-set rows on either side, the difference in height creating a central nave. Entirely roofed with stone slabs, the hypostyle hall would have been completely dark but for the narrow slanting shafts of light admitted by the clerestory windows located along the nave; some of their stone grilles are still visible.

The decoration was begun under Seti I, whose fine raised reliefs adorn the northern part of the hall; the southern half was completed by Ramesses II in his characteristic heavy, sunk style. Remnants of the original brilliant paintwork survive on some of the capitals and architraves. Well-preserved carvings on the southern wall include scenes of Ramesses II receiving Jubilees from Amun and the Theban Triad (west side) and having his name inscribed on a leaf of the sacred Persea tree by the god Thoth (east side). The exterior walls of the hypostyle hall are covered in battle reliefs; those of Seti I on the northern side are particularly interesting.

At the eastern end of the hall, the **third pylon**, the work of Amenhotep III, is little more than a bulky ruin. Investigation of its interior, however, has yielded the substantial remains of earlier buildings, including two complete shrines, now re-erected in the Open Air Museum. Nearby is the southern red granite **obelisk of Thutmose** I, 23 m (75 ft) high. Modelled on the *Benben*, the sacred fetish of the solar deity Re of Heliopolis, pairs of such obelisks were often placed in front of temple pylons during the New Kingdom. The **fourth** and **fifth pylons**, now largely destroyed, were also constructed by Thutmose I; between them his daughter Hatshepsut erected her own pair of obelisks in celebration of her Jubilee. Each obelisk, 27.5 m (90 ft) high, was cut from a single piece of red Aswan granite weighing 325,120 kgs (320 tons). Their pinnacles, sheathed in precious electrum, were intended to reflect the first rays of the sun; piercing the sky above the temple buildings, they must have created a powerful impression among the general populace, who were excluded from the temple proper. Although her successor, **Thutmose III**, encased Hatshepsut's obelisks in masonry in his attempts to obliterate her memory, his action only served to preserve them in pristine condition; today the northern obelisk can be

Luxor Museum, slab from a red quartzite sanctuary at Karnak: Queen Hatsheput (left) presents a pair of obelisks to Amun. (New Kingdom, Eighteenth Dynasty).

viewed in its original site, while the upper part of the southern obelisk has been moved to a spot beside the sacred lake.

The **sixth pylon**, also the work of Thutmose III, precedes his **Hall of Annals**, where he is represented embraced by Amun on two exquisitely carved granite pillars, the southernmost representing the lotus of Upper Egypt and the northernmost the papyrus of Lower Egypt. Immediately behind is the granite sanctuary, dating to the reign of Philip Arrhidaeus and comprising two chambers, originally closed with doors at the eastern and western ends. The west-facing room was the shrine, accommodating the divine image of Amun, while the god's portable bark rested on the pedestal in the chamber behind. There are some well-preserved painted scenes on the sanctuary's exterior walls.

The scattered blocks of granite and alabaster lying in the court behind the sanctuary are all that now remains of the original Middle Kingdom Temple of Amun, although a fine painted limestone Osiride figure of **Senusert I** found here can now be seen in the Luxor Museum. Beyond is the **Festival Hall of Thutmose III**, built to commemorate his Jubilee. Measuring 44 m (144 ft) by 17 m (55 ft), it comprises a columned hall surrounded by suites of chapels, cult rooms and stores. Approaching from the direction of the sanctuary, the visitor faces the southwestern side aisle of the hall, which appears as a colonnade of square pillars surmounted by an architrave bearing a fine symmetrical inscription listing the royal names and titles.

Entry to the Festival Hall is via an antechamber in the southwestern corner, which leads into the **columned hall**. This unusual structure consists of twin side aisles of square pillars flanking a higher central nave supported by a unique type of column representing a kind of tentpole. Since Thutmose III was well-known for his martial exploits, it has been suggested that this hall was intended to represent his campaign tent; an alternative explanation may be that it emulates an archaic type of temporary shrine. As in the hypostyle hall, the difference in height between the nave and side aisles creates a clerestory zone in which windows were set.

Thanks to a recent cleaning, much of the bright paintwork on the architraves and capitals is now visible; of especial interest are the crude figures of saints executed when the hall was reused as a church during the Christian era. Many of the surrounding chambers are in a ruinous condition, but visitors are often shown the so-called '**Botanical Garden**', with its low raised reliefs recording the exotic fauna and flora encountered by Thutmose's army during his Levantine campaigns. The four papyrus-bundle columns at the centre of the room display exceptional refinement. The exit is from the rear, via a wooden walkway running over the inner retaining wall to a point immediately behind the back of the temple proper.

As in the late temples, this was the focal point of the god's public cult, and the area is strewn with the remains of 'Hearing Ear' images and shrines, through which the general populace could direct their prayers and petitions to Amun. One such image, an alabaster dyad representing Thutmose III with a deity—no doubt Amun himself—survives in a shrine just to the south. To the east an impressive gateway of Nectanebo I rises out of the overgrown rubble. Just beyond was the site of a vast sun-temple of Akhenaten, dismantled by Horemheb to provide filling for his pylons; part of a reconstructed wall of this temple is displayed in Luxor Museum.

A short distance west is the **sacred lake**; filled by ground water, it is equipped with staircases used during purification rites and waterborne rituals. On the southwest side, a low covered passage connected the lake with the temple **fowl-yard**, allowing Amun's sacred birds access to the water. At the western corner of the lake is a colossal granite **scarab** of Amenhotep III, removed from his mortuary temple on the west bank of the Nile.

The transverse axis of the temple begins in the court situated to the northwest of the sacred lake. The **seventh pylon**, located at its southern end, was erected by Thutmose III. Otherwise, there is little remarkable about the court, whose chief interest lies in the fact that over 17,000 buried bronzes and sculptures—now in the Egyptian Museum—were discovered here in the early years of this century. Access to the remainder of the transverse axis is restricted by ongoing conservation work, but a good view of its courts and pylons can be obtained from the footpath running south to the Temple of Khonsu. The **eighth pylon**, begun under Hatshepsut, was completed by Thutmose III and his son **Amenhotep II**; six colossal statues of various dates from Amenhotep I to Amenhotep II abut its southern face. The **ninth** and **tenth pylons** are both the work of Horemheb, who had them filled with the dismantled blocks of Akhenaten's nearby temple. From here, the processional route continued, via an avenue of sphinxes, to the Precinct of Mut.

TEMPLE OF KHONSU

Tucked away in the southwest corner of the precinct enclosure, the Temple of Khonsu is seldom visited—a great pity, as it is a beautifully-preserved example of a small late New Kingdom temple. It was probably founded by **Amenhotep III**, whose avenue of sculptured rams—the sacred animals of Amun—linked it with Luxor Temple. The present structure, measuring 125 m (410 ft) in length, is mainly the work of **Ramesses III** and **IV**, with additions by later kings, and is built on the standard New Kingdom plan. Facing south, the approach to the temple is via a well-preserved gateway of **Ptolemy III** and a pillared arcade which has almost completely disappeared. The **pylon**, measuring 31.9 m (104 ft) wide and 17.2 m (56 ft) high, was decorated by the priest-king **Pinedjem I**. His ambitious predecessor, **Herihor**, had been responsible for the reliefs in the **peristyle court** in which, for the first time, a priest dared to represent himself on the same scale as the reigning monarch. This court is surrounded on three sides by a double colonnade of papyrus-bud columns, which is elevated at the northern end to form a portico. The transverse **hypostyle hall** has eight papyrus columns; the four at the centre have open capitals and are flanked by two pairs of shorter columns with bud capitals to create the effect of a nave. The **sanctuary**, a free-standing shrine of red granite, is open at both ends. Originally built for Amenhotep II but usurped by **Ramesses IV**, it is the oldest part of the building. Behind it is a small hall with four columns and a pedestal for Khonsu's portable bark. A nearby staircase leads to the **Disc Chapel** on the roof, an excellent vantage point for a panoramic view of the site.

TEMPLE OF PTAH

As one of the great national deities, it was natural that Ptah, the creator god of Memphis, should have his own cult temple within Egypt's foremost religious foundation. Begun by Thutmose III and extensively expanded under the Ptolemies, the Temple of Ptah is reached via a path running from the north side of the Temple of Amun. Oriented east-west, it is entered via a series of six gates, the outermost dating from the Ptolemaic period and the innermost from the reign of Thutmose III. The inner chambers comprise a vestibule with two columns and three sanctuaries for the Memphite triad—mummiform Ptah, his lioness-headed spouse **Sekhmet** and the funerary deity **Nefertum**.

OPEN AIR MUSEUM

During the course of Karnak's 2000-year history, old temple buildings were continually being removed to make way for new ones, and the dismantled blocks were commonly reused as foundations or filling for the new constructions. Located to the north of the first court, the Open Air Museum contains a fascinating assembly of architectural fragments recovered from the site, including the two shrines found inside the third pylon of Amenhotep III—the White Chapel of Senusert I and the Alabaster Chapel of Amenhotep I.

The **White Chapel** is of importance as one of the few surviving examples of Middle Kingdom temple architecture. Built as part of Senusert's Jubilee celebrations, it takes the form of a raised kiosk accessible by shallow ramps. Open at either end, the chapel contains a granite pedestal for the divine image; the flat roof is supported by square pillars and crowned by a cavetto cornice. It is constructed of fine white limestone, the stark design relieved by carvings of exceptional quality. The nearby **Alabaster Chapel** of Amenhotep I, an austere rectangular roofed shrine, is simpler still, but its marriage of pure line with the opulence of lightly-carved white

Karnak, Open-Air Museum: The White Chapel of Senusert I. (Middle Kingdom, Twelfth Dynasty).

alabaster is most satisfying. Also worthy of note are the blocks from a red quartzite sanctuary of Hatshepsut, well-carved despite the difficulties of working such hard stone; one fine example, representing Hatshepsut presenting a pair of obelisks to Amun, is displayed in the Luxor Museum.

LUXOR TEMPLE

LUXOR

Among the most appealing of Egyptian monuments, the present temple was begun by Amenhotep III on the site of a Middle Kingdom structure, and later extended by Ramesses II. Facing north, the temple connects with a processional way leading from Karnak 3 km (2 miles) away; the conspicuous bend in its axis was necessary to correct this alignment. Closely associated with Karnak, Luxor Temple was known in ancient times as the

93

'Southern Harem', where Amun was worshipped in his fertility aspect, and every year, the image of Amun of Karnak would travel southwards in a magnificent water-borne procession to meet Amun of Luxor as part of a great celebration known as the Opet Festival.

On land, the processional route is lined with an **avenue of sphinxes** erected by Nectanebo I, leading to the pylon, built by Ramesses II; this originally measured 24 m (79 ft) high by 65 m (213 ft) wide, and is famous for its reliefs depicting episodes from the Battle of Kadesh, which took place between the Egyptians and the Hittites around 1275 BC. Two **obelisks** and six colossal statues, two seated and four standing, originally fronted the pylon; the seated figures and one of the standing figures remain *in situ* along with the eastern obelisk, but the easternmost standing statues were removed to Paris together with the western obelisk, which now graces the Place de la Concorde. The trapezoidal **first court** is also the work of Ramesses II, whose colossal standing figures punctuate the double colonnade. The eastern colonnade has not been fully excavated due to the presence of the mainly nineteenth-century **Mosque of Abu el-Haggag**, whose elevation from the temple floor demonstrates the level to which the temple was formerly buried. In the northwest corner of the court is a small triple **bark shrine** dating from the time of Hatshepsut and Thutmose III; rebuilt by Ramesses II, its refined papyrus-bundle columns contrast dramatically with the heavy papyrus bud columns of Ramesses' own colonnade.

Leaving the first court, the visitor passes between two colossal statues of Ramesses II seated on thrones whose sides are carved with the *sema-tawy* emblem, symbolic of the unification of the Two Lands. Behind is a magnificent **processional colonnade**, comprising fourteen enormous papyrus columns whose open capitals conceal abaci carved with the cartouches of Tutankhamun. The lightly-carved reliefs on the walls of the court also date to the short reign of the young king and depict episodes from the Opet festival. The pylon at the end of the colonnade, which would have formed the original temple façade, has been destroyed, so entry is directly into the **court of**

Luxor Temple, Court of Amenhotep III: double colonnade of papyrus-bundle columns. (New Kingdom, Eighteenth Dynasty).

Amenhotep III, whose elegant double colonnade of papyrus-bundle columns testifies to the skill of the royal architect **Amenhotep, son of Hapu**. At its southern end is the **hypostyle hall**, comprising 32 columns arranged in four rows of eight.

The small court behind was originally another columned hall, but underwent major modifications during the Roman period, when it was converted into a **chapel** of the Imperial cult, used by the soldiers of the garrison whose quarters can be seen between the temple and the Corniche. The columns were removed, and the doorway to the temple's inner chambers closed off by an apsidal recess flanked by Corinthian columns. The reliefs of Amenhotep III were plastered over and repainted; these later paintings are now very damaged, but figures of emperors can be distinguished in the niche.

Behind the Roman chapel is the **Hall of Offerings**, its roof supported by four columns; the next room was originally very similar, but during the reign of Alexander the Great its columns were removed to make room for a small free-standing **bark shrine**. The suite of rooms behind the shrine, though not so well preserved, are of interest because they comprise the Opet, or 'Harem'—the private apartments of Amun which gave the temple its name and within which its secret rites were enacted. The central **sanctuary**, which has four columns and a pedestal for the god's shrine, is flanked by a pair of two-columned chapels and preceded by a **second hypostyle hall**, with twelve columns. Before leaving the temple, it is worth visiting the **Birth Room** of Amenhotep III, located on the eastern side of the temple, which features reliefs of the king's divine conception and birth, designed to bolster his rather questionable claim to the throne.

Luxor Temple: Hall of Amenhotep III adapted to a chapel of the Roman Imperial Cult.

LUXOR–WEST BANK

From the earliest times, the ancient Egyptians had associated the western horizon with the realm of the dead, and thus wherever possible had located their cemeteries to the west of their settlements. Accordingly, when the Theban rulers of the Eleventh Dynasty decided to be buried in their native city, they selected a location on the Nile's west bank, a choice which was to determine the future site of the royal necropolis. Known as 'The Place of Truth', it eventually extended over 7.5 km (4½ miles), and was used for all royal burials from the Seventeenth Dynasty to the end of the Twentieth Dynasty. As in ancient times, a visit to the cemeteries requires a river crossing; ferries operate from landings along the Corniche.

It was the early New Kingdom rulers who developed the typical Theban rock-cut royal tombs of the Valley of the Kings and the Valley of the Queens, together with the

(Opposite) Valley of the Kings, Tomb of Seti I: Relief of Seti I with the goddess Hathor. (New Kingdom, Nineteenth Dynasty). Musée du Louvre, Paris.

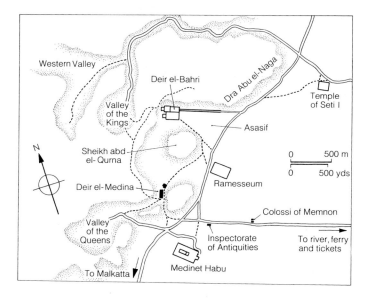

The Theban necropolis

97

mortuary temples, which for the first time were located away from the burial site. With this change came an alteration in the purpose and function of these temples; ceasing to be mere offering-places for the dead king's spirit, they began to resemble state cult temples with the addition of suites of chapels for the deified ruler and for various funerary deities. Such temples were built for use during the king's lifetime; from the Nineteenth Dynasty, when Thebes was no longer the capital, they usually incorporated modest residences for the monarch's use during protracted festivals.

The Eighteenth Dynasty kings, however, did reside in Thebes, and Amenhotep III actually located his palace on the west bank, at Malkatta; a huge establishment almost 1 km (½ mile) in length, it encompassed royal residences and audience halls, a temple of Amun, kitchens, work-shops, stores, and servants' quarters as well as a vast T-shaped harbour which doubled as a pleasure-lake. Although some fragments of the palaces' brightly-painted walls remain *in situ*, the buildings are today reduced to their lowest courses, and special permission is required to visit the fragile mudbrick remains.

Life in western Thebes during the New Kingdom was probably as far removed from the silence of the grave as can be imagined. Apart from the villages of the palace servants, there were, as today, settlements of farmers who cultivated the fertile land, the houses of priestly and administrative staff around the temple compounds, and at Deir el-Medina an entire town for the royal tomb-builders. Death was, for many in New Kingdom Thebes, a living, and while the Thebans had a positively Victorian relish for the things of the tomb, they did not subscribe to the concomitant gloom. Perhaps the best expression of their optimistic attitude can be found in the tomb paintings of families happily passing eternity in each other's company. In the same spirit was the annual festival known as 'The Beautiful Feast of the Valley', when the images of the Karnak Triad were taken across the Nile to rest in the mortuary temple of the current ruler, accompanied by the citizens of Thebes wearing their finery to picnic and spend the night among the tombs of their ancestors.

Located in a natural bay of the limestone cliffs, the site of Deir el-Bahri provides a dramatic setting for the Eleventh Dynasty funerary complex of Montuhotep I, the Eighteenth Dynasty Temple of Hatshepsut, and located between the two, the temple of her successor, Thutmose III; the latter, though largely ruined, has yielded fine reliefs and sculptures, some of which are displayed in the Luxor Museum. Facing east, the best time to visit the temples is at sunrise, when the early light suffuses the façades with a golden glow.

TEMPLE OF MONTUHOTEP I

Currently under restoration, the tomb-temple of Montuhotep I was greatly damaged by rock falls from the cliffs behind, and its exact form has been the subject of some debate. Aligned with the temples of Karnak, it bears some similarity to earlier royal tomb complexes, comprising a valley temple, a causeway and a mortuary temple, which in this case included the royal tomb. A shaft in the forecourt led to underground chambers possibly originally intended for the tomb, but which probably served as a cenotaph—when excavated, only a painted limestone seated statue of the king, carefully wrapped in linen, was discovered; it is now displayed in the Egyptian Museum. The earliest known monumental building in Upper Egypt, the temple was a major element in Montuhotep's ambitious city plan. Its innovatory design consisted of a central square structure surrounded by a columned hall, fronted by porticoes and approached by a ramp, giving the impression of rising terraces. The innermost part of the temple, including the royal burial chamber, was cut into the cliff behind.

TEMPLE OF HATSHEPSUT

Having assumed the throne on the death of her husband, Thutmose II, Hatshepsut was one of the few women to have ruled Egypt in their own right. Her temple, built chiefly as a memorial for herself and her father Thutmose I, was located immediately behind their tombs in the Valley of the Kings. It also served as a sanctuary of

DEIR
EL-BAHRI

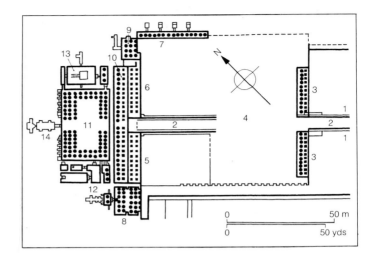

Deir el-Bahri, Temple
of Hatshepsut
1. Lower Terrace
2. Ramp
3. Lower colonnade
4. Middle Terrace
5. Punt colonnade
6. Birth colonnade
7. Colonnade
8. Hathor Chapel
9. Anubis Chapel
10. Osiride
    colonnade
11. Upper terrace
12. Mortuary suite
13. Altar Court
14. Sanctuary

Deir el-Bahri, Temple
of Hatshepsut:
Façade. (New
Kingdom, Eighteenth
Dynasty).

Amun, and included shrines for Hathor and **Anubis**, in
addition to an open-air court for the solar cult. Built of
fine limestone, and constructed on three levels linked by
sloping ramps, its design—the work of Hatshepsut's
cherished architect **Senmut**—was clearly influenced by the
nearby temple of Montuhotep I, but far surpasses its
neighbour in the sense of lightness and spaciousness which
it conveys. However, like the temple of Montuhotep, it
was seriously damaged by rock falls, and as seen today is
largely a reconstruction executed by the Polish National
Academy of Sciences.

Approached from its valley temple by a **causeway** lined

with sphinxes, the temple's lower terraces were preceded
by large forecourts, lush with ponds and avenues of trees;
the roots of one pair are visible in the concrete wells near
the entrance kiosk. The lower **colonnade** terminates at
either end with huge Osiride figures of the queen. Its
barrel-vaulted roof is supported by semi-square piers,
with an inner row of fluted polygonal columns: a
particularly elegant form, this type of column was
obviously favoured by Senmut, as it is extensively used
throughout the temple. The reliefs are very damaged, but
it is worth trying to decipher those in the southern
colonnade, which depict the transport by river of two huge
obelisks from the royal granite quarries at Aswan.

The **middle terrace** consists of a colonnade of square
pillars flanked by chapels for Hathor on the south and
Anubis on the north; on the north side of the court there is
also a fine colonnade of fluted polygonal columns. The
carvings in the colonnades are well preserved and retain
much of their original colouring, despite defacing carried
out first under Thutmose III, the legitimate heir of
Thutmose II, who upon his belated accession removed all
traces of Hatshepsut's image, and then under Akhenaten,
who disfigured all the images of Amun—these latter,
however, were later restored under the Ramessides. The
reliefs in the **southern colonnade** commemorate Hatshepsut's trading expedition to the people of Punt—believed to
be in modern Somalia—a meeting which probably took
place on the shores of the Atbara early in the 15th century
BC. Scenes depicted include the distinctive local houses,
built on stilts amid groves of coconut palms, the arrival of
the Egyptian delegation and their reception by the king
and queen, the exchange of goods, the embarkation and
transport of the exotic cargo—which included gold, apes
and incense trees in pots—and finally its presentation by
Hatshepsut to her 'Divine Father' Amun.

Adjoining the colonnade to the south is the **chapel of
Hathor**, worshipped here in her funerary aspect of the
'Lady of the West'. On the façade, she is represented in
bovine form licking Hatshepsut's hand, while on the
southern wall of the hall inside she suckles the queen. The
ceiling of this hall, now missing, was supported by

columns with Hathor capitals. The **shrine** itself is cut into the cliff behind and is preceded by a small hypostyle hall.

The **northern colonnade**, which has an inner row of fluted polygonal columns, is devoted to reliefs intended to support Hatshepsut's claim to the throne by depicting her conception and birth as the legitimate—male—child of Amun. Although many of the scenes are badly damaged, it is possible to discern the conception scene where Amun, seated on a bed with Hatshepsut's mother Ahmose, offers her the *ankh*, the sign of life. Later, the ram-headed creator god **Khnum** fashions Hatshepsut and her *ka* on his potter's wheel, after which Ahmose, her pregnant condition depicted with the utmost delicacy, is conveyed to the

Deir el-Bahri, Temple of Hatshepsut, Upper Terrace: Osiride colonnade. (New Kingdom, Eighteenth Dynasty).

birthing chair. After the delivery, the child is presented to Amun, who acknowledges it as his own before the other gods. Adjoining the colonnade to the north is the **shrine of Anubis**, the jackal-headed god of embalming. It comprises a hall with twelve fluted polygonal columns; on the west is a narrow corridor leading to a small sanctuary with a statue niche. The colours on the painted reliefs, which represent Hatshepsut and Thutmose III offering to Anubis and other funerary deities, are exceptionally well preserved; the fine star-spangled ceiling is particularly noteworthy.

The colonnade of the **upper terrace** (access restricted at present) is supported by colossal Osiride pillars representing Hatshepsut, which produce a fine dramatic effect. The view towards the great pylon of Karnak, 5 km (3 miles) away across the river, is equally impressive. Beyond the granite doorway in the colonnade is a peristyle court surrounded by fluted polygonal columns. On the northern side of the court is a complex dominated by an open court with an altar for the worship of the sun god, while on the south is a suite of chapels dedicated to funerary deities and the royal mortuary cult. The sanctuary, dedicated to Amun, is on the west. Originally comprising two rooms, a third chamber, dedicated to the deified architects Imhotep and Amenhotep son of Hapu, was added during the Ptolemaic period—surely a fitting tribute to Senmut's finest achievement.

THE SECRET TOMB OF SENMUT
A short distance east of the temple's first court is the entrance to the secret tomb of Senmut, whose burial chamber would have lain under the court of his royal mistress's monument. Those prepared to make the difficult descent down the steep, unlit corridor will find a small chamber with incomplete reliefs and paintings, including a striking portrait of Senmut; the astronomical ceiling is particularly interesting. A staircase by the south wall leads down to two more rooms with unfinished decoration.

TOMBS OF THE ASASIF
The large mudbrick pylons visible in the plain east of

Hatshepsut's temple, known as the Asasif, invariably provoke curiosity among visitors. They belong to the tombs of Twenty-sixth Dynasty nobles, only one of which, that of **Pabasa**, is open to the public. All, however, have similar plans, comprising a pylon, a long staircase descending, via a vestibule, to an open, pillared court cut from the bedrock, beyond which is a covered, pillared hall and sometimes a small chapel. The tomb shaft and burial chamber lie beneath. Many of the interesting reliefs of domestic and agricultural activities found in these tombs have been removed to the Egyptian Museum.

THE COLOSSI OF MEMNON

The Colossi of Memnon. (New Kingdom, Eighteenth Dynasty).

Virtually all that remains of his mortuary temple, which was quarried away in antiquity, these colossal seated statues of Amenhotep III once fronted its main entrance. Today they stand in splendid isolation beside the road from the ferry to Medinet Habu and the Valley of the Queens. Measuring almost 18 m (59 ft) high, the figures represent the king, flanked by his mother, Mutemwia, and the 'Great Wife' Tiye. Due to damage caused by the earthquake of 27 BC, the northern colossus used to emit strange musical sounds each day at dawn, presumably the result of expansion in the stone. Whatever its cause, copious Greek graffiti on the statue's left foot testify to the appeal the phenomenon held for tourists of the Graeco-Roman era, who identified the figure with Memnon, son of Aurora. Modern visitors, however, cannot hear the statue sing, as repairs carried out under **Septimius Severus** early in the third century AD silenced its voice forever.

TEMPLE OF SETI I

The remains of the Temple of Seti I are located close to the village of Qurna. Very little survives of the first two pylons and their courts, and entry is through a portico into the **hypostyle hall**, which has six papyrus bud columns, and is lined with small chapels. Decorated jointly by Seti and his son Ramesses II, the reliefs here are executed in sandstone, and thus are not so fine as those in Seti's temple at Abydos, or his tomb in the Valley of the Kings. The central part to the temple is dedicated to Seti, and the southern part to his father Ramesses I, whose short reign had allowed him no time to construct his own temple. In plan, the inner chambers of the temple bear some resemblance to those of the upper terrace of Hatshepsut's temple, having a central sanctuary dedicated to Amun, a suite on the south for the ancestral cult, and on the north an open court with an altar for the worship of the solar deity. While not among the most spectacular monuments of the west bank, the Temple of Seti I has the advantage of being little visited, and provides a rare haven for peaceful contemplation.

Oriented east-west, the Ramesseum—the mortuary temple of Ramesses II—is aligned with Luxor Temple on the opposite bank of the Nile. Built on the conventional temple plan, it comprises two pylons, two colonnaded courts, a hypostyle hall, a series of antechambers and subsidiary rooms, a bark shrine and a sanctuary. In addition, there was a modest palace on the south of the first court, which connected with the court by means of a **Window of Appearances**. A small temple to Ramesses' mother, Muttuya, adjoined the north side of the hypostyle

THE RAMESSEUM

1. First Pylon
2. First court
3. Palace buildings
4. Fallen colossus
5. Second Pylon
6. Osiride colonnade
7. Second court
8. Temple of Muttuya

(See over)

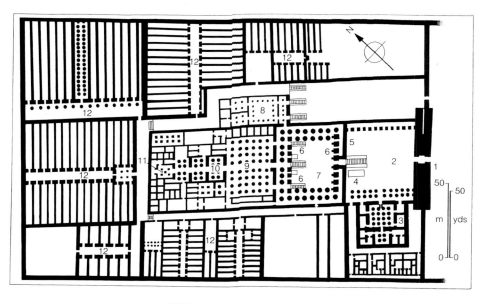

The Ramesseum: Vaulted mudbrick storage magazines. (New Kingdom, Nineteenth Dynasty).

hall. Behind the temple are numerous well preserved vaulted mudbrick storage magazines. Entry to the temple today is via the **second court**, lined with headless Osiride pillars of Ramesses which are seen to their best advantage in the moody shadows of early morning or late afternoon. To the east are the **ruined pylons**, carved with reliefs which include scenes from the battle of Kadesh. Scattered around the western end of the first court lie the shattered remains—feet, hands, broken limbs—of a colossal seated **granite figure** of Ramesses, originally some 17 m (55 ft) in height. The portico leading into the **hypostyle hall** is approached by three ramps, originally flanked by colossi; inside, only 29 of the original 48 sandstone papyrus bud columns survive. The ceiling of the room beyond boasts well preserved astronomical scenes.

However, the Ramesseum's chief claim to fame is as the **Tomb of Ozymandias** (a corruption of *User-Maat-Re*, Ramesses' coronation name) made famous by Diodorus and—much later—by Shelley. Even today, the lonely grandeur of its ruins makes it one of the most atmospheric sites in Egypt.

MEDINET HABU

(*Cont. p. 107*)

Approached from the east, the temple complex of Medinet Habu appears more like a fort, with its high crenellated stone walls and fortified gate: features which were to prove useful during the 12th century BC, when Thebes came under attack from bands of marauding Libyans. The most easily defended site in the district, it also assumed the role of the local economic and administrative centre, sheltering a vast collection of dwellings, storehouses, offices and workshops within its massive mudbrick inner walls. As at Karnak, the religious monuments were constructed over a very long period, in this case between the Eighteenth Dynasty and the Roman era, although the mortuary temple of Ramesses III belongs to his reign alone.

THE HIGH GATE

The complex was approached, as usual, by a canal from the river; visitors entering the temple today pass over

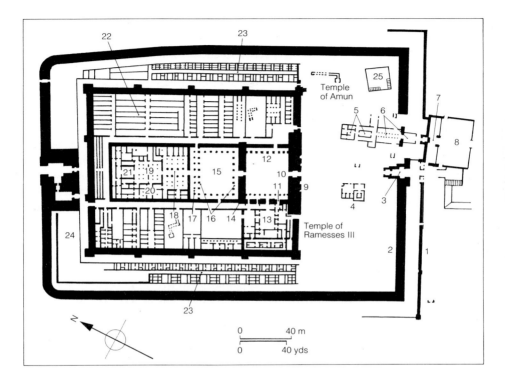

Temple of Amun

Temple of Ramesses III

0   40 m

0   40 yds

N

what remains of the quay. The high fortified gate originally measured about 22 m (72 ft) in height, and may to some extent have been inspired by contemporary Syrian military architecture. It fulfilled a double purpose, incorporating on the one hand defensive features such as its sloping base and the arrow slots hidden behind the stone consoles of prisoners' heads; while on the other, the upper levels, with their large rectangular windows, served as a retreat for the royal family during their visits to the temple. This dual function is reflected in the relief decoration; the carvings on the exterior depict mainly military scenes, while inside, Ramesses III is shown relaxing with the ladies of his harem. Ironically, it was probably here, in the thirty-first year of his reign, that some of these same women attempted to assassinate the king. Although he survived long enough to see the culprits caught and punished, Ramesses was dead within a month,

Temple of Ramesses III
9. First Pylon; 10. First court; 11. Window of Appearances; 12. Royal statues; 13. Palace; 14. Second Pylon; 15. Second court; 16. Osiride colonnade; 17. Portico; 18. Hypostyle hall; 19. Inner chambers; 20. Osiris suite; 21. Sanctuary; 22. Storage magazines; 23. Housing; 24. House of Butehamun; 25. Sacred Lake

Medinet Habu,
Temple of Ramesses
III: The High Gate.
(New Kingdom,
Twentieth Dynasty).

from causes which to this day remain the subject of speculation.

TEMPLE OF AMUN

Just inside the entrance to the north is the small Temple of Amun, a classic example of the growth of an Egyptian temple over many reigns. As always, the **sanctuary** area was constructed first, in this case by Hatshepsut; it comprises six interconnecting chambers, the innermost containing a large stone naos. In front of the sanctuary is a **bark shrine**, open on the east and west and surrounded by a roofed **ambulatory** enclosed on three sides by pillars. The work of Thutmose III, the reliefs on the northern wall depict the king participating in the temple foundation ceremonies. The **columned hall** to the east of the ambulatory was originally built by the Nubian pharaohs of the Twenty-fifth Dynasty, but was replaced by the present structure in the Ptolemaic period; the **pylon**, however, is of Twenty-fifth Dynasty date. Abutting its eastern side is a **portico** dating from the Saite period, but usurped by Nectanebo I of the Thirtieth Dynasty. Opposite the portico are the remnants of the Ptolemaic **pylon**, whose grand gateway is crowned with a splendid cavetto cornice adorned by a brightly-painted winged disc. The final addition, a spacious **forecourt**, dates from the reign of the Roman emperor **Antoninus Pius**.

THE CHAPELS OF THE DIVINE VOTARESSES

To the south of the Temple of Amun is a row of three tomb-chapels dating to the Twenty-fifth and Twenty-sixth Dynasties and belonging to the Divine Votaresses of Amun; powerful priestesses who were regarded as the living consorts of the divinity, these women were also members of the royal family and served as their representatives in Thebes. The basic plan of the chapels comprised a forecourt with a columned portico, an inner columned hall and a sanctuary area, with the interments beneath the floor. Above the entrance of one, an inscription exhorts passers-by to pray for the deceased, promising blessings to those who comply—and divine retribution to those who do not!

THE TEMPLE OF RAMESSES III

The mortuary temple of Ramesses III is of orthodox design and is closely modelled on the Ramesseum. Adjoining the first court on the south was a small **palace**, which was used by the living king during festivals and served after his death as a symbolic residence for his spirit. Built in two separate stages, the lower courses of the second phase have been reconstructed to convey some idea of its plan. The apartments included a throne room and audience hall in addition to private quarters, among which were a bedroom and bathroom for the king. The palace was roofed with barrel vaults; the sockets for their beams can still be discerned on the southern wall of the temple, above the **Window of Appearances** which connected it with the palace. Here, in the **first court**, the king would appear on a balcony—symbolically 'trampling' the prisoners' heads on the console below—to receive tribute or distribute honours. Nearby reliefs depict members of the court watching the ceremonial wresting matches common on such occasions. On the colonnade opposite is a row of huge engaged statues of the king.

The **second court** is surrounded by colonnades of papyrus bud columns on the north and south and Osiride pillars on the east and west; the western colonnade is raised to form a **portico**, which has an inner row of papyrus bud columns. In contrast to the martial scenes found in the first court, the reliefs here focus on the

Medinet Habu, Temple of Ramesses III: Exterior view. The remains of the palace buildings are visible on the left of the picture. (New Kingdom, Twentieth Dynasty).

religious festivals of the temple. During the Christian era, this court was converted into a church by the Copts, who were responsible for the damage to the Osiride figures. The rooms beyond are in a very poor condition, having been used as a quarry in antiquity, but comprised the normal sequence of hypostyle halls, vestibules and chapels. The **sanctuary** was, as usual, dedicated to Amun, and in keeping with the funerary nature of the temple, separate suites of rooms were dedicated to Osiris and Re-Harakhty.

The exterior of the temple is covered with carvings in sunk relief; the royal names and titles were cut exceptionally deeply, presumably to discourage usurpation by later monarchs. The **pylon**, measuring 65 m (213 ft) wide by 27 m (88 ft) high, depicts Ramesses III in the conventional attitude of striking captives, while the north and west walls are occupied by lively scenes of land and sea battles; on the south wall is an enormous calendar listing the temple festivals. Surrounding the temple are the mudbrick remains of its secular buildings; particularly noteworthy is the remnant of the house of **Butehamun**, a scribe from Deir el-Medina who moved here when the village was abandoned during the reign of **Ramesses IX**. Lying at the back of Ramesses' temple, only two rooms of the house survive, but it is easily identified by its white columns.

THE VALLEY
OF THE
KINGS

From the time of Thutmose I to the end of the New Kingdom, all the rulers of Egypt were interred in the Valley of the Kings, a remote *wadi* located to the west of the cliffs of Deir-el-Bahri. The *wadi*—a dry water course—has two arms, the Western Valley where the tombs of Amenhotep III and Ay were found, and the Eastern Valley, which accommodates the majority of the monuments. Sixty-two tombs have been discovered so far, though not all belonged to kings, the privilege of a burial in the Valley having occasionally been granted to high officials.

Not all of the tombs in the valley are open to the public, but enough can be visited to form an impression of their stylistic development. The earliest accessible tomb is that of **Thutmose III**, secreted in a remote cleft of the valley wall. After descending its steep corridors, the 'God's Passages', one encounters a deep well, once filled with limestone rubble; it may have been designed to draw off water from the flash floods which periodically devastate the valley, but its name, the '**Hall of Hindering**', suggests that its magical function was to ward off intruders, whether physical or spiritual. Should tomb robbers have penetrated this far, they would have encountered an apparent dead end, the doorway having been plastered over and painted to match the walls. Had its presence been detected, the room beyond (which would have been the burial chamber in the earliest tombs) had been made to look like an incomplete burial chamber. Here the axis of the tomb makes a right-angled turn, the stairway to the true burial chamber beneath being concealed in a corner of the floor. This latter room was known as the '**House of Gold**', for reasons that will be obvious to readers who have seen the gilded shrines and golden funerary equipment of Tutankhamun in the Egyptian Museum.

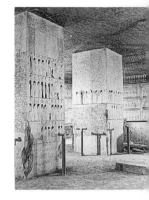

Valley of the Kings, Tomb of Thutmose III: Burial chamber. (New Kingdom, Eighteenth Dynasty).

Here, the beautiful oval chamber has two central pillars and four side chambers for grave goods. The walls are adorned with paintings resembling a papyrus scroll, and the cartouche-shaped red quartzite sarcophagus, carved with the figures of goddesses, remains *in situ*. The tomb of Amenhotep II is similar in plan to his father's, but is laid out more regularly, having a rectangular burial chamber with six pillars and four side rooms; a sunken recess at the far end accommodates the sarcophagus. The decoration— texts from the *Amduat*, the 'Book of What is in the Underworld'—is also similar to that of Thutmose III, but the drawings are by comparison rigid and formal.

The most famous tomb in the valley is that of **Tutankhamun**, discovered intact by Howard Carter in 1922, thanks to its having been buried under an enormous heap of rubble created by the excavation of the tomb of Ramesses VI above. Comprising just four small rooms, the tomb was probably intended for the vizier **Ay**—who succeeded Tutankhamun onto the throne—and was hurriedly adapted upon the young king's unexpected death. The only decorations are some hastily-executed paintings in the burial chamber, in which Ay is depicted performing the Opening of the Mouth ceremony on Tutankhamun's mummy; these paintings have suffered badly from the volume of visitors in the tomb, necessitating conservation work. By far the most impressive tomb of this period is that of Ay's successor, **Horemheb**. The deepest in the valley at 105 m (115 yds) long, it is famous for its brightly-painted reliefs; those left unfinished in the burial chamber clearly illustrate the different stages of execution.

Universally esteemed as the finest in the valley, the tomb of **Seti I** set the pattern for all later tombs in terms of the disposition of the religious texts and scenes intended to protect the king on his journeyings in the Underworld; as one would expect, these are executed, with Seti's typical delicacy and attention to detail, in fine coloured bas-reliefs. By this date, the tomb plan had been extended and the well-room reduced to a mere symbolic vestige, while the burial chamber had been elaborated into a high vaulted chamber, here decorated with a magnificent star map. This ongoing simplification of plan reached its logical conclusion in the tomb of **Merneptah**, where the basic elements of the tomb were rearranged along a single straight corridor. All the later tombs in the valley broadly conform to this type, while at the same time there was a tendency to excavate increasingly larger monuments. Among the most interesting examples are those of Ramesses III, with its splendid façade of sculptured bulls-head standards and its painted side-chambers for grave goods, the tomb of Ramesses IV, which retains its gargantuan sarcophagus, and the tomb of Ramesses VI, with its glorious astronomical ceilings.

THE VALLEY OF THE QUEENS

The burial site of the royal wives and children, the tombs of the Valley of the Queens are smaller, simpler versions of those found in the Valley of the Kings. The finest belonged to **Nefertari**, the beloved Chief Wife of Ramesses II; unfortunately, its beautiful paintings have suffered enormous damage from the rising water table, and the tomb is currently closed for conservation. Most of the other monuments date from the Twentieth Dynasty, and three of these are presently open to the public. Visitors are usually shown the tomb of **Amenhirkhopshef**, a son of Ramesses III, who even named his children after those of his hero, Ramesses II. Comprising two passages and an unfinished burial chamber, it is decorated with fine painted reliefs representing Ramesses III presenting the prince to the various underworld deities. The tomb of **Khaemwese**, another son of the same king, is decorated in similar fashion, although here the plan is slightly more elaborate and the burial chamber has been completed. Although badly damaged, the tomb of **Titi**, an obscure Twentieth Dynasty princess, is perhaps the most interesting of all. Approached by a long corridor, the central hall of the tomb has three small side-rooms delicately painted with mythological scenes. The **western chamber** probably contained the princess's canopic jars, which are depicted on the southern wall; the western wall has a delightful scene of the cow goddess Hathor in her aspect of Lady of the West, emerging from the Western Mountain, believed to mark the entrance to the Underworld.

Thanks to its location in a remote desert valley, the village of the royal necropolis workers at Deir el-Medina is among the very few ancient habitation sites to be preserved in good condition. Established during the reign of Thutmose I, the village underwent considerable expansion during the reign of Seti I, but was finally abandoned in the time of **Ramesses IX** of the Twentieth Dynasty, when its isolated situation made it vulnerable to Libyan raids and civil disorder. The extraordinary amount of documentation recovered from the site in the form of ostraca included letters, legal documents and laundry-lists, songs, stories and sketches, prayers, poems and pornography, which together have enabled scholars to piece together a vivid picture of the villagers' life. The workmen themselves spent eight or nine days of the ten-day week away at their work in the Valley of the Kings or Valley of the Queens, where they passed their nights in temporary camps, returning to the village only at

DEIR EL-MEDINA

Deir el-Medina:
Limestone ostracon
bearing a sketch of a
mason executed by
one of his colleagues.
(New Kingdom).
Fitzwilliam Museum,
Cambridge.

Plan of a typical Deir
el-Medina house
 1. Door to street
 2. Entrance room
 3. Shrine
 4. Living room
 5. Column
 6. Divan
 7. Entrance to cellar
 8. Bedroom
 9. Passage
10. Bench
11. Kitchen
12. Oven
13. Mortar
14. Stairs to cellar
15. Stairs to roof

weekends. During the week, therefore, the town was the province of the women, who enjoyed the luxury of state-supplied domestic help, cleaners and laundrymen being allocated to households on a rotation basis. The remote location of the village, chosen in a rather naïve attempt to preserve the secrets of the royal tombs, meant that all the community's needs, including food, drink and clothing, had to be brought up from the valley. On several occasions during the Twentieth Dynasty, the workmen responded to disruptions in these supplies by striking—the earliest recorded industrial action!

THE VILLAGE

The entrance and oldest part of the town lies on the northeast, ending where the main street makes a right-angled bend; the district southwest of this was constructed during the Ramesside period. Of almost seventy houses in the village, a dozen have been identified as belonging to known families; in some cases their names are painted on the doorposts. Constructed of mudbrick on stone foundations, the basic plan of the houses comprises an entrance hall with a raised shrine, a living room with a brick divan and one or more wooden columns supporting the ceiling (the stone bases are still visible in many houses) and an open-air kitchen area with a clay oven and stone mortar. Stairways led down to cellars for the storage of valuables and household commodities, and up to the upper storeys, which incorporated bedrooms and additional storage space. The interior walls were plastered and painted: traces of the colour can still be discerned here and there. It is such fragile survivals which lend the site its poignancy, for nowhere is the modern visitor closer to the

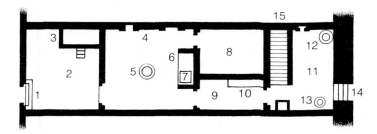

114

ordinary people of ancient Egypt. Wandering the narrow streets, one can almost hear the voices of the children who were born in the little houses and played in the alleys, grew up, married, laughed and worked, ate and drank beer, and finally went to their rest in tombs made by their own hands.

Deir el-Medina, Tomb of Sennedjem: Burial chamber. Sennedjem and his wife worship the gods of the Underworld. (New Kingdom, Nineteenth Dynasty).

THE TOMBS

Perhaps because of their occupation, the village workmen were more aware than most of the need to prepare for the afterlife. They were also uniquely placed to equip themselves with burial places of the highest quality, since by bartering their services among the community, they were able to marshal all the skills necessary for the construction, decoration and furnishing of their tombs. The outer part of these comprised an open court, a portico and a small mudbrick pyramid over an inner chapel, while a concealed pit led to a vaulted burial chamber. Unusually, the burial chambers are decorated, and even more unusually the subjects chosen are a variety of mythological scenes, clearly inspired by those found in the royal tombs.

115

For many visitors, these tiny, gem-like chambers are the highlight of the west bank monuments. At present, only two are accessible: the tomb of **Sennedjem**, located just a few metres from his home in the southwest corner of the village, and that of **Anherkhau** nearby. The eastern end of Sennedjem's chamber is dominated by a scene of the tomb owner and his wife engaged in ploughing, sowing and reaping in the Fields of Iaru, the Egyptian equivalent of the Elysian Fields, while elsewhere the couple are shown venerating various funerary deities. Anherkhau's tomb paintings are distinguished by their bright gold background, typical of the late Ramesside era.

THE TEMPLE OF HATHOR

To the northeast of the village is the small well-preserved Ptolemaic Temple of Hathor, which overlies several New Kingdom foundations. Extremely simple in plan, it comprises a small hypostyle hall with two Hathor columns, a vestibule and a triple sanctuary, and is enclosed by well preserved pan-bedded walls.

TOMBS OF
THE NOBLES

Among the most appealing monuments of Egypt, there are over 400 private tombs, mainly dating from the New Kingdom, scattered about Luxor's west bank. Most, of course, are badly damaged, having been reused by local residents as houses, stores and stables, and few are presently accessible. However, a particularly well-preserved group of New Kingdom tombs, situated on the hillside of Sheikh abd el-Qurna near the Ramesseum, is kept open for the public. These tombs are divided into three groups—the Village group at the bottom of the hill, the Lower Enclosure on its northern slops, and the Upper Enclosure to the west, uphill from the village.

In general, the Theban private tombs of the New Kingdom comprise an open forecourt preceding a T-shaped chapel surmounted by a small brick pyramid; a shaft located in the court or chapel led to an undecorated burial chamber cut into the rock below. The chief appeal of these tombs lies in their lively painted scenes of everyday episodes in the lives of their owners.

The oldest tomb in the village group is that of **Userhet**, comprising a small, T-shaped chapel with a statue niche at the far end. Among its wide variety of paintings is a banquet scene, an innovation introduced in the New Kingdom as a device to include the tomb owner's family and friends in the scheme of decoration. The finest paintings, however, are found in the tomb of the royal astronomer **Nakht**, which has recently been restored. Two tombs of the group, those of the royal scribe **Khaemhet** and the vizier **Ramose**, date from the reign of Amenhotep III, and are decorated in the superb raised relief typical of the period. The tomb of Ramose featured a large transverse hall with thirty-two columns and an inner hall with eight columns. The high quality of the workmanship is probably attributable to the fact that the tomb was built for Ramose by his brother **Amenhotep**, the Chief of Works at Memphis. Spanning the reigns of Amenhotep III and Akhenaten, the exquisite relief decoration is partly traditional and partly in the revolutionary Amarna style. It was left unfinished at the time of Ramose's death, essential scenes having been hastily added in paint on the southwest wall.

The tombs of the Lower Enclosure are closed at present, but two very interesting tombs in the Upper Enclosure are accessible. The tomb of **Rekhmire**, vizier of Thutmose III, is one of the most fascinating monuments of ancient Thebes, providing priceless glimpses of the official aspects of court life. The central arm of the T-shaped chapel is exceptionally long and high, its western wall covered with scenes depicting life in the temple workshops at Karnak.

A little higher up the hill is the tomb of the Major of Thebes, **Sennefer**, whose tomb, dating from the reign of Amenhotep II, is different in that it comprises a painted antechamber and pillared burial chamber, roughly hewn from the rock. The decoration, however, is remarkably sophisticated. Perhaps in reference to Sennefer's duty as overseer of the gardens of Amun, an enormous painted vine, heavy with bunches of grapes, snakes across the undulating ceiling, which is also adorned with brightly-coloured imitation mats.

Sheikh abd el-Qurna, Tomb of Sennefer: Decorated burial chamber. (New Kingdom, Eighteenth Dynasty).

THE SOUTH AND
ASWAN

Just south of Luxor, the Nile resumes its normal south-north course and the landscape becomes increasingly arid until, at a point just south of Edfu, the familiar limestone scenery of the north finally yields to the southern sandstone. From here the landscape changes dramatically, as the river, leaving behind the green expanses of fields, cuts through high gorges, or glides past rolling dunes of yellow sand dotted with spiky dom palms. The sky is an unrelenting blue, and the temperature soars as the latitude nears the Tropic of Cancer. At Aswan, scattered granite outcrops mark the First Cataract of the Nile, the historical boundary of Egypt; until the recent completion of the tourist road to Abu Simbel, the only land communications to the south from here were the ancient desert caravan routes.

The region abounds in remains from both the earliest and latest periods of ancient Egyptian history. Located on the west bank of the Nile, approximately 30 km (18½ miles) south of Esna, is the site of Kom el-Ahmar, known as Hieraconpolis to the Greeks and Nekhen to the Egyptians, which with its twin town of Nekheb (modern El-Kab) on the opposite bank, was one of the earliest urban settlements and the predynastic religious centre of Upper Egypt. The island of Elephantine, at modern Aswan, has also been inhabited since prehistoric times. Straddling the boundary of Egypt and Nubia, its ancient name, *Abu*, was also the word for ivory, reflecting its importance as a major crossroads of the Saharan trade routes. On the east bank a second settlement, Syene, grew up around the granite quarries. There was in addition a garrison, part of Egypt's elaborate defences against possible attacks from the south. During the Graeco-Roman period a flurry of temple-building in Upper Egypt, expressing the determination of Egypt's foreign rulers to maintain a high profile in the remote corners of their

(*Opposite*) Edfu, Temple of Horus: view along the main axis from the hypostyle hall to the sanctuary. (Ptolemaic Period).

empires, produced the great monuments at Esna, Edfu, Kom Ombo and Philae, where the Temple of Isis remained an important pilgrim centre well into the Christian era.

ESNA

Located on the west bank of the Nile, 55 km (34 miles) south of Luxor, Esna's Greek name, Latopolis, was derived from the Nile Perch, *Lates Niloticus*, which was venerated in the locality. Like Aswan, the city's wealth came from trade, having served until the end of the last century as the Nile terminus of one of the important Sudanese caravan routes. Of its numerous ancient monuments, all that now survives is the Roman hypostyle hall of a temple dedicated principally to the ram-headed potter god **Khnum**, together with the temple quay, which is still in use. Partly cleared by the French archaeologist Mariette during the last century, the temple remains are now 9 m (30 ft) below modern street level due to the accumulation of occupation debris; its sandstone reliefs have suffered badly as a result of seepage from the surrounding houses, which lack modern drainage.

Containing 24 columns, the **hypostyle hall** measures 32.8 m (108 ft) by 16.4 m (54 ft), and was decorated by a series of Roman emperors between the first and third centuries AD; a reminder of their less savoury activities can be found in the group of **Septimius Severus** and his sons located in the southeastern corner, where the figure of Geta was erased following his assassination by his elder brother Caracalla. Facing east, towards the river, the façade of the hall consists of columns linked by screen walls surmounted by a uraeus frieze. The central door has a split lintel, a useful feature which enabled the frequent processions entering and leaving the temple to pass without lowering the divine standards, which were carried aloft on poles. Many of these festivals are detailed in the calendrical texts inscribed on the columns, whose chief architectural interest lies in their magnificent composite capitals; these are seen to their best advantage in the early morning, when long shafts of pale light penetrate the hall's lofty interior.

On the east bank of the Nile, 32 km (20 miles) south of Esna, the location of El-Kab, ancient Nekheb, is heralded by the appearance of its towering mudbrick city walls. The cult centre of the vulture goddess **Nekhbet**, the tutelary goddess of Upper Egypt, Nekheb was nonetheless overshadowed by its twin town Nekhen until the New Kingdom, when it took over the role of provincial capital from its neighbour.

Apart from a cluster of ruined houses and temples in the southern corner, little of the city itself survives. However, it is well worth climbing the ramparts simply to gaze out across the overgrown site, for few locations in Egypt convey such a sense of sheer antiquity. Truly awesome, the twelve metre thick walls enclose an area of approximately 31 ha (76½ acres). The entrance is on the northeast, via one of the original gateways, whose dimensions seem to mock human scale; inside, a ramp just to the south leads to the top of the wall.

In the cliffs half a kilometre (⅓ mile) to the north is a group of nobles' tombs; dating from the New Kingdom, they consist of simple vaulted rock-cut chapels. Four tombs are generally open to the public: that of **Ahmose** son of Ibana, is famous for its biographical text detailing battles with the Hyksos during their period of occupation. Two others, those of Ahmose's grandson **Paheri** and of **Renni** (both Mayors of Nekheb) have an unusual range of painted reliefs. Northeast of the town enclosure, in a deserted *wadi*, is a little-visited group of rock-cut chapels and stelae dating from various periods, appealing chiefly for the lonely charm of their setting.

EL-KAB

Inhabited at least since Old Kingdom times, the city of Edfu, located on the west bank of the river, 52 km, (32 miles) south of Esna, is best known today for the magnificent Ptolemaic Temple of Horus, the falcon-headed god of kingship. Located approximately 1 km (⅔ mile) west of the Nile, its colossal sandstone pylon dwarfs the houses that have clustered around it, encroaching on the sacred precincts. It had been almost completely buried

EDFU

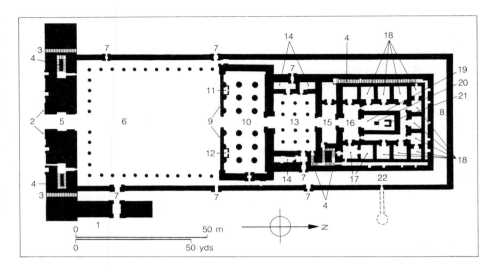

under the town until the 1860's, when it was partially cleared by Mariette, and it was not until the beginning of the present century that complete clearance and restoration was carried out.

The **Temple of Horus**, is the most complete and best preserved temple in Egypt. It is also the best documented, thanks to the copious foundation and building texts inscribed on its walls. These inform us, for example, that the construction and decoration of the temple spanned in total 180 years—from 237 BC to 57 BC—a twenty-year delay having been incurred by the disturbed political situation. Appropriately enough, the plan of the temple is virtually identical to that of Horus' spouse, Hathor of Dendera, which was intentionally modelled on Edfu. From the visitor's point of view, the two temples complement each other well, for while the roofs and crypts visible at Dendera are here inaccessible to visitors, the pylon and peristyle court never constructed there can be seen at Edfu in their completion.

Entry to the site is, unimpressively, from the rear of the temple, and it is necessary to walk around the well-preserved inner enclosure wall to the vast forecourt before being able to appreciate the full dramatic effect of its façade. Just outside the court is a birth house of the same type as that at Dendera, but rather more ruined. The massive **pylon**, 79 m (259 ft) wide by 35 m (115 ft) high, is conventionally adorned with images of the 'pharaoh' **Ptolemy XIII** striking captives and offering to the gods, in affirmation of his role as defender of Egypt and guarantor of its stability. The great **gateway** is crowned with a concave cornice adorned with a winged disc, a symbol of Horus which recurs throughout the temple. As the main temple door, this would only have been opened to allow the passage of the divine processions during temple festivals, such as the Feast of the Beautiful Meeting, the annual visit of Hathor of Dendera to her husband's temple for the celebration of their sacred marriage. Episodes from this festival are represented in the reliefs of the lowest register on the southern wall of the **peristyle court**.

The court itself is surrounded on three sides by porches supported by 32 columns with a variety of elaborate capitals arranged symmetrically in pairs. Like most temples, Edfu was built over earlier religious foundations; numerous blocks from a New Kingdom temple previously on the site were recently discovered in the paving of the court and are displayed nearby. While the present structure—unusually—faces south, the earlier temple was conventionally oriented towards the river; a door on the east side of the court led, via a pylon of Ramesses III, to the original processional way, now buried under the modern town. At the northern end of the court, the

Edfu: The pylon, Temple of Horus. (Ptolemaic period).

interior of the hypostyle hail is shielded from view by columns linked by screen walls; the entrance was flanked by an enormous pair of granite falcons, one of which survives intact, a reminder of the importance of statuary in Egyptian temples.

The lofty ceiling of the **first hypostyle hall** is supported by 18 columns with composite capitals; as at Esna, their texts in the main recount the temple festivals. An unusual feature is the pair of tiny rooms built onto the interior of the screen wall. The chamber on the west probably served as a vestry, while that on the east was used as a small library for religious texts, whose titles are listed in the inscriptions; niches for the papyrus scrolls can be discerned in the interior. The chief point of interest in the hall, however, is the fine series of reliefs depicting the temple foundation ceremonies, a series of archaic rituals clearly related more closely to early building practices than to those of the time—as, for example, where the king is shown making mudbricks.

Only at Edfu is it possible to fully experience the masterly engineering of light and space inherent in the design of the Egyptian temple. Ahead, in the **second hypostyle hall** or Festival Hall, the floor is already higher, the roof lower, the chamber narrower. The only light streams in slender threads from slits in the ceiling. The sole focus is the small, unlit **sanctuary**, the holy-of-holies, whose empty granite naos once housed the divine image inhabited by the 'living god'. In front of it is the pedestal for Horus' **sacred bark**, a modern replica of which is displayed in the chapel behind the sanctuary.

The Festival Hall is as usual lined with service rooms, stores for the liquid and solid offerings being located on the east and west respectively. Visitors are often shown the room known as the 'Laboratory', where incense and unguents were prepared for temple use; the walls are covered with recipes, and with charming reliefs showing offerings of flowers and fragrant plants, as well as a fine array of perfume vessels. From either side of the hall, doorways lead into the **ambulatory** between the side of the temple and its inner enclosure wall; on the east is a staircase leading to the **well** which supplied pure water for the temple rituals. Used by the priesthood to facilitate movement around the temple, the ambulatory may also have been accessible to privileged laymen at certain times. The sunk relief decorations are certainly of a semi-public nature; the most interesting, located on the inside of the western exterior wall, relate episodes from a ritual play entitled 'The Triumph of Horus'. Enacted annually at Edfu, the drama—in which Horus and his human embodiment, the living king, defeat the forces of evil personified by Seth in the form of a hippopotamus—symbolized the cosmic struggle between the forces of order and chaos.

GEBEL SILSILA

Although seldom visited, travellers on Nile cruises in particular may be interested to note the location of the ancient sandstone quarries at Gebel Silsila, 48 km (30 miles) south of Edfu. Extending for approximately 2 km (1 mile) on the west bank of the Nile and 1 km (⅔ mile) on the east, these quarries supplied the bulk of the stone used in the great monuments of Upper Egypt. Apart from the quarry workings, the site is distinguished by numerous rock-cut stelae and shrines, mainly dating from the New Kingdom, some of which are very elaborate.

KOM OMBO

Due to an eastward shift in the course of the Nile, the temple of Kom Ombo, 70 km (43 miles) south of Edfu, now enjoys what is surely the most dramatic location in Egypt, perched among emerald fields of sugar-cane above the eastern bank. It is at its most beautiful in the late afternoon, when the rays of the setting sun cast long shadows in its ruined halls, colouring the sandstone a ruddy gold.

Dating from the Ptolemaic period, the temple is unusual in being dedicated to two gods, **Harwer**, or **Horus the Elder**, and the crocodile-headed Nile god **Sobek**. While the majority of the cult chambers were shared by the deities, the eastern half being dedicated to Sobek and the western half to Harwer, each had his own sanctuary and processional way. The temple has a number of other double features, including a double inner enclosure wall,

Kom Ombo, Temple
of Harwer and Sobek
1. Pylon
2. Outer enclosure
   wall
3. Outer
   ambulatory
4. Inner enclosure
   wall
5. Inner ambulatory
6. Main entrances
7. Side entrances
8. Peristyle court
9. First hypostyle
   hall
10. Second
   hypostyle hall
11. Vestibules
12. Twin sanctuaries
13. Staircases to roof
14. Hearing Ear icon

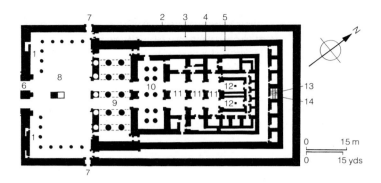

Kom Ombo, Temple
of Harwer and
Sobek: view along
the double axis to the
twin sanctuaries.
(Ptolemaic Period).

which creates an inner and an outer ambulatory around the sanctuary area. The outer ambulatory was the province of the pilgrims who flocked to the temple seeking healing from Horus 'The Good Doctor'; its pavements are covered with the graffiti they scratched to pass the time—names, games, gods, trees, ships and always feet—their own feet, pointing towards the sanctuaries, enabling them to stand in the gods' presence forever. As usual, the cult focus of the temple was located immediately behind the sanctuaries; here it comprised a small **statue niche** flanked by images of Sobek and Harwer, and equipped with carvings of ears which enabled the deities to 'hear' their supplicants. Nearby, on the opposite wall is

126

a famous **panel** which appears to represent a variety of medical instruments.

Behind the sanctuaries is a suite of small rooms whose half-finished decoration furnishes a good illustration of the stages in the carving of raised relief. The inner apartments of the temple are much ruined, but the elegant proportions of the **hypostyle hall** can still be admired, and some pleasing relief carvings can be found here and there. When excavated, the underground crypts visible around the sanctuaries were discovered to be stuffed with mummified crocodiles sacred to Sobek; some examples are displayed in the small **Chapel of Hathor** to the east of the temple. To the west is a large circular **well**, accessible by staircases and connected to a cistern and a rectangular basin. Some writers have suggested that the well may also have served as a pool for the sacred crocodiles, an appealing theory which as yet lacks conclusive evidence. In addition there is a ruined **birth house** in front of the temple.

The city of Aswan, 40 km (25 miles) south of Kom Ombo, nestles attractively beside the Nile, against a dramatic backdrop of the desert cliffs and granite islands of the First Cataract. The modern name of the town is derived from *swenet*, the ancient Egyptian word for trade, and even today, Aswan's heritage as a caravan town is reflected in its splendid bazaar, packed with exotic African spices. It has also remained a garrison town, although the modern soldiers who protect the High Dam today definitely belong to a different age from the border guards of antiquity.

ASWAN

ELEPHANTINE

The site of the first settlement in the district, the island of Elephantine is reached by a ferry running from the southern end of the Corniche. The majority of the monuments, which on the whole are very ruined, are clustered at the southern end of the island, around the remains of a temple dedicated to Khnum; they include the vaulted mudbrick tombs in which the sacred rams of the god were interred. The best preserved building is the **Nilometer**, a steep stone staircase descending into the river, which was used to measure the level of the annual inundation. Similar installations, many of them in use until modern times, were set up along the river; as the height of the inundation was crucial to the harvest, it was often used in ancient times in calculating the level of taxation, which was levied as a proportion of the crop. Nearby is a small museum (closed on Mondays) devoted to local archaeological finds dating from prehistoric times onwards. The granite rocks of the island and its vicinity are covered with inscriptions and royal cartouches of different periods; aficionados of graffiti can find a wealth of ancient inscriptions on the island of Sehel, further upstream.

QUBBET EL-HAWWA TOMBS
With that unerring Egyptian instinct for a dramatic location, the nobles of Elephantine chose a high sand-stone bluff on the west bank of the Nile for the site of their rock-cut tombs. The modern name of the site, which translates as 'Dome of the Wind', derives from the domed tomb of a Muslim saint visible on the summit. Access is by boat: there is a ferry from the northern end of the Corniche. A lonely spot, seldom visited, the stiff climb up to the tombs is amply rewarded by the magnificent panorama of the town and islands below. Dating from the Old Kingdom to the Roman period, few of the tombs are now in good condition. One of the more remarkable is the double tomb of the father and son **Mehu** and **Sabni**, whose steep twin causeways can be seen from the opposite bank. Dating from the reign of **Pepi II**, the chapel contains 18 roughly-cut columns and has false doors on the west wall; there are also some wall paintings, executed, like the architecture, in a rather crude provincial style. The tomb of **Harkhuf**, from the same reign, is far simpler, comprising a courtyard and chapel with four pillars; its chief interest lies in the delightful commemorative text describing how he brought a dancing pygmy from the Sudan to the royal court in Memphis. Two other monuments of interest are the Twelfth Dynasty tombs of **Sarenput I** and

his grandson **Sarenput II**. The chapels of these are far more elaborate; that of Sarenput II is particularly sophisticated, comprising a pillared hall, a corridor lined with mummiform statues of the deceased and a second small pillared hall with a statue niche.

GRANITE QUARRIES

Exploited from remote antiquity for their beautiful red and black granite, there are numerous ancient quarries in the Aswan district. Visitors are most often taken to the Northern Quarries, where the star exhibit is a huge **unfinished obelisk**, 41.75 m (137 ft) long, which if completed would have weighed almost 12,200 kgs (1200 tons). Possibly dating to the reign of Hatshepsut, work on the obelisk was abandoned when a flaw in the stone was discovered. Although this accident must have been viewed as a tragedy at the time, it has provided modern archaeologists and engineers with much valuable information concerning ancient quarrying techniques, which chiefly seem to have relied on continuous pounding with heavy balls of dolerite, an exceptionally hard stone.

Aswan: the unfinished obelisk.

PHILAE

Unlike most of the major cult centres of Egypt, the Temple of Isis at Philae does not appear to have been an ancient foundation, as the earliest remains discovered there date from the Twenty-fifth Dynasty. The site seems to have developed as an adjunct to a shrine of Osiris on nearby Biga Island, but had by the Roman period become the foremost pilgrimage centre of Egypt. Philae also has the distinction of having been the last functioning temple of the ancient religion, serving the cult of Isis until closed down by **Justinian** in AD 551.

During the 19th century, Philae again became a centre of pilgrimage, this time for a new breed of Nile tourists. However, at the beginning of the present century, the construction of the first Aswan Dam condemned its temples to partial submersion for most of the year, and with the prospect of the High Dam, they seemed doomed to total annihilation. Fortunately, the technology evolved for the rescue of the Abu Simbel monuments was

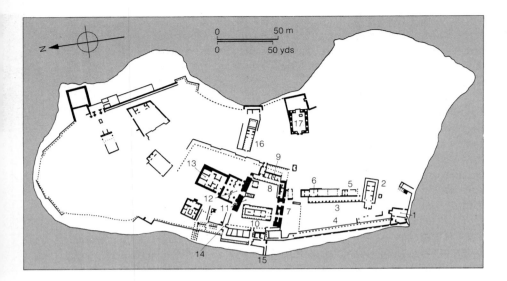

Philae, Temple of Isis
1. Kiosk of Nectanebo
2. Temple of Arensnuphis
3. Eastern colonnade
4. Western colonnade
5. Chapel of Mandulis
6. Chapel of Imhotep
7. First Pylon
8. Court
9. Service rooms
10. Birth house
11. Second Pylon
12. Hypostyle hall
13. Sanctuary
14. Gateway of Hadrian
15. Nilometer
16. Temple of Hathor
17. Kiosk of Trajan

adaptable to Philae's situation, and in 1980 the relocated temples reopened to the public on the nearby island of Agilkia, which was landscaped to match the original; it can be reached by boat from the nearby Tourist Harbour.

Modern visitors disembark at the southern end of the island, not far from the original landing stage. On the southwest is the earliest structure on the island, a **kiosk of Nectanebo I**, while to the north is the ruined Ptolemaic temple of the Nubian deity **Arensnuphis**. Between the two is the entrance to the forecourt of the Temple of Isis, bounded on the east and west by **Roman colonnades**; the columns display a fine variety of composite capitals, and the back wall of the western colonnade has windows which once overlooked Biga Island. Behind the eastern colonnade are two small chapels dedicated to **Mandulis**, a Nubian solar deity, and the deified architect **Imhotep**.

Dating to the late Ptolemaic and Roman periods, the **Temple of Isis** was the main monument on the island. It has a distinct bend in its axis, probably the result of constraints of space; a **gateway of Ptolemy II** close to the first pylon is oriented east-west, suggesting that the buildings in this area were originally arranged quite differently. The towers of the present **first pylon** were

built by **Ptolemy XII** around an existing doorway of
Nectanebo I; on the eastern wall inside is an inscription of
1799 recording the presence of the Napoleonic Survey. A
door in the western tower leads directly to the **birth house**,
unusually located in the temple's first court. Built by
Ptolemy VI, with additions by later rulers, it consists of a
columned portico, two vestibules and a sanctuary; some
fine reliefs here illustrate the mythology of the birth of
Horus, who is shown on the north wall as a falcon
emerging from the marshes of the Delta. Like other birth
houses of the period, it is surrounded by an **ambulatory**
formed by screen walls linking columns with elaborate
Hathor capitals. On the east of the court is a suite of five
service rooms fronted by a **colonnade of Ptolemy VIII**. The
granite outcrop in the northeast corner forms part of the
original surface of the island; the fact that it was left *in situ*
may indicate that it was considered in some way sacred.

Philae, Temple of Isis:
view from the west.
(Graeco-Roman
Period).

The **second pylon** is also the work of Ptolemy VIII and,
like his colonnade, it was decorated by Ptolemy XII.
Beyond, the transverse **hypostyle hall** is unusual in that its
southern section lay open to the sky. Unfortunately,
between the damage wrought by the Christians who
converted the hall into a church in the sixth century and
that done by the temple's resident bird population, the
effect of what must once have been an impressive
chamber has been seriously marred. The **sanctuary**,
preceded by three vestibules, is a simple rectangular room
flanked by a pair of side chapels; the naos is missing, but
the pedestal for the sacred bark of Isis remains *in situ*. As
in other temples, there are crypts beneath the floors, but
access to these, and to the roof, is restricted at present.

Among the numerous ruined structures to the east of
the temple is a **gateway of Hadrian**, which is ornamented
with bizarre and fascinating carvings of local mythology.
On the north wall, the source of the Nile, generally
believed to be beneath Biga Island, is represented by a
scene of a Nile god, inside a rocky cave protected by a
snake, engaged in pouring out water from vases. A little
to the south is the temple's **Nilometer**. On the west of the
island is the tiny **Temple of Hathor**, built by Ptolemy VI
with later additions. Comprising only a small forecourt

Philae, Temple of Isis:
Trajan's Kiosk.
(Roman Period).

and hall, the temple was left unfinished, but it is nonetheless a charming structure. In keeping with the goddess' role as patroness of music, the court has some delightful reliefs of priests and deities playing musical instruments. Nearby is the elegant **Kiosk of Trajan**, which was conceived as a formal entrance to the temple complex. A large rectangular structure, open on the east and west, it comprises 14 columns, linked by screen walls, supporting an architrave. There may originally have been a wooden roof, but the building is clearly uncompleted; parts of the walls have been left unfinished and only a few reliefs have been carved. From its forecourt there are pleasant views across the lake, where the remnants of the coffer dam used to protect the temples during relocation, mark the site of the now submerged original Philae Island.

NEW KALABSHA

The site of New Kalabsha is located on an island in Lake Nasser, a short distance southwest of the High Dam. When the water in the lake is low, it is possible to cross on foot; at other times it is necessary to negotiate a passage with one of the local boatmen. The monuments here were relocated from other sites in Nubia as part of the salvage campaign following the construction of the High Dam, but surprisingly the site remains little known and seldom visited; it is therefore possible to enjoy the temples and the lake vistas in perfect peace and solitude.

TEMPLE OF KALABSHA

The original site of Kalabsha, ancient Talmis, was about 50 km (31 miles) south of Aswan, on the west bank of the Nile. The temple, dedicated to Mandulis, was the largest of its type in Nubia, measuring approximately 74 m (243 ft) long by 33 m (108 ft) wide. These proportions are unusual, and the normal temple plan has also been much simplified here; during relocation, the rectangular grid on which it was constructed came to light. Built on a New Kingdom foundation, the present structure dates mainly from the reign of **Augustus**, but the outer wall encloses two earlier chapels, located in the northeast and southwest corners; one may have served as a birth house and both probably date from the Ptolemaic period.

The temple was approached from the well preserved **Roman quay** on the east of the island, which leads, via an impressive causeway over 30 m (33 yds) long, to the main entrance in the temple **pylon**. At the original site the closeness of the river made it necessary for the pylon to deviate a little from the main axis, and compensation was made by shortening one of its towers. Behind is a **peristyle court**; only eight of its original 14 columns survive. At the western end, columns linked by screen walls separate the court from the hypostyle hall beyond. The transverse **hypostyle hall** has eight columns, and precedes two vestibules, each with two columns; on the south of each is a staircase leading to the roof. The **sanctuary** beyond is large in proportion to the temple, and originally had two columns. A well preserved **ambulatory**, with lion-headed water spouts, surrounds the temple's inner apartments.

KIOSK FROM QERTASSI

Nearby, to the south, is a pretty little Roman kiosk from Qertassi, originally 40 km (25 miles) south of Aswan. It comprises a single small chamber, whose roof was supported by four columns with floral capitals; the main entrance, on the north, is flanked by a pair of Hathor columns.

BEIT EL-WALI TEMPLE

At the age of 22, while still his father's co-regent, the young Ramesses II was entrusted with his first military command—an expedition to subdue a minor revolt in Nubia. In commemoration of its successful conclusion he ordered the excavation of a rock-cut temple at Beit el-Wali, near the original site of Kalabsha; it has now been re-erected at the northwest of the new site. Although its mudbrick pylon is missing, the rest of the temple, comprising a narrow forecourt, a vestibule with two columns and a sanctuary, is well preserved. The campaign itself is recorded on the southern wall of the court, where Ramesses is represented leading the chariot charge against the rebellious Nubians and, following the victory, receiving tribute—great heaps of gold and ivory, and processions of exotic birds and animals.

OUTLYING SITES

In comparison to the Nile Valley, far less is known of the towns and monuments of Lower Egypt. This is due not only to the high water table, which has waterlogged sites, destroying monuments and impairing excavation, but also to the high density of population, which has led to sites being used as sources of ready-quarried stone and *sebakh*. Thus of such famous cities as Sais—the Twenty-sixth Dynasty capital—and the Ramesside capital of Per-Ramesses, virtually nothing remains. However, recent excavations at Buto, the cult centre of **Wadjet**, the cobra goddess of Lower Egypt, suggest that exciting discoveries may lie in the future.

ALEXANDRIA AND THE DELTA

ALEXANDRIA

The same may well be true of that most celebrated city of the Delta, Alexandria, where comparatively few excavations have been carried out. Laid out by Dinocrates of Rhodes, and admiringly described by classical writers, including Strabo, Alexandria was once known as the Queen of the Mediterranean. Even in its decline it was a splendid city: a contemporary account of the arrival of the Arab conqueror Amr in AD 642 describes how his invading troops were obliged to shield their eyes from the dazzle of the marble buildings!

Following his conquest of Egypt in 332 BC, **Alexander** planned the city as the capital of his vast empire, but did not live to see it, as he died just nine years later while on campaign in Persia. His tomb, the Soma, like so many of the famous Alexandrian monuments—the Library, the Museum and the Lighthouse on Pharos Island—has been lost, its last traces buried beneath the grey concrete blocks of the modern commercial city. The scanty remains excavated to date include a Roman odeon, fragments of the Serapeum—a temple complex dedicated to Serapis—

(*Opposite*) Abu Simbel, Great Temple: Rock-cut façade with colossi of Ramesses II. (New Kingdom, Nineteenth Dynasty).

Alexandria, Kom el-Shuqafa catacombs. (Roman period).

and several cemeteries, whose tombs are decorated in a weird blend of Greek and Egyptian styles; most notable among these are the **catacombs of Kom el-Shuqafa**, dating to the first two centuries of Roman rule. Every effort should be made to see the **Graeco-Roman Museum**, whose excellent collections provide tantalising glimpses of the city's vanished glories.

TANIS AND BUBASTIS

Two sites of interest in the eastern Delta are San el-Hagar, ancient Tanis, and Bubastis, near modern Zagazig. Bubastis was the cult centre of the feline goddess **Bastet**, and the principal remains there are found in the vicinity of her ruined temple compound; these include the ruins of smaller temples and some late New Kingdom tombs. Tanis was the native city of the kings of the Twenty-first and Twenty-second Dynasties, and most of its monuments date from their reigns. The site is marked by a massive mudbrick enclosure wall, originally 10 m (33 ft) high and 15 m (49 ft) thick. Inside, reused blocks of all periods litter what were once the precincts of the Great Temple of Amun.

The most important finds at the site, however, were the six royal tombs discovered virtually intact by the French archaeologist Pierre Montet in 1939. Located for security reasons within the temple enclosure, no superstructures were found, but the underground chambers, some of them decorated, were well preserved.

Overshadowed by the outbreak of the Second World War, this thrilling discovery—rivalling that of the tomb of Tutankhamun—went largely unnoticed, and even today few visitors are aware of the magnificent collection of jewellery and funerary equipment, including gold masks and silver coffins, which was recovered from the site and is now displayed in the Egyptian Museum.

SINAI

Between the Old Kingdom and the New Kingdom, the Sinai peninsula was significant to Egypt as the source of copper ore and turquoise; numerous stelae and rock inscriptions mark the areas of mining activity, such as the Wadi Maghara in southwest Sinai. Located close to the turquoise mines at Serabit el-Khadim, the most important ancient monument is a ruined temple dedicated to Hathor, 'Lady of Turquoise'.

THE OASES

Inhabited since prehistoric times, the oases of the Western Desert were under Egyptian control more or less continuously from the Old Kingdom onward, forming a useful buffer zone between Líbya and the Nile Valley.

Located on the ancient trans-Saharan caravan routes, their chief economic importance was commercial, though agriculture played a secondary role. The earliest surviving monuments belong to the Old Kingdom, but the majority of remains date from the Third Intermediate Period onward; many are in an excellent state of preservation, thanks to the dry climate of the oases and their natural isolation.

The oases of **Kharga** and **Dakhla**, to the west of Luxor, are the most accessible, and abound in monuments of various periods, from the Old Kingdom tombs of **Balat** to the well preserved Persian period temple at **Hibis**. To the north, **Bahriya** and **Farafra** are much less accessible, and have little of architectural interest to offer; they are recommended only to the intrepid. The remotest, and perhaps the most fascinating oasis is **Siwa**, located deep in the desert, close to the Libyan border. An ancient Berber settlement with its own language and culture, it will appeal to travellers who like to seek out the furthest outposts of civilization. Siwa's scattered monuments are not well preserved, but the temple at **Aghurmi**, where Alexander the Great consulted the Oracle of Ammon, and the late rock-cut tombs of Gebel el-Mawta are of historical interest.

NUBIA

South of Aswan, the ancient land of Nubia stretches deep into modern-day Sudan. From the Old Kingdom onward, Egyptian rulers exploited the area as a source of minerals, wood and mercenary soldiers—but above all they sought gold, on which the wealth of their empire was founded. The construction of the Aswan High Dam in the 1960's and the subsequent creation of Lake Nasser signalled the destruction of much of Nubia and the irretrievable loss of many of its monuments. However, other more fortunate buildings were salvaged in an international rescue programme of unprecedented scale, carried out under the auspices of UNESCO. These include two other groups of reconstructed monuments, both located on Lake Nasser's western shore, at Wadi el-Sebua, 140 km (87 miles) south of the High Dam, and at Amada, another 40 km (25 miles) further south. There is no provision for visitors at present, but it is hoped that access will improve in the future.

ABU SIMBEL

The most spectacular feat was the removal and relocation of a pair of massive rock-cut temples of Ramesses II at Abu Simbel on the west bank of Lake Nasser, near the Sudanese border. The larger of the two, the **Great Temple**, is approached from a forecourt at whose western end is the temple's vast façade, measuring 35 m (115 ft) wide by 30 m (98 ft) high; substituting for the conventional pylon, it is fronted by four colossal **seated figures** of the king, each 21 m (69 ft) in height. Inside, a **pillared hall** with side chambers and eight standing royal figures replaces the peristyle court, and precedes the orthodox sequence of pillared hall, vestibule and sanctuary. Reliefs in the first two chambers concentrate on Ramesses' military exploits, and include episodes from the Battle of Kadesh. The temple was so oriented that twice a year the rays of the sun penetrated the darkness of the **sanctuary** to illuminate a group of four **seated statues** carved into its rear wall. Representing the king with the three great national deities, the figures are rather worn and can be difficult to identify. From left to right they are: Ptah of Memphis, Amun-Re of Thebes, Ramesses II and Re of Heliopolis.

The **Small Temple** was dedicated to the goddess Hathor, and to Ramesses' beloved wife, Nefertari. On the façade, which comprises four colossal **standing statues** of the king and two of the queen, she is accorded the exceptional compliment of being represented on the same scale as her husband—compare the proportions here with the tiny figures of wives and children clustered around Ramesses' feet on the façade of the Great Temple! In plan, Nefertari's temple is far simpler, comprising a hall with six Hathor pillars, a vestibule with side chambers and a sanctuary with a niche containing a statue of Hathor in her bovine form.

CHRONOLOGY

Adapted from Murnane, W J, *The Penguin Guide to Ancient Egypt*, 1983

Dates refer to regnal years and should be regarded as approximate. Only major kings and those mentioned in this work have been included.

PREDYNASTIC PERIOD 5500–3150 BC

	Early settlements
	Development of agriculture
	Copper smelting and pottery
	Pit burials

EARLY DYNASTIC PERIOD 3150–2686 BC

Narmer	United Egypt
	Capital at Memphis
	Narmer Palette
	Development of writing
First Dynasty 3050–2890	Mastabas at Saqqara and Abydos
Second Dynasty (2890–2686)	

OLD KINGDOM 2686–2181 BC

Third Dynasty (2686–2613)

Djoser (2668–2649)	Step Pyramid complex
Huni (2637–2613)	Meidum Pyramid

Fourth Dynasty (2613–2498)

Sneferu (2613–2589)	Egyptian control of Nubia
	Dahshur Pyramids
Khufu (2589–2566)	
Khafre (2558–2532)	Giza Pyramids
Menkaure (2532–2504)	
Shepseskaf (2504–2500)	Mastabet el-Fara'un

Fifth Dynasty (2498–2345)

Userkaf (2498–2491)	Pyramids at Saqqara and Abusir
Sahure (2491–2477)	Sun Temples at Abu Ghurab
Niuserre (2453–2422)	
Unis (2375–2345)	Pyramid complex and mastabas at Saqqara

Sixth Dynasty (2345–2181)

Teti (2345–2333)	Pyramid and mastabas at Saqqara
Pepi I (2332–2283)	Pyramids at South Saqqara
Pepi II (2278–2184)	Decline of royal power
	Tombs of Mehu and Sabni, and Harkhuf, at Aswan

CHRONOLOGY

FIRST INTERMEDIATE PERIOD 2181–2040 BC

Seventh and Eighth Dynasties (2181–2160)

Ninth Dynasty (2160–2130)   Capital at Heracleopolis

Tenth Dynasty (2130–2040)

MIDDLE KINGDOM 2040–1782 BC

Eleventh Dynasty (2133–1991)	Theban challenge to the Heracleopolitan rulers
Montuhotep I (2060–2010)	Reunification of Egypt
	Capital at Thebes
	Funerary complex at Deir el-Bahri
	Tombs of Khety and Baqet at Beni Hassan
Twelfth Dynasty (1991–1782)	
Amenemhat I (1991–1962)	Capital at Ittawy
	Tombs of Amenemhat and Khnumhotep at Beni Hassan
Senusert I (1971–1928)	White Chapel at Karnak
	Tomb of Sarenput I at Aswan
Amenemhat II (1929–1895)	Tomb of Sarenput II at Aswan
Senusert III (1878–1841)	Domination of Nubia
Amenemhat III (1842–1797)	

SECOND INTERMEDIATE PERIOD 1782–1570 BC

Thirteenth Dynasty (1782–1650)	Separatist movements in Delta (Fourteenth Dynasty)
Fifteenth Dynasty (1663–1555)	Hyksos kings rule from Avaris
	Nubian independence
	Sixteenth Dynasty of 'Lesser Hyksos' rulers
Seventeenth Dynasty (1663–1570)	Theban challenge to the Hyksos

NEW KINGDOM 1570–1070 BC

Eighteenth Dynasty (1570–1293)	
Ahmose I (1570–1546)	Expulsion of the Hyksos
	Capital at Thebes
Amenhotep I (1551–1524)	Alabaster shrine at Karnak
Thutmose I (1524–1518)	Expansion of empire
	First royal tomb in the Valley of the Kings
	Foundation of the Workmen's Village at Deir el-Medina
	Obelisks at Karnak
Thutmose II (1518–1504)	
Hatshepsut (1498–1483)	Co-regency with Thutmose III
	Punt Expedition
	Temple at Deir el-Bahri

	Temple of Amun at Medinet Habu
	Obelisks at Karnak
	Eighth Pylon at Karnak
Thutmose III (1504–1450)	Consolidation of empire in Asia
	Hall of Annals at Karnak
	Festival Hall at Karnak
	Tomb of Rekhmire at Thebes
	Seventh Pylon at Karnak
Amenhotep II (1453–1419)	Tombs of Sennefer and Userhet at Thebes
Thutmose IV (1419–1386)	Tombs of Menna and Nakht at Thebes
Amenhotep III (1386–1349)	Weakening of empire
	Luxor Temple
	Colossi of Memnon
	Tombs of Khaemhet and Ramose at Thebes
Amenhotep IV/Akhenaten (1350–1334)	Atenist heresy
	Capital moved to Akhetaten
	Defacement of earlier religious monuments and suppression of other cults
	Erosion of northern empire
Tutankhamun (1334–1325)	Restoration of the cult of Amun
	Capital re-established at Thebes
Ay (1325–1321)	Throne passes to Tutankhamun's ministers Ay and Horemheb
Horemheb (1321–1293)	Second, Ninth and Tenth Pylons at Karnak
	Tomb at Saqqara
Nineteenth Dynasty (1293–1185)	Royal burials in the Valley of the Kings and Valley of the Queens
Ramesses I (1293–1291)	Horemheb bequeaths throne to his minister Ramesses
Seti I (1291–1278)	Hittite Wars
	Temples at Abydos and Qurna
	Hypostyle Hall at Karnak
Ramesses II (1279–1212)	Capital at Per-Ramesses
	Temple at Abydos
	Battle of Kadesh
	Egyptian-Hittite peace treaty
	Pylon and First Court at Luxor Temple
	Ramesseum
	Nubian monuments
	Tomb of Sennedjem
Merneptah (1212–1202)	Invasion of Libyans and Sea Peoples crushed
Seti II (1199–1193)	Internal dynastic struggles
	Bark Shrine at Karnak
Twentieth Dynasty (1185–1070)	Royal burials in the Valley of the Kings and Valley of the Queens
Ramesses III (1182–1151)	Further invasions by Libyans and

	Sea Peoples
	Temples at Karnak and Medinet Habu
	Economic problems
	First tomb builders' strikes
	Harem conspiracy
Ramesses IV (1151–1145)	Tomb of Anherkhau at Deir el-Medina
Ramesses VI (1141–1133)	Internal disorder
	Priests of Amun extend their control over Upper Egypt
Ramesses IX (1126–1108)	Tomb robbery scandals and strikes
Ramesses XI (1098–1070)	Internal chaos and economic collapse
	Loss of southern empire
	Smendes rules from Tanis
	Viceroy of Nubia seizes Thebes
Herihor (1080–1072)	High priest of Amun expels Nubian Viceroy and assumes rule of Upper Egypt, claiming the title of King
	Nubian independence

THIRD INTERMEDIATE PERIOD 1069–525 BC

Twenty-first Dynasty (1069–945)	Capital at Tanis
	Priest-King Pinedjem I at Thebes
	Royal burials at Tanis
Twenty-second Dynasty (945–712)	Libyan rulers
	Priest-King Harsiese at Thebes
	Royal burials at Tanis
Twenty-third and Twenty-fourth Dynasties (818–712)	Breakdown of centralised government and Nubian encroachment in Upper Egypt
Twenty-fifth Dynasty (772–656)	Nubian kings
Taharqa (690–664)	Kiosk at Karnak
	Assyrian invasions
Twenty-sixth Dynasty (664–525)	Capital at Sais
	Chapels of the Divine Votaresses at Medinet Habu
	Nobles' tombs at Asasif
	Tomb of Amun-Tefnakhte at Saqqara

LATE PERIOD 525–332 BC

Twenty-seventh Dynasty (525–404)

Cambyses (525–522)	Persian rulers—Egypt absorbed into the Achaemenid Empire
Darius I (521–486)	Temple of Hibis
Xerxes (485–465)	Egyptian revolt
Darius II (423–405)	

Twenty-eighth Dynasty (404–399)	Egyptian independence
Twenty-ninth Dynasty (399–380)	Ephemeral Egyptian Dynasties
Thirtieth Dynasty (380–342)	Last dynasty of Egyptian rulers
Nectanebo I (380–362)	Birth house at Dendera
	Kiosk at Philae
	First Pylon at Karnak
	Sphinx Avenue at Luxor
Thirty-first Dynasty (342–332)	Persian rule resumed

GRAECO-ROMAN PERIOD 332 BC-AD 323

Alexander the Great (332–323)	Foundation of Alexandria
	Bark chapel at Luxor Temple
Philip Arrhidaeus and Alexander	Sanctuary at Karnak
II (323–305)	Tomb of Petosiris at Tuna el-Gebel
Ptolemaic Dynasty (305–30)	
Ptolemy I (323–282)	Ptolemy assumes rule of Egypt, taking royal title in 305
Ptolemy II (285–247)	Temple of Isis at Philae
Ptolemy III (246–222)	Temple of Horus at Edfu
Ptolemy IV (221–205)	Temple at Deir el-Medina
	Rebellion in Upper Egypt
Ptolemy V (205–180)	Temple at Kom Ombo
Ptolemy VI (180–145)	Temple of Khnum at Esna
Ptolemy VIII (170–116)	Fragmentation of the kingdom: Interdynastic struggles for the throne, with frequent changes of ruler
	Increasing Roman influence
Ptolemy IX (116–80)	Temple of Hathor at Philae
Ptolemy X (110–88)	Temple of Hathor at Dendera
Ptolemy XII (80–51)	
Cleopatra VII (51–30)	Defeat at the Battle of Actium
Roman Emperors (30 BC-AD 323)	
Augustus (30 BC-AD 14)	Roman annexation of Egypt
	Temple at Kalabsha
Tiberius (14–37)	
Claudius (41–54)	
Nero (54–68)	
Vespasian (69–79)	
Titus (79–81)	Catacombs at Kom el-Shuqafa
Domitian (81–96)	
Nerva (96–98)	
Trajan (98–117)	Birth house at Dendera
	Kiosk at Philae
Hadrian (117–138)	
Antoninus Pius (138–161)	
Marcus Aurelius (161–180)	
Septimius Severus (193–211)	
Geta (209–211)	
Caracalla (209–217)	
Diocletian (284–305)	

ARCHITECTURAL GLOSSARY

Abacus (pl **abaci**) bearing slab placed on top of a capital to support the architrave.

Aisle lateral division within, for example, a hypostyle hall.

Ambulatory enclosed walkway, sometimes roofed, around a temple.

Architrave horizontal stone beam supporting a ceiling.

Arcuate method of construction dependent on the principle of the arch (cf trabeate).

Bark shrine small chapel or kiosk to accommodate the portable bark on which a divine image was carried in procession.

Barrel vault vault in the form of a half-cylinder.

Bas-relief low raised relief carving.

Batter inclined face of a wall.

Birth house small temple for the celebration of divine birth rituals.

Capital crowning part of a column.

Cartouche elongated version of the hieroglyph for eternity, used to enclose royal names.

Causeway raised way or passage connecting the parts of a religious complex.

Cavetto cornice concave moulding, semicircular in section, used as the crowning element of walls, doorways, pylons, etc.

Cenotaph monument to a person buried elsewhere, symbolic tomb.

Clerestory in a hypostyle hall, the zone created by the difference in height between the taller columns flanking the central nave and those in the body of the hall; windows set in this zone.

Colonnade row of columns supporting an architrave.

Colossus (pl. **colossi**) over-lifesize statue, usually of a god or king.

Corbel projecting block supporting a beam or other horizontal member; a series of corbels, each projecting beyond that below, can be used to create an arch or vault.

Cornice uppermost projecting moulding of an entablature, wall, etc.

Criosphinx mythical creature with the head of a ram and the body of a lion.

Crypt in a temple, a concealed chamber beneath the floor or within the thickness of the walls.

Dais raised platform for a throne, etc.

Disc chapel small kiosk with a removable roof for the exposure of divine images to sunlight.

Dyad statue of a couple, usually husband and wife.

Engaged column column attached to a wall.

Entablature the superstructure borne by a colonnade: in Egypt this generally comprised an architrave, torus moulding and cavetto cornice.

False door stele in tombs, a dummy door intended to allow the passage of the deceased's spirit between the burial chamber and offering chapel.

False vault vaulted ceiling created by hollowing the underside of a flat roofing slab.

Hypostyle hall many-columned covered hall.

***Ka*-statue** in tombs, a statue of the deceased which could be occupied by the *ka*, or spirit double.

***Kheker* frieze** decorative frieze found over doors, at the top of walls, etc, probably derived from bundles of reeds tied together.

Kiosk small, open-sided pavilion used in religious rituals or as a way-station.

Lintel horizontal beam bridging an opening.

Mammisi see Birth house.

Mastaba free-standing tomb with a rectangular brick or stone superstructure and subterranean burial chamber.

Mortuary temple in the royal funerary complexes of the Old Kingdom, an offering temple abutting the pyramid tomb; from the New Kingdom, a memorial temple primarily serving the cult of a dead monarch.

Naos (pl. **naoi**) shrine to house a divine image; sometimes used to describe the sanctuary area of a temple.

Nave central division of a hypostyle hall.

Niche small recess, eg. for a statue.

Nilometer staircase descending into the Nile to facilitate the measurement of the annual inundation.

Obelisk tall, monolithic stone pillar, square in section, with sides tapering to a pyramidal apex.

Osiride pillar pillar with an engaged colossal figure of the king in the form of the god Osiris.

Palace-façade niching decorative motif on mastabas, sarcophagi, etc, derived from the buttressed mudbrick exteriors of early palaces.

Pan-bedding technique of building mudbrick walls in separate sections to enable them to survive ground movement during the inundation.

Parapet wall around the edge of a roof, lake, etc.

Peristyle court open court surrounded by a roofed colonnade.

Pier solid masonry support.

Pilaster a shallow pier or rectangular column attached to the face of a wall.

Portcullis stone sliding stone slab used to block a tomb shaft or passage after burial.

Portico in tombs or temples, a roofed entrance porch supported by columns.

Propylon free-standing gateway preceding a pylon.

Pylon Ceremonial gateway comprising twin towers with battered walls flanking a central entrance.

Pyramid royal funerary monument of masonry, rubble or mudbrick faced with stone. From the Fourth Dynasty onwards, the pyramid had a square base and four sloping triangular sides meeting at a single apex.

Pyramidion miniature pyramid: the capstone of a full-scale pyramid, the uppermost part of an obelisk or a mudbrick addition to a private tomb.

Sacred lake lake belonging to a temple, used for purification and waterborne rituals.

Screen wall non-load bearing partition wall.

Serdab in a tomb, a sealed chamber containing a statue of the deceased.

Sphinx mythical creature with the head of a human and the body of a lion.

Split lintel lintel above a doorway having a central gap to allow the passage of standards, etc.

Stele (pl. **stelae**) stone slab with figures and inscriptions. There are two categories: funerary stelae, found in tombs, and votive stelae which were placed in temples and elsewhere.

Temenos enclosure wall.

Torus moulding semicircular or cylindrical moulding employed on the corners of walls and around doorways, stelae, etc.

Trabeate method of construction dependent on the post-and-lintel principle (cf arcuate).

Uraeus frieze frieze of uraei, or royal cobras, surmounting temple walls, etc.

Valley temple in a funerary complex, a riverside temple linked by a causeway to the monument located in the desert.

Vault arched structure forming a roof or ceiling.

Way station see Bark shrine.

Window of Appearances elevated balcony where the king would appear before his subjects.

SELECT BIBLIOGRAPHY

Badawy, A. *A History of Egyptian Architecture*. Vol i, Giza, 1954, Vols. ii-iii, Berkeley and Los Angeles, 1966–68

Baines, J and Malek, J. *Atlas of Ancient Egypt*. Oxford, 1980

Bierbrier, M. *The Tomb-Builders of the Pharaohs*. London, 1982

Cambridge Ancient History. Vols. i-ii, Cambridge, 1970–75 (includes comprehensive bibliographies)

Clarke, S. and Engelbach, R. *Ancient Egyptian Masonry*. London, 1930

Edwards, I.E.S. *The Pyramids of Egypt*. 2nd ed.

London, 1961

Habachi, L. *The Obelisks of Egypt*. Cairo, 1984

James, T.G.H. *An Introduction to Ancient Egypt*. London, 1979

Lauer, J-Ph. *Saqqara, Royal Cemetery of Memphis*. London, 1976

Lloyd, S. and Müller, H.W. *Ancient Architecture*. London, 1974

Lucas, A. *Ancient Egyptian Materials and Industries*. 4th ed., J.R. Harris, ed. London, 1962

Murnane, W.J. *The Penguin Guide to Ancient Egypt*. London, 1983

Robins, G. *Egyptian Painting and Relief*.

Aylesbury, 1986

Schäfer, H. *Principles of Egyptian Art*. E. Brunner-Traut, ed., J. Baines ed. and trans. Oxford, 1986

Smith, W.S. *The Art and Architecture of Ancient Egypt*. 2nd ed., revised by W.K. Simpson. Harmondsworth, 1981

Spencer, A.J. *Death in Ancient Egypt*. Harmondsworth, 1982

Trigger, B.G. et al, eds. *Ancient Egypt: A Social History*. Cambridge, 1983

Uphill, E.P. *Egyptian Towns and Cities*. Aylesbury, 1988

ACKNOWLEDGEMENTS

The author wishes to express her gratitude to Mr George Hart of the British Museum and to Mrs Lorna Oakes for their patience in reading the text and for their many helpful comments and suggestions. Thanks are also due to Mr Martin Stone and Miss Ruth Webb, who checked the Arabic and Greek transliterations, and to the staff of the British Museum, especially the unsung heroes and heroines of the Information Service. All errors, naturally, remain the author's own. Travel within Egypt was facilitated by Mr Tamer el-Narsh of Trans Egypt Travel, Cairo, Mr Tarek Imam of Eastmar Travel, Cairo, Miss Kate Couling of Hayes and Jarvis (Travel) Ltd in Luxor, Miss Beverley Newman of Isis Travel, Cairo and Mr and Mrs Midhat El-Masry of Balloons Over Egypt in Luxor. Above all, I am indebted to my family and friends for their unfailing support and encouragement; special thanks go to Dr Bernard O'Kane and Mrs Amina O'Kane for their generous hospitality in Cairo. Lastly, but by no means least, I would like to thank my Egyptian colleagues, too numerous to name individually, for their kindness, companionship and good humour.

Photographs
British Museum: pp. 9, 17, 18, 20; Cairo Museum: pp. 3, 42, 60; J. Allan Cash Photo Library: p. 136; Peter Clayton: p. 13; David Couling: jacket photograph and pp. 4, 33, 82, 86, 93, 94, 95, 100, 102, 104, 106, 108, 109, 131; Fitzwilliam Museum, Cambridge: p. 114; Robert Harding Photo Library: p. 6; Hirmer Fotoarchiv, Munchen: p. 71; A. F. Kersting: pp. 72, 118; Louvre Museum: pp. 80, 96; William MacQuitty International: pp. x, 129; James Morris: pp. 7, 42, 45t, 45b, 51, 53, 54, 58, 62t, 62b, 64, 66, 74, 88, 115, 123, 126, 132; Museum of Fine Arts, Boston: p. 50; Delia Pemberton: p. 15; Ronald Sheridan Photo Library: pp. 87, 117, 134; Wim Swann: pp. 33, 77; Werner Forman Archive: pp. 23, 34, 111.

Plans
The majority of plans in this book have been adapted from *The Penguin Guide to Ancient Egypt*, William J. Murnane. In addition, the following sources have provided the basis for certain plans in this book. The author and publishers acknowledge with gratitude permission from the relevant copyright-holders for this use. Every effort has been made to trace copyright-holders; it is hoped that any omission will be excused.

Aris & Phillips, *Pharaoh Triumphant: The Life and Times of Ramesses II*, K. A. Kitchen, 1982, pp. 25, 105; British Museum Publications, *Ancient Egyptian Designs*, E. Wilson, 1986, p. 11: Cambridge University Press, *Ancient Egypt – A Social History*, B. G. Trigger et al. 1983, p. 30; Dover Publications, *Life in Ancient Egypt*, A. Erman, 1894, pp. 11, 12; M. V. Seton Williams, *Ptolemaic Temples*, Private Publication, 1978, p. 12; Thames & Hudson, *Egypt to the end of the Old Kingdom*, C. Aldred, 1965, pp. 23, 24.

INDEX

INDEX

Murder at La Marimba

Murder at La Marimba

A SOUTH BRONX MYSTERY

CARSON WOLFE

ST. MARTIN'S PRESS   NEW YORK

MURDER AT LA MARIMBA. Copyright © 1984 by Carson
Wolfe. All rights reserved. Printed in the United States
of America. No part of this book may be used or
reproduced in any manner whatsoever without written
permission except in the case of brief quotations
embodied in critical articles or reviews. For
information, address St. Martin's Press, 175 Fifth
Avenue, New York, N.Y. 10010.

Library of Congress Cataloging in Publication Data

Wolfe, Carson.
   Murder at La Marimba.

   I. Title.
PS3573.0496M8   1984   813'.54   83-17610
ISBN 0-312-55285-8

First Edition

10 9 8 7 6 5 4 3 2 1

ONE

Ricky Betancourt's dice had rolled craps tonight. There he lay on the hospital cot, police surrounding him, blood oozing from a nasty wound in his belly, and handcuffed to the bedrail, when he should have been home in his own bed dreaming of his wedding next week to Eloida.

"Jesus Christ," he muttered as he glanced down at the shredded twenty-dollar embroidered shirt he had just bought for the disco, "where the fuck am I?" The cop nearest him, tall, thin, and carrot-faced, with a fringe of mustache covering narrow lips, heard him and barked, "You ain't nowhere, spic, and you ain't goin' nowhere good, either—hell if you die or the clink for the next twenty years if you live."

Ricky looked up at Patrolman Bob Powers and decided he'd better shut up. He had been busted a couple of times before and knew Powers's type. One wrong word, and the guy would swing his nightstick across your groin or poke your balls till they rattled. No, better to shut up, even if he had no idea what Powers was talking about. What the hell were they trying to pin on him now? He concentrated, and started to recall blurred images from the past two hours. Oh,

1

yeah, same old pattern: just when I thought I had the brass ring, everything got screwed up. He remembered winning the dance contest, the argument in the disco, the guys getting ballsy with the Dominicans because of the rod, the fight downstairs, pulling the rod, getting stabbed, and blacking out. "Shit, just my luck—they're gonna send me up for getting stuck!" And then he drifted off.

Ricky Betancourt was indeed a hard-luck guy. First of all, any Rican carrying a French name has deuces for openers. His father, after presenting his mother with Ricky and his three brothers and a sister, opted out when Ricky was five and left them to the tender ministrations of the New York City Department of Welfare. About three years later one Jesus Valdez brought the career of the senior Betancourt to a sudden end with a deft upward flick of a switchblade, which managed to sever Betancourt's liver approximately in half.

Ricky had always been small, and by the time he was nineteen bad and insufficient nutrition and Puerto Rican genes had given him a height of 5'5", a weight of 120 pounds, and a bad case of acne. He was first arrested at fifteen for stealing at Woolworth's, thrown out of school at sixteen for stealing from the principal's office, and did six months at Spofford during the same year for stealing a car.

Actually, Ricky wasn't a bad kid. He just got caught every time he tried to do something for someone. The Woolworth caper resulted from his trying to get some Tylenol for his mother, who had commissioned him to rescue her from one of her migraines, but had, in her

2

distress, forgotten to provide the money.

When he got caught in the principal's office, he was only trying to help his friend Angel by retrieving the letter from the principal to Angel's mother telling of Angel's latest epileptic seizure.

As for the stolen car, he was not even among the original "perpetrators," as the police like to say, but was offered a lift by some of his friends. When the cops started the sirened chase along the back streets off Southern Boulevard and through Crotona Park a hasty conference among the six fugitives in the car revealed that Ricky was the only occupant still eligible for treatment as a juvenile offender. When the police finally caught up with the stolen car, there was Ricky sitting alone behind the wheel. Ricky kept his promise and spent the six months at Spofford without revealing the names of his friends in the car.

After he got out, he hung around, did some numbers running, peddled some pot, and otherwise tried to become a member in good standing of society. But nothing lasted. The numbers guy he worked for was bankrupted to death by the mob and the pusher was arrested by the police and sent up. Ricky Betancourt, at the age of eighteen, had few prospects, no money, and no hope for the future: a typical ghetto kid. Then he met Eloida. Now, Eloida was a nice-looking girl with huge brown eyes, short bobbed hair Buster-Browned over her forehead, a Colgate smile, and not one brain in her head. The best thing Eloida had going for her was her mother.

Maria Fuentes had realized early on that her only

child, Eloida, was going to need considerable help surviving the booby traps of the Bronx ghetto. To that end
she had carefully selected Ricky Betancourt out of a
welter of eager suitors and steered Eloida into a ro-
mance with him. She had a feeling that Ricky was special, of that she was certain, and he proved it, when
with her help and Carlito's, Ricky passed the test and
received his high school equivalency certificate. She
had him enrolled in Bronx Community College the day
before she announced the engagement of her daughter
to him. She left very little to chance.

Dr. John Stevens was talking to Powers and his partner, Woody Fertig, outside the Jewish Memorial Hospital emergency room. "The knife victim is stable. No
vital organs damaged. I've stitched him up and the
only sequella he'll suffer is a sore belly for the next few
weeks. The other boy was D.O.A. As a matter of fact,
rigor mortis was beginning to set in by the time I was
able to look at him. You know what's peculiar about
that dead boy?"

"No, doctor," Powers replied, "what's peculiar
about the dead boy?"

"He's got two bullet wounds in his chest, so close
together they could be twins."

"I wonder," Woody Fertig asked his partner, "if that
last shot I heard when you were running into the alley
was meant for the stiff rather than for you?"

"Naw." Powers scowled. "I told you when I got into
the alley one of the spic's friends took a pot shot at me.
The stiff was already down on the ground. Anyhow,"

he continued, "I found one slug in the alley, and I bet it fits the gun we found on the spic."

At that moment Ricky was wheeled out. Powers stopped the attendant, bent down over Ricky, and whispered, "You're gonna live, little spic, and you're gonna do some hard time—I'm gonna see to that."

Ricky blinked his eyes once, then closed them and thought: "So what the hell else is new?"

TWO

Maria Fuentes called Carlito as soon as she found out. Maria was nothing if not decisive. For most of her thirty-seven years she had been forced to make decisions on her own, and she was acting almost on instinct. Still, this news had really rocked her. The last thing in the world that she expected from Ricky was for him to be in police custody in the hospital, charged with shooting someone. Could she have been mistaken about him? She didn't think so. Her instincts about Ricky had to be right. She couldn't live with that kind of mistake. Well, mistake or not, she was committed to him now.

Maria had noticed Ricky last year when he was part of a group of young machos sniffing around Eloida. Despite his small stature, he seemed to be the leader of the group. He was the one with all the ideas, he made the plans, and they listened to him. She managed to catch him alone a couple of times, found out how street-wise he was and, more important, found out that he really had the smarts. A kid like that could be molded, trained, educated. *"Mierda!"* Carlito had said. "He can read as well as college kids." That decided her. She let Ricky move in with her and Eloida, had Eloida fitted with a diaphragm, showed her how to use it, and then closed her eyes when Ricky crept from the sofa bed in the living room to Eloida's bed and then back out again.

In the meantime, she got all kinds of material from the Board of Education for him to study for his equivalency, got Carlito to come over two nights a week to help him, and fed him some decent food. She knew he could pass at the first crack, and he didn't disappoint her. The only thing that bothered her was his connection with his gang. That's why she planned the wedding. She figured being married would keep him home evenings. Still, every once in a while he had to cruise with his pals. She decided not to pull the reins tight yet. Let him tomcat around every once in a while. Well, tomcatting had sure gotten out of hand.

Calling Carlito was a decision Maria made after much careful thought. Carlito—Carlos Rivera, attorney at law—had been her sometime lover for the last three years. Each of them knew the score, wanted no permanent attachments, and respected each other's independence. Maria was an R.N. at Lincoln Hospital in the South Bronx, and Carlito's office was near Third Avenue, two blocks from the hospital. The geographical proximity made it easy for them to meet, whether it was for a romantic tryst or a spaghetti dinner. The

6

thing was that if she retained Carlito to represent Ricky she would have to pay him the same fee as any of his other clients. She had too much respect for him and too much pride in herself to allow herself to be anybody's *puta*. The only favor she would ask would be that he permit her to pay him out over a period of time. Hell, he was used to that; almost every one of his clients paid that way anyhow. But he was a good lawyer, even if he didn't get the respect he deserved in the courts because he was Puerto Rican. And he knew Ricky—knew him better than anyone except her. He was the man for the job.

When the phone rang in Carlito's office his secretary, Lisa, picked it up, bent her frizzy hairdo to meet the phone halfway so her arthritic left arm wouldn't have to reach too far, shifted her licorice into her cheek, and said, "Mr. Rivera's office, can I help you?" The stubby fingers of her huge hand did an acrobatic number between the hold button, the buzzer, and the intercom as she informed her boss: "Ms. Fuentes on twenty-two."

Carlito smiled into the phone. *"Querida mia! Como esta?"*

"Don't querida mia me," Maria growled. "This call is strictly business, so talk English."

Carlito couldn't suppress a chuckle. One of the things he had learned during the three years he and Maria had been seeing each other was that smooth, sweet Spanish was reserved for private, intimate, soul-baring, love-talking, life-searching moments. English was used to discuss the weather, work, or business.

7

"Okay," he breathed, "what's up?"

"I want an appointment to see you at the office. Ricky's been knifed. He's in the hospital and he's being charged with shooting another kid."

"Is he hurt bad?" Carlito gasped.

"No, I've got some friends over at Jewish Memorial—the cops are crawling all over him. He has a stomach wound that's superficial—no vital organs involved." She hesitated a moment and then plunged ahead. "Carlito, I want you to represent him. But no favors—I want a regular fee arrangement. Figure out how much down and how long you can give me to pay it out. Be fair is all I ask."

"All right, all right, Maria, relax. God knows I understand how you feel. I'm free now, how soon can you get here?"

"I'll be there in ten minutes. 'Bye."

Carlito waited till she had disconnected and then jammed the receiver down angrily. "Damn that bitch!" He shoved his chair back, lurched erect, and pounded his fist into his palm. With his green eyes flashing beneath a café-au-lait brow, his fine wavy silver hair cascading over his forehead, his broad shoulders tensed under the elegant gray pin-striped vested suit, he was a caged tiger. In court at moments like this, court clerks, adversaries, witnesses, even judges, were awed by the raw power of the man under the civilized clothing. Because he was prematurely gray and always wore gray suits in court, the court officers among themselves called him The Gray Bantam.

Carlito strode over to the window behind his desk,

8

A SOUTH BRONX MYSTERY

CARSON WOLFE

ST. MARTIN'S PRESS   NEW YORK

Library of Congress Cataloging in Publication Data

Wolfe, Carson.
   Murder at La Marimba.

   I. Title.
PS3573.0496M8   1984   813'.54   83-17610
ISBN 0-312-55285-8

First Edition

10 9 8 7 6 5 4 3 2 1

flung it open, took a couple of deep breaths, and slowly regained his civilized veneer. When the hell was Maria going to stop fighting him and understand just how much she meant to him? At thirty-five he had played the singles game long and hard. With his high cheekbones hinting at Aztec ancestry somewhere along the line, his choirboy smile that projected the naïveté that was still somehow part of his personality, and the magnetism of his animal grace and physique, he had seduced many a woman juror into a vote for acquittal. Outside the courtroom he didn't even have to try.

But with Maria Fuentes it was different. No chance of seduction there. Maria would never allow that concept to enter their relationship. It was true that she had been attracted to him. But when he started to play his macho games, and strike his lawyer poses, she saw right through him. And, honest woman that she was, she told him, and scolded him for his hypocrisy. She saw through the veneer, and what she found underneath—the idealism, the sensitivity, the tentativeness and fear of failure that stoked the fire of his outward furies—all this she liked; and then loved. It was she, then, who called the tune, she who decided when, where, and how they were to consummate their passion. And Carlito had come to realize that this was no one-night stand, no quickie screw. But Maria had Eloida, and until Eloida was provided for, Maria was making no commitment. For three years Carlito had been waiting, and with Ricky doing so well, he figured it was just a matter of a little more time. And now

9

Ricky was facing what? Murder—attempted murder? It didn't even matter—conviction on either one would destroy Maria's plan for Eloida and his plan for Maria. *Mierda!*

The intercom buzzed. He turned, lifted the receiver.

"Ms. Fuentes is here to see you."

"Fine, send her in."

Maria was a dark Puerto Rican with a wide, full-lipped mouth, broad nose, and deep black eyes. Her hair fell down over her shoulders in two thick plaits. Carlito always knew Maria's moods from the way she wore her hair. She was tall for a woman—the same height as Carlito, and when they went out dancing or to the theater she combed the fine, silky mass back off her face, fastened a glittery barrette at each temple, and let it flow down her back to her waist. When she worked, it was braided and either coiled over each side of her head or into a bun at the nape of her neck. She did not have conventional good looks, but that hair, together with the poised arch of her trim, athletic body, created an aura of regal femaleness that always attracted notice and comment from women as well as men.

Carlito moved to her side, took her arm, pecked a swift, respectful kiss on her cheek, and led her to the chair facing his desk. "Tell me as much as you know, and try to include everything," he urged.

Maria sat erect and poised, starting right in: "Ricky left the house at eight-thirty last night. He told Eloida he was going to a disco with his pals. Eloida says he had a gun. I've never seen it. At two this morning,

10

Angel Colon, one of his buddies, rang our bell. When I let him in he told us there had been a fight at the disco—La Marimba, at 183rd and Broadway. That Ricky had used the gun in the fight and that another kid had been shot. After that someone knifed Ricky and Angel ran away and came straight to us."

Carlito frowned and bit his lower lip. "La Marimba," he mused, "that's Dominican territory. No wonder they got into trouble. Did you ask Angel why they went there?"

"I asked Angel a lot of questions," she snapped, "but couldn't get a damn thing more out of him; he was shaking like a wet puppy. And then Eloida started crying. I told him to go home and stay there and wait for a call from me. Then I checked the hospitals and found out Ricky was at Jewish Memorial. The rest you know."

"Is Ricky ambulatory?"

"He may not be ambulatory, but he's going to be sent down to 100 Centre Street for a court appearance tonight."

"Okay, I'll be there." He paused. "How much money can you raise for bail?"

"I can get a thousand by tonight, and there's eight hundred on deposit with Val-Jean for the wedding. Plus I've got five hundred with me for your fee. Is that all right?"

"No need to worry just now about my fee," he said, rushing on before she could voice the protest growing in her throat. "You see, I can take an assignment of bail from you to pay my fee. So the main thing is to try

11

to gather as much money as we can for bail. Now I'll call Victor Valencia at Val-Jean's and get your deposit returned so that we'll have that eight hundred dollars to add to the five hundred. That gives us twenty-three hundred. It probably won't be enough—but we'll see what judge we get. If Jacoby or Wentworth is sitting we might swing it." He didn't add that he had $2500 he intended to pitch in, if it would help get Ricky out. "Why don't you go and make your arrangements and meet me back here at five? We'll drive down together."

"Okay." Maria nodded. "And I'm bringing Eloida with me. After all, she's his fiancée and he should see her in court and know that she's behind him." She stood up, squared her shoulders, walked to the door of the office, turned to Carlito, and said, *"Muchas gracias, querido. Tu eres un hombre muy guapo,"* and strode out.

Carlito glowed: Spanish in the office from Maria! That was a first. One hell of a man, eh? Well, he sure hoped so.

THREE

Carlito steered Maria through the front doors of 100 Centre Street, the home of the Manhattan Criminal Court. "It's ugly and cold-looking from the outside," Maria remarked.

"You ain't seen nothin' yet," Carlito retorted. "As I told you on the way down, the arraignment court is a snake pit."

He had never taken any special notice of the archi-

12

tectural niceties of any of the courthouses in New York; to him they all represented the bullring, and he became the torero as he entered. He recognized a kind of heady elation, the accelerated pulse rate and the pumping of adrenalin into his skull, that accompanied him into every courtroom he worked. He hadn't ever admitted it to anyone but himself, but he reveled in the combat of the trial court—that one-on-one, knock-'em-down, drag-'em-out, hand-to-hand battle of wits and intellect with the enemy.

Carlito led the two women through the large vestibule, past the round information desk to the far end of the building. There, just inside another bank of doors that exited from the back of the courthouse to Baxter Street, was the arraignment courtroom, known as AR1. A large number of relatives and friends of the defendants milled outside. Underlying all the different accents and languages that filled the corridor was an atmosphere of fear, uncertainty, anguish, and anger that hung so heavily it had a taste, smell, and touch all its own. This is where it all starts, for every arrested citizen must be presented within forty-eight hours and AR1 is where every defendant is first brought. Here, he first appears before a judge; hears for the first time the formal charges lodged against him, and the presentment of the bones of the case by the assistant district attorney, and the demand for high bail. The defendant and his family usually have not had time to hire a lawyer, or make arrangements to have him appear at arraignment, so most defendants are represented by lawyers from the Legal Aid Society. In any one session, each Legal Aid lawyer will be representing twenty to thirty clients, none of whom he knows. He will have spent three or four minutes interviewing each defendant in the holding pens behind the courtroom, and then be expected to make an intelligent rebuttal to the district attorney. After listening to arguments on both sides, experienced judges base their bail decisions on such realities as the amount of money available from the defendant and his family, the current jail capacity, and the size of the current calendar. Only a very few deal with the basic legal question posed by bail applications: How likely is the defendant to return to court to answer the charges? So, bail in AR1 is a lottery.

Carlito pushed through the crowd and found seats for Eloida and Maria in the second row behind the one reserved for the police. He then left the courtroom, turned right into the clerk's office, and filed his notice of appearance. He was in luck. Ricky's case was just being put on the calendar, and he was handed a copy of the complaint in the case. The clerk told him Ricky was already in the holding pen, so he hurried back to tell Maria. On the way he scanned the complaint, and his worst fears were confirmed: Murder. One Pablo Alvarado had been shot to death and Ricky was accused of using a .38 Smith and Wesson to accomplish the deed. The complaint added those most ominous words, "weapon recovered," which meant the alleged murder weapon was in the hands of the police.

Carlito sat down beside Maria and shoved the complaint at her. Maria frowned, read it, and sighed. "So

14

okay, it's murder, and they say he did it. Now it's up to you to prove he didn't."

"No, Maria, it isn't that way at all. My job is not to prove Ricky innocent at all. My job is to prevent them from proving he's guilty. And that's a big difference." At that moment Powers and Fertig entered the row in front of them reserved for police and sat down. Carlito's intuition, along with his familiarity with court procedure, made him guess that these cops were here on Ricky's case. He got out of his seat and walked to face them, knowing policemen never like to be approached from behind. "Hello, Officer," he said to Powers. "Are you on the Betancourt arrest?"

"Yeah," Powers answered.

"My name is Carlos Rivera, and I've been retained to represent him."

"How about that," Woody said admiringly. "He's got a retained lawyer at arraignment? I wouldn't've expected that!"

"It ain't gonna do him any good!" spat Powers. "We got him dead to rights." Powers stood up, looked down at Carlito, and said, "You talk his language, counselor. Better tell the little spic to cop a plea."

Carlito began to fume, but caught himself: Just a minute, Carlito—this isn't the time to tangle with him. Mark him down for later—on the witness stand, where it counts. Carlito shrugged and smiled at Powers. "Well, maybe—*quien sabe?*" he said, letting Powers know he had caught the insult. "What I really wanted to ask you is how my client is doing. I understand he was wounded also."

"Got a superficial knife wound in the belly," Fertig replied, smiling. "That's the least he has to worry about."

"Have you made an arrest of the perpetrator of the knife wound, *amigos?*" Carlito asked, his eyes glinting with the sarcasm.

"Why, no," Powers replied. "Your boy was the only one left on the street with the stiff. When we got there all them other Latinos had disappeared." Carlito smiled as Powers bit his tongue. Damn it! the policeman brooded. That little spic lawyer got me talking too much. And in front of witnesses, too.

In the meantime, Carlito filed that important bit of information in his brain: No witnesses on the scene when police arrived.

At that moment two corrections officers, each holding Ricky by an arm, led him to a chair inside the dock. Ricky was completely bent over, both manacled hands over his stomach, his face ashen. Carlito heard Eloida gasp and cry out. Ricky raised his head and tried to smile; two front teeth were missing, and the effect was the grimace of a death mask. As Eloida fainted, the clerk called, "People versus Ricardo Betancourt." The last glimpse that Carlito got as he turned to face the judge was Patrolman Woody Fertig carrying Eloida in his arms up the courtroom aisle, with Maria following fast behind.

F O U R

The arraignment was over in minutes. Powers was identified as the arresting officer who had signed the complaint. Carlito waived the reading of the complaint and then the assistant D.A. made his pitch for no bail. Carlito made his reply, telling the judge what a bright, accomplished person Ricky Betancourt was, produced the contract with Val-Jean's on the wedding arrangements, the printed invitations to church, and Ricky's recently earned high school equivalency certificate. The assistant D.A. countered with Ricky's prior record of conviction as a Youthful Offender for stealing a car. Carlito replied by voicing chagrin that the Y.O. record had not been sealed, and the judge interrupted to say that as learned counsel well knew it was proper for the D.A.'s office to refer to Y.O.s on bail applications. It was a familiar charade, the outcome never in doubt. The judge set bail at $100,000 bond, and when Carlito remonstrated once more, lowered it to $50,000 cash bail. It made no difference: Ricky would have to stay in jail until the trial.

Ricky had been permitted to remain seated during the arraignment process and, after asking the judge's permission for a courtroom conference with his client, Carlito went to the far corner of the dock with Ricky and sat down next to him. "Listen to me, Ricky. Don't say anything—just listen. Can you hear me—under-

17

stand me?" Ricky nodded through a low moan. "I've demanded that they hospitalize you. You'll probably be sent to Bellevue for two or three days. Then it's out to Rikers. You are not—and I mean positively *not*—to talk to anyone about what happened."

"Okay, Mr. Rivera."

Carlito continued: "From now on we'll talk in Spanish, and keep your voice low." He shifted into Spanish, putting his head next to Ricky. "The first thing I must know is what kind of a gun you were carrying."

"It was a twenty-two, nickel-plated. Cheap."

"Was it loaded?"

Ricky looked at Carlito as if he were a kindergartener. "Sure it was loaded, Mr. Rivera. What kind of fool would I be to carry a gun without ammo? I wasn't trying to commit suicide."

"Have they given you a paraffin test?"

Ricky looked puzzled. "What's that, Mr. Rivera?"

"They dip your hands in hot wax, and then they let it harden. After it's hard they peel it off."

"No, sir, they didn't give me no test like that at all."

"Were you conscious when they arrested you? Did you see the policeman who made the hit?"

"No," Ricky replied, sighing. "You see, after I got stuck and fell down, a bunch of them Dominicans jumped me, knocked my teeth out, and really punched me out. The first thing I remember is coming to in the emergency room."

"Did you find any wax on your fingers after you woke up? They could have done the test while you were out of it," Carlito persisted.

18

"Maybe they did, but I didn't find no wax, like you say," and he lifted his hands, still shackled, to Carlito's face. Carlito grabbed Ricky's hands and quickly slid a fingernail under Ricky's nails to see if he could find some remnants of wax. As he was doing it, a corrections officer grabbed Carlito's shoulder and growled, "C'mon, Counselor, you know you're not supposed to be touching the prisoner."

Carlito turned to the guard, shot him a contemptuous glare, and responded—all the while continuing his inspection—"What the hell are you doing? As an attorney, I'm an officer of the court, and you're interfering with my conference with my client."

"Yeah, well maybe you're trying to slip him something. How do I know, maybe you're carrying a gun?"

"The only way you can find out is to place me under arrest. Want to try it?" Carlito sneered. He had completed his inspection of Ricky's fingernails and found no trace of wax. He sighed. "C'mon, Officer, let's not argue. Here, see? I'm not touching him. Let me finish my interview." The guard relented and stepped back again. Carlito turned back to Ricky. "How many shots did you fire?"

Ricky shook his head as he replied, "No, man, I never shot that gun—I lifted it to keep them Dominicans off me, but I never shot the gun."

Carlito grabbed Ricky's chin, pulled his face full to him as if to kiss him and hissed: *"Who did? Man, who did? Quien?"*

"No se. I don't know—someone grabbed it from behind me. Then I got stuck and went down. I don't re-

member hearing no shots, man—*no recuerdo eso.*" He looked Carlito in the eye. *"No recuerdo."*

Carlito dropped his hand and smiled. Maria had been right again. The kid hadn't done it. Carlito was convinced. "Okay, now give me the names of your gang that went to the disco with you."

Ricky began counting: "Angel Colon. Pancho Perez. Luis Esteban. And me. There were four of us."

"Were you the only Ricans at La Marimba last night?"

"Hell no, there were at least five or six others. They weren't with us, but I recognized them."

"Try to remember their names, Ricky—give it to me."

"Gee, Mr. Rivera, I ain't feeling so hot, the bandage feels wet and my belly hurts. It's hard to think." Ricky's eyes were glazing with pain and fatigue.

"Just give me that," Carlito pleaded. "I need to get a jump on the cops. Try, Ricky—try!"

"Miguel Fernandez, Jesus Torres . . ." he faltered. "I'm sorry—this pain in my belly's too much. They're the only ones I can remember," and he dropped his head.

Carlito moved back, motioned to the corrections officer to take the prisoner. They lifted Ricky off his seat and began to move him back to the pens. Suddenly Ricky stopped, turned his head, and called to Carlito: *"Yo recuerdo un otro*—one more."

Carlito bounded forward. *"Quien es*—who is it?"

"Pablo," said Ricky. "Pablo Alvarado."

Carlito's eyes opened wide. "But Ricky!" he called.

It was too late—Ricky was out of the courtroom and the heavy door to the pens had closed. "Dammit!" Carlito muttered at the closed door. "Pablo Alvarado is the man you're accused of killing!"

FIVE

Woody Fertig looked down at Eloida in the little room next to the clerk's office while the paramedic was reviving her. What a sweet-looking little girl. I could've had a daughter like that if I had ever gotten married. Woody Fertig, fifty-five and balding, was ready for retirement. A gentle giant of a man, he seemed miscast as a policeman and, indeed, he was. As a youngster he had tried professional baseball and failed (good hitter but too slow, they decided), selling trimmings and buttons in the garment center and failed (not aggressive enough), and in desperation had taken the police exam. He managed to pass that with the aid of veterans' points added to his score and became a policeman at the age of twenty-five. For about thirty years he had plodded through his job, making no waves and few friends. Now in his last tour before retirement he was paired with Bob Powers, a thirtyish, foulmouthed, racist anti-Semite (Woody, although he could speak no Yiddish, always pronounced it ontasem*it*, the way his father had). He had nothing in common with this Cossack and considered this assignment the most onerous of the Joblike depredations visited upon him by his superiors. He had only six months to go to become eligible for the thirty-year retirement, but since being paired with Powers, each day seemed a month and each month a year.

He bent down, took Eloida's hand in his, and said, "How's it going, kid—you feeling better?"

Eloida looked away shyly, and then turned her head to find Maria. But Maria had decided that Eloida was being well taken care of, between the paramedic and Fertig, and had returned to the courtroom. "I'm so ashamed to do that in front of Ricky. I hope I didn't upset him."

"Don't worry, I don't think he noticed. He sure has his own troubles. Is he your boyfriend—brother?"

"He's my fiancé," she said, while some color returned to her cheeks. "We were supposed to get married next week. Do you think the judge will let him out for the wedding?"

"I'm afraid not, little girl, unless your lawyer is very persuasive or you're very rich. By the way, what's your name?"

"Eloida," she replied. "Eloida Fuentes."

"Eloida," he repeated. "That's a pretty name. How old are you?"

"I'm nineteen." She looked at his hand still clasping hers and he hurriedly dropped it. "Ricky didn't shoot anybody, you know," she suddenly blurted. "He couldn't have."

"He had a gun, there were bullets fired from it, and another boy is dead." Fertig counted on his fingers as he repeated the litany.

Eloida was becoming more animated and mimicked

Fertig's counting. "It wasn't Ricky's gun, somebody else used it, and Ricky wouldn't shoot one of his friends."

Fertig's look of puzzlement put a road map of wrinkles and creases across his broad face. "How do you know it wasn't his gun?"

"Because I saw the gun he left the house with and it wasn't no .38 Smith and Wesson like the paper says. Some people think I'm dumb, but I know the difference between a Saturday night special and a .38 Smith and Wesson."

Fertig was appalled. She hadn't even realized that she had made a very damaging admission. "Look, I think we should end this conversation right now. As a matter of fact, it never happened. I'm going to get your mother." And he shambled away as fast as discretion would allow.

He met Maria and Carlito in the vestibule outside the courtroom, told Maria that Eloida was better, and rushed away to the men's room, where he locked himself in a booth and sat down to think. He had managed to survive thirty years on the job because of his ability to detach himself, take no position for or against, and stay out of controversy. Now, in an instant, the babbling of a stupid child had forced him to take sides. On the one hand, his duty required him to report the conversation with Eloida to the assistant D.A. in charge of the case. On the other hand, he hated Powers and his attitudes, and, more important, he had been captivated by the very naïveté of Eloida that had exposed her, and not only didn't want to hurt her, but felt that

23

somehow he should help her. He knew that whatever he did, he was now committed to one side or the other. Hell—he'd make no decision tonight. Sleep on it: the A.D.A. was gone already, and the information could wait. He slapped his thigh, left the bathroom, and continued right out of the building into the night.

Back in the courthouse, Carlito was discussing with Maria the information he had obtained so far: "On the debit side we have the following: one, Ricky admits carrying a gun; two, he admits being in a fight with the Dominicans at the club; three, he was unconscious when the police arrived and for a considerable period of time thereafter. On the credit side: one, Ricky denies he had a .38 caliber gun; two, no witnesses were present when the police arrived; three, no paraffin test has been administered yet; four, we have the names of Ricky's friends who were there; and five, the dead boy is not a Dominican but a Rican from Ricky's barrio."

Maria frowned. "I'm not sure I understand all the credits and why they are credits. But if you say so, I believe it."

"Do you really, Maria?" Carlito smiled at her. "You're not always so ready to take what I say without question or argument."

"Not in this case, Carlito. This is your profession, and as far as I'm concerned, you're one of the best." She cradled his arm against her breast. "So what's our next step?"

Carlito felt the warmth of her body go straight to his loins, gave her a long kiss right there outside of AR1

and said, "Go call Angel Colon. Let's see him tonight.
After that I have plans for us."

"So do I," she murmured, "but they may be different from yours."

S I X

Bob Powers stepped out the back door of the courthouse onto Baxter Street, hunching his shoulders
against the chill of the night air. He crossed the street
to the little park on the other side of which he had
parked his car. As he entered the path through the
park, a familiar figure approached him.

"*Buenas noches*, Beepie. How you are?"

"Fine, Joe. What the hell are you doing here?"

"How many times I tell you it's Jose, not Joe. The
boss wants to talk to you."

"I don't give a shit, Joe, and I don't like Beepie, either."

"But that's your initials, *verdad?* B.P. iss Beepie. You
got your car here, no?"

"Listen, I'm tired, I been in court all day with a
homicide, I don't feel like seeing the boss. I'm going
home."

"But Beepie, that why the boss want to talk. Alvarado, Pablo Alvarado, you know him. He's dead in
an alley. And who finds him, our pal Beepie, *verdad?*"

"Okay, I'll come. I knew I'd hear about this. Might

25

as well take care of it now. You want to come in my car?"

"How else I know you see the boss, eh?"

"Okay, but you keep your trap shut, see? You call me Beepie one more time and I'll toss you the hell out."

"Okay Beepie, I'm quiet like mice."

The two strode through the park to Powers's 1972 Chevrolet in total silence, Jose keeping slightly behind Powers, who walked as if he were alone. When Powers opened the door, Jose went into the back seat. "Is more better this way. I sit in back more comfortable, and you no try no tricks on me."

Powers looked at the little brown man with slate blue eyes and laughed. "I guess you didn't survive all these years by being careless, Joe, but shit, I ain't going to try nothing with you."

"You never know, Beepie. There's Alvarado in the alley."

Powers got in the car and started the motor. He realized it was no use arguing with Jose. He was there to make sure Powers got to the boss right away.

The boss, Anselmo Lovato, looked like anything but a local Mafioso. The keynote to Anselmo's personality was moderation. He was of medium height and weight and dressed neatly and conservatively. He lived in a five-room apartment on Anderson Avenue in the Bronx, on the third floor of a six-story building. The apartment itself was a combination of browns, ochres, and beiges with furnishings that were completely unremarkable. To the outside world, Anselmo Lovato was the model of working class decorum. To his intimates and family he was the hardworking, demanding chief of the South Concourse rackets who controlled all gambling, dope, prostitution, and loan sharking in his little fiefdom, and whose very mediocrity found favor with the Mafia. His lack of ostentation and apparent satisfaction with his present station in life, combined with his delivery of substantially more profits to the organization than any of his predecessors had produced, engendered a feeling of comfortable safety in his Mafia superiors.

When Powers was ushered in, Lovato looked up from the T.V. news program he was watching and waved him to a seat next to him. They sat in silence for the next five minutes, Lovato completely intent upon the program, Powers fidgeting nervously. Finally, Lovato pushed a button on the remote control he was holding and set it down on the table in front of him as the television went dark.

"Good evening, Police Officer Powers. Thank you for coming to see me." Lovato was always polite and formal. Especially with people he was annoyed with.

"Look, Lovato, I know you're angry about Alvarado getting bumped, so why don't we get right to it."

Lovato sighed. "Some people have no patience. It is a sign of bad upbringing. Were you brought up badly, Patrolman Powers?"

"Keep my family out of this, will you?" snarled Powers.

"Ah, but that's just it. It is family we are discussing. Pablo Alvarado was a member of my family here, even

27

if not a blood relative, and certainly connected to you in a way, was he not?"

Powers jumped up, his face turning red. "Alvarado has no connection to me—you understand? To me he was a nothing!"

"Calm down, Officer Powers, calm down." Lovato smiled benignly. He had elicited the expected reaction. "Tell us what you know of what happened to Pablo Alvarado."

"Alvarado was at a disco in Washington Heights. A fight broke out between two gangs of kids. One of the kids started shooting everyone around. Pablo caught two bullets in the heart."

"And that's it?" asked Lovato.

"That's it," replied Powers. "I answered the call with another cop and by the time we got there it was all over and Alvarado was dead."

"It's not that simple," hissed Lovato. "One, the disco is not my territory, and Alvarado should not have been there. Two, Alvarado is not a kid to get mixed up in a stupid fight about girls." Lovato had started counting on his fingers and now continued. "Three, the boy who is accused of the murder is Ricky Betancourt, a runner for my predecessor, the late lamented Ivan DeJesus, and finally, it is you of all people who find Alvarado dead in an alley while the boy Ricky is stabbed in front of the disco."

Powers looked startled. "So that's why he did it, the kid was settling an old score."

"I don't believe it, Officer Powers—at least not yet." Lovato stood up, started to pace the room, clasping his hands behind him. "Betancourt has no history of violence. When he worked for DeJesus he was merely a runner. But if someone was trying to run my territory?" He shrugged his shoulders. "*Quien sabe?*" He turned back to Powers. "But you finding Alvarado—that puzzles and troubles me. You are a cop and a gringo and I don't understand you."

"I had nothing to do with killing Alvarado—by the time I got there he was dead. Don't you understand?" Powers's face had reddened again.

"Well, maybe," Lovato stared at him intently and finally continued: "Okay, right now I believe you. We're asking around, and we'll see. But let me tell you, your credit line is dead. We take no bets from you, and you can't borrow a penny from anybody."

"To hell with you, Lovato," Powers growled. "I paid you back every penny I owed."

Lovato permitted himself a small grin. "Did you ever think it could be any other way? Now go, please, I'm missing the newscast."

Powers stumbled into his house an hour later, his breath reeking from the three quick ones he had downed after leaving Lovato. His wife, skinny and birdlike, was waiting up for him.

"Your sister's been calling. Three times already."

Powers rolled his eyes heavenward and sighed, "Oh shit."

SEVEN

Maria called and reached Angel's mother, who told her Angel was not home. Maria was annoyed. She had instructed him to stay there and wait for her phone call. Well, he was almost eighteen and not her kid, and she couldn't expect him to obey her. Still, it was a little unsettling. She turned to Carlito and told him. "What do you think?" she asked.

"Ask her if he said when he was coming back."

"I did, she says she doesn't know."

Carlito looked at his watch: eight-thirty. "Tell her we'll be there at eleven tonight. If Angel comes home before then, tell him to wait there for us."

Maria nodded and relayed the message and then entered into a long conversation with Mrs. Colon. When she came away from the phone she explained: "It's all over the barrio that Ricky's arrested and Pablo Alvarado is dead. Everybody's taking sides. Half the people say they don't believe Ricky did it. The other half say Ricky must have done it by accident. Incidentally, she's not too happy about our coming at eleven. She has two younger children, and their bedtime is ten. Anyhow, she's among the half that didn't believe Ricky did it, and she'll keep Angel there for us when he comes home."

"Then let's get Eloida and have some dinner. We're right near Chinatown. Let's drop in on Han's and see what specials he has tonight."

30

"Great, but remember, it's Dutch treat."

"Okay, okay, Ms. Independent. Tonight it's Dutch."

When they reached the room where Eloida had been taken they found her sitting comfortably, mesmerizing the paramedic with her radiant charm. "Can I see Ricky before we leave?" she asked.

"No," Carlito told her, "he's back in the holding pen. But he gave me a message for you and told me to give you this," and Carlito took her in his arms and kissed her. "Now come on, we're going to have some dinner."

Maria went over to Eloida, took her by the hand, and said, "Listen, Carlito and I have to be running around seeing people after dinner. Why don't you call Titi Josefina and see if you can spend the night there. We'll be out late, and I don't like the idea of your being home alone."

"That's a good idea," Carlito echoed. "Besides, if you're at home you'll be getting a million phone calls asking about Ricky, and I don't want you talking to anybody about the case. *Entiende?*"

"Sure I understand." Eloida nodded. "Anyhow, I like Josefina. I suppose I can tell her?" Josefina was Maria's sister-in-law.

"Now listen, Eloida," Carlito said. "Don't tell Josefina anything. Particularly I don't want you talking about Ricky leaving the house last night with a gun."

"Oh, oh, sure, I won't say anything." Eloida seemed crestfallen as she walked over to make the call to her aunt.

"Was I too tough with her?" Carlito asked. "I know

she's very sensitive, but I didn't expect that reaction."

"Don't worry, in a few minutes she'll be chirping happily again," Maria assured him. But Eloida didn't chirp, and retained her somber expression all the way to Han's.

Ming Toy Han operated a delightful Chinese restaurant on Bayard Street. Two steps down from the sidewalk, and you found yourself in a small replica of a Chinese drawing room. Unlike his competitors, Han did not try to make up for lack of space by crowding tables together like sampans in Hong Kong harbor. The service was quiet and efficient. The two waiters, Freddy and Lonnie, were Han's nephews, Yasmine, the cashier, was a cousin's daughter, and Han and his wife ran the kitchen. Maria had been touted to the restaurant by the proprietor's son, Charles Yin Han, who had been a surgical resident at Roosevelt Hospital when she worked there. She had introduced Carlito to the place on one of their early dates, and they had been adopted by the elder Han immediately. He supervised all their meals, barely letting them order for themselves. There had been one or two disasters (Carlito's stomach did backflips at the thought of fried tofu), but on the whole they were fed well at Han's.

Shortly after they arrived Han seated them at a small round table behind an exquisitely ornamented Chinese screen, and announced the he had a Peking duck that would just suit the three of them. Still Eloida seemed upset.

"Okay, Eloida, you've done or said something you shouldn't have," Maria probed. "So you might as well tell me. You know it's going to come out sooner or later."

Huge tears welled in Eloida's eyes and streaked down her cheeks. Not a sound came out of her. Carlito was always struck by the irony that an independent, strong-willed, consciousness-raised feminist like Maria could rear a daugher as helpless and unprepared for life as Eloida. Or was it an irony?

"Well, I was just defending Ricky," she finally wailed. "I didn't know I was doing anything wrong," and went on with her teary recital of her conversation with Fertig.

"*Basta! Cállate*—shut up! *Stúpida!*" Each word spat through his tight lips as Carlito stood up. He raised his arm above his head as if to hammer down on the table but was suddenly riveted by the hot stare of Maria's black eyes. The tigress defending her cub. He lowered his arm, pushed his chair back under the table, and stalked out of the restaurant.

Maria sat with one hand on Eloida's arm and didn't even watch him go. When Han brought the duck, she served Eloida first and then herself, and began to eat.

EIGHT

Carlito stepped out of the restaurant, leaped up the two steps to the sidewalk, and crashed head-on into two elderly tourists. It would have been calming to him to stride down the street and work out his anger that way, but Chinatown at dinnertime is no place for striding. Narrow streets, tourists, and Chinese shop-keepers combine to keep the pace slow and the direction meandering. By the time he had worked himself back to the small park on Baxter Street, he had spent his rage by ducking and pivoting to avoid running other people down. He sat on a bench in the park to weigh the implications of Eloida's story.

First, he had to assume the Fertig would tell the A.D.A. Since the A.D.A. had the story there were two things he would do: (1) Look for other caliber shells in the area of the shooting (2) Look for a gun other than the .38. But if the bullets in the body of the dead man were .38 the A.D.A. would certainly not find it necessary to reveal the presence of other caliber slugs found in the neighborhood.

It seemed to Carlito as he pondered that perhaps this information would not be welcomed by the A.D.A. If the A.D.A. already had a case relying on the finding of a .38 on the defendant, the presence of another gun would only complicate the case. Except—what if—and the thought that suddenly, inexplicably entered Carlito's brain at that moment made him laugh aloud. People in the little park turned their heads at the noise. Carlito, not at all embarrassed, looked around and shouted, "Ladies and gentlemen of the jury: what if—" and laughed himself right out of the park, back toward Han's.

By the time he returned to the table, Maria and Eloida had finished their dinner. Carlito's rages were always short-lived, and Maria knew he had recovered as he walked toward them. Well, another reason for not marrying. He had never been physically violent in his rages, but the raw seam of that brute animality had appeared ready to burst a moment ago. If she had been his wife, would he have restrained himself as he did, or would that arm have come crashing down on her? She waited for him to speak.

"*Perdones, querida*. I'm sorry I yelled at you. *Da me un besito.*" And he kissed first Eloida and then Maria.

Maria held the dinner check toward him. "Your share is one-third."

"But I didn't eat anything."

"That's not our fault. Han brought a big Peking duck that was almost too much for us. I suggested a Dutch treat, I didn't offer to pay for your dinner."

Carlito grinned. Maria had forgiven him and had made penance easy. He wished he could have atoned for some of his other rages as easily. "Fine with me. Let's go."

Carlito had Maria take the wheel as they headed for the Bronx. He wanted a chance to think, and Maria was an excellent driver. While Maria threaded her way up the F.D.R. Drive, his mind kept returning to the problem of the .38 Smith and Wesson. Maybe Angel would have some answers.

They dropped Eloida at Titi Josefina's, waiting for the signal that she had reached the apartment before they continued to Angel's house.

Angel Colon lived with his father and mother and two younger sisters in a courtyard complex of five buildings on Morris Avenue that had once been the pride of the neighborhood, straddling the corner of

35

165th Street. Built in the 1920s, each building consisted of four apartments on each of five floors, with no elevators. The Colons lived on the fifth floor with windows facing the courtyard, which was now used as a playground for the army of children inhabiting the complex. Inside, the families shared their apartments with the armies of roaches and mice who disported themselves as if they paid the rent. Mr. Colon was an invalid confined to a wheelchair except for an occasional walk to the bathroom with the aid of a four-pronged cane. His paralysis was the result of permanent damage to his lower spine suffered when struck down on a dark winter night by a hit-and-run driver.

The Colon apartment was spotless, with all the furniture covered by yellowing plastic. Here and there were sharp slashes in the plastic and deep gouges in the upholstery underneath, a result of the appetites of manic rodents who could find no other goodies in the sterile environs of the apartment. When Maria and Carlito entered the living room they found not only Angel but also Pancho Perez and Luis Esteban, the other boys who had been at the disco with Ricky. Carlito had mixed feelings about finding them all together in the apartment. On the one hand, it saved him the trouble of hunting up each one separately. But it also assured that, accurate or not, he would get a single recital of the events of last night with each boy reinforcing the other's account.

Angel Colon was a tall, thin, nervous boy of seventeen, the youngest of the group, who never sat for more than a fleet moment in any one place, pacing the floor between the living room and kitchen during most of the interview.

Carlito sat down, pulled out his legal pad, and began the interview. He asked them to describe the entire evening, starting from the moment they first met with Ricky. He wasn't particularly concerned with the details leading up to the fight with the Dominicans, knowing he would drag every minute item from Ricky. But he wanted them to start talking freely, getting into the narrative flow, so he took few notes on the pad, preferring to rely on his impeccable memory. What he wanted to get at was where each of them was when the shots were fired. Surprisingly, he encountered the first disagreement between them on this point. Luis and Pancho said they had left the disco first and that Ricky and Angel were right behind. When they were surrounded by the Dominicans, Luis and Pancho were cut off from Ricky and Angel. Neither of them had seen Ricky knifed. They had seen Ricky pull the gun and told Carlito that they had broken and run when the crowd fell back. But they both were certain that when Ricky pulled the gun, Angel was right behind Ricky.

Angel, however, claimed that when they were accosted by the Dominicans outside the door of the disco, he was in turn cut off from Ricky, pushed to the side, and was not close to him. Angel had also seen Ricky pull the gun, and he, too, had fled when the Dominicans fell back. All had heard shots moments later, but none had seen whether it was Ricky actually firing the shots. Disagreement also existed as to how

many shots had been fired, the estimate ranging between three and six. All confirmed that the gun was a
.22 nickel-plated Saturday night special. None knew
where that gun was now. All knew Pablo Alvarado,
the dead boy, but no one could place him close enough
to Ricky to have been shot accidentally.

They described Alvarado as being older—about
twenty-one—and the tough guy in the barrio. He was
built for it, too. At six feet, two hundred pounds, a Tai
Kwan Do brown belt, he threw his weight around. Nobody liked Alvarado much, but nobody crossed him,
either.

Carlito peered at the three boys. He decided not to
tell them about the .38 found on Ricky. What he did
say was, "Look, guys, I need you to help me with
Ricky. Are you with it?"

"Sure!" they all responded.

"Hey, man, Ricky's my best friend," Angel added.

"Okay, then first thing tomorrow morning I want
you guys to go to Broadway where La Marimba is, and
I want you to look all over the area for spent slugs. If
you find any, bring them to me."

"Cool, man, that's easy," said Angel.

"No matter what you find or don't find, don't talk to
anybody but me about it. Agreed?"

They all shook Carlito's hand as he got up. Maria
was in the kitchen with Mrs. Colon and winked as she
saw Carlito. After thanking Mrs. Colon, they left, es-
corted down the four flights by the three boys. As they
approached Carlito's car, Carlito held Angel by the
arm, delaying him just enough so that the two boys

and Maria moved ahead. "Angel, if you really want to help Ricky, I need to have Ricky's gun. Don't bother to tell me you don't know where it is. I heard that already. But I know that you know. Just get it to me—no questions asked. You get me that gun, Angel—" and, he added for effect, "or else."

NINE

Titi Josefina Fuentes, Maria's sister-in-law, was a woman who had survived the hard way. A heroin addict at the age of eighteen, a methadone addict and the mother of three illegitimate children by the time she had reached thirty, she had finally kicked the habit and picked up the threads of her life. Within five years of her thirtieth birthday, she had found a job as a receptionist in a Bronx real estate office, recovered her children from the Bureau of Child Welfare, and turned her back on the welfare system. Now forty-five, she was a solid pillar of her Pentecostal church, dominating her family with strict if benign authority. No liquor or cigarettes were permitted in the Fuentes household, and any kind of oath or obscenity was rewarded with an instant invitation to leave.

When Eloida entered Titi Josefina's apartment, her aunt had a glass of hot milk ready and waiting for her, despite her protestations that hot milk and Peking duck just didn't go together.

"Tell me what happened in court, Eloida," Josefina asked as Eloida grudgingly set herself to the task of sipping the hot milk. As Eloida recounted the events of the evening, she was surprised at how knowledgeable Josefina was about courtroom procedure.

"Listen, I grew up in the streets," Josefina said. "I know the courts A to Z. I never want to see myself there again."

"Anyway," Eloida went on, "I shouldn't be surprised you understand me even better than my mother."

"Why do you say that?" countered Josefina.

"Because my mother thinks I'm so simple I can't figure out how to handle my life. You know better than that, don't you, Titi?"

"Yes, I do, Eloida, but you put a different face to me than to your mother."

"I know," Eloida responded, grimacing as she sipped the milk, "but, when she started pushing Ricky at me, how could I tell her that Ricky and I had already decided we wanted each other? And when she decided that I should try to get a job at Alexander's, what was the point in telling her I had already made an appointment for an interview? As it is, I got the job—it all worked out fine." Eloida stood up. "Well, Titi—I tried the milk, but it won't go down. Save it for me, and I'll drink it tomorrow." Eloida moved into the living room and began making up the open sofa bed where she always slept when she stayed over. "Where's Cousin Clara?"

"She'll be in soon. She went to a movie with some friends," responded Josefina.

Clara was the youngest of her children and the only

one still living with her. Even at twenty-two it was obvious Clara would not marry. She showed no interest in men, her preference at the moment being confined to eighteen- and nineteen-year-old girls.

Eloida got undressed, put on a pair of Clara's pajamas that Josefina gave her, and got into the sofa bed. "Is it all right to watch T.V.?" she asked.

"Of course," replied Josefina. "I'm going to bed too. Tell Clara we'll all have breakfast with her tomorrow."

After watching the eleven o'clock news Eloida began to doze in front of the television set. She didn't hear Clara come in and was awakened by the feel of Clara's cool hand on her brow.

"How are you, chiquita?" murmured Clara as she sat looking down at Eloida while she brushed Eloida's bangs back from her forehead.

Eloida sat up, gently taking Clara's hand from her head and kissing it lightly. "I'm fine, Clara. I'm sleeping over tonight."

"So I see," said Clara. "You look better in my pajamas than I do. But how come you always wear a bra and panties when you stay here? Wouldn't you be more comfortable without them?"

Eloida looked straight at Clara with an open stare of innocence and said, "Because I love you dearly, cousin, and I want us to be dear friends as we are. It is out of consideration for you. Good night, Clara dear."

Clara sighed and stood up. "I'm sorry, Eloida. Please forget I said that. *Buenas noches.*"

Eloida switched off the television after Clara went to

41

her room, and turned on her side. What, she wondered, would her mother have said to Clara in that situation? Eloida smiled. One of these days I'll tell Mami about Clara—but not yet.

TEN

As Maria drove to her apartment, Carlito sat silently cracking his knuckles. She knew it would be useless to talk to him now. He was immersed in the sea of his subconscious, too far away for any communication.

Maria lived on the Grand Concourse, the Bronx's once elegant street, in a middle income building refurbished and maintained by federal funds allocated during the Carter administration. It had tight security, including a television intercom and doorman.

Each remained silent as Maria pressed the elevator button for the eighth floor. Carlito was still far away, never considering the novelty that this was to be the first time he and Maria would be in her apartment alone. In the tiny foyer she flicked a switch that lit up the spacious living room like a stage set, and Carlito, still distracted, headed for the wine red, multi-cushioned sofa and sank into it with a sigh. It was a dramatic room, a combination of ultra modern and traditional Mediterranean: dark oak latticed tables, dark oak caned chairs upholstered in sand velvet, an Aztec rug with reds and blacks and beiges warring endlessly in a pattern of symmetrical fascination. The room's drama was softened by sand-colored nubby draperies that pulled across the wide expanse of windows. One wall was covered by a floor-to-ceiling bookcase with a stereo cabinet built in and giant speakers hung strategically on opposite walls. An assortment of cheap Picasso, Braque, and Monet prints in wide, beautifully crafted frames hung on the sand-colored walls. These frames, begun in a casual crafts workshop by Maria, had turned into a passionate hobby.

As Maria approached Carlito with a small tole tray bearing two crystal goblets of Puerto Rican white rum, he became aware of her and of where he was for the first time since they had left the Colon apartment.

He sipped the rum, then leaned back and closed his eyes, murmuring, "This is about as close to heaven as I ever expect to get. If only I wasn't so damned hungry!" A moment later he sensed Maria's presence hovering over him, and opened his eyes to see Maria dangling a Chinese take-out carton in front of his nose. "What the hell is that?"

"If you had any sense of smell at all, *amigo*, you'd realize that this is your share of Han's Peking duck."

He snatched the carton from her, opened the top flap, and gazed in lascivious delight. "How about that—I knew there was a reason I loved you."

"If you can bear to part with it for a little while, I'll heat it for you along with some rice and beans I have left over from lunch."

"Gladly, *querida*, gladly."

Maria put the duck and the rice and beans into ovenware dishes and slid them into the oven. "Now, this will take about fifteen minutes to heat. I've put the timer on. Use this potholder to take them out. I've set the table for you. Do you think you can manage?"

"Probably, but I don't promise to manage it well. Except the eating part, that is. Are you leaving me here all on my own?"

"I, *querido*, am going to take a shower. Try to bear up while I'm gone." Maria turned, went to her bedroom, and shut the door. A few moments later she crossed through the living room into the bathroom dressed in a bulky terry robe. Carlito sighed, sipped his rum, and waited for the timer to ring.

After he finished eating, he cleared the table and washed the dishes, then returned to the sofa with his rum. Maria had still not emerged from the bathroom, so he turned on the stereo and played Maria's favorite album—Callas singing Carmen at La Scala. Halfway through the first act Maria walked solemnly out of the bathroom. To Carlito she was a vision of sensuality. She wore a long red Chinese caftan split to the thigh on each side. Her hair fell to her waist in soft waves, and her eyes glowed like sparkling charcoal embers. She picked up her glass of rum, sat down next to Carlito, and rested her head on his shoulder. Carlito held her, gently caressing her cheek while they listened together. As the record ended and the stereo shut itself off, Carlito lifted her from the sofa and carried her into the bedroom.

Their lovemaking was slow and tentative at first, as if they were really too tired to expend the energy. But these two had been together too many times to rush headlong into the heights of their passion. They understood and respected each other's needs and reactions too well to skip any of the delightful steps along the way. Their path was point and counterpoint, weaving in and out of embraces, pacing slowly and surely as their passion mounted. Finally, as if at a prearranged signal, they quickened their pace and climaxed together in the paroxysms of final and shared fulfillment.

Hours later, Carlito sat smoking a cigarette, while Maria was once again in the shower. The repetition of the act of love had seemed different tonight. It had been familiar and yet new. New because without discussing it, each understood that tonight there would be no hurried dressing, no need to drive Maria back to her apartment, no need for them to retire to separate beds. Tonight, for the first time, they would spend the whole night together in Maria's bed. Carlito marveled at the realization that never in their three years together had they ever gone away for a weekend, that never had Maria stayed over at his apartment, nor he at hers. Maria had insisted she could not leave Eloida alone for the whole night or ship her off to Josefina. Well, things were finally changing.

Let all the macho guys have their docile, subservient women, he mused. Maria's feminism meant having pride in her body, respecting her sexuality, sharing lovemaking so totally that maleness and femaleness merged into one thick love knot. He'd settle for that any time.

Maria returned to bed and he cradled her in his arms. "What are you thinking?" she whispered.

"I'm thinking about your money—the $2,300 cash I'm carrying around that we didn't use for bail money. Give me your savings passbook and I'll deposit it for you first thing tomorrow."

"No, *mi amor*," she replied, her voice hardening, "you will do no such thing. Tomorrow you will take the cash and deposit it as the down payment of your fee."

"But Maria, you know I don't require such a down payment. Especially not from you."

"Especially from me, *mi vida*. If you don't take it, it will spoil this whole night for us. Don't you see, you must keep the money or I'll feel disgraced, dishonored. Like I was your whore for the money."

Carlito understood at once. Proud Maria would never consider taking back the money after tonight. He kissed her gently and sighed. "You are too much for me, Maria! I give up." They nestled gently against each other and closed their eyes.

Damn! Carlito pondered. Could she have planned the whole thing just to make sure I kept the fee? And fell asleep still wondering.

ELEVEN

Maria sat at the edge of her bed braiding her hair. Carlito was in the kitchen preparing breakfast. Maria was confused. She had always thought that she would never again consider marriage. But having awakened that morning all entangled with the feel and smell of

Carlito and being cradled and cuddled in the early hours by this strong and gentle man had made her feel she had indeed missed something precious. The problem was that her first marriage had been a disaster. Not that her husband, Francisco, had been such a terrible man, but he wasn't anything wonderful, either. They had married much too young, and she had become pregnant almost immediately. Very quickly marriage became a stifling cage where she felt trapped. Francisco's death in Vietnam had liberated her. The insurance money had enabled her to enroll in college to study for a nursing degree, and the government pension payments and support allocations for Eloida had provided the financial cushion to make it possible.

Of course, everything was different with Carlito. He respected her intelligence and had enough of his own not to feel threatened by her. He was a passionate lover, yet considerate and confident enough to be adventurous in his lovemaking, always ready to try new ways for them to find pleasure in each other. His philosophy of life matched hers in more ways than had any other person's she had ever met. In short, why not marry him?

The sharp ringing of the telephone interrupted her reverie. It was Mrs. Colon, frantically trying to locate Angel. He had not returned to the house after walking down with Carlito and Maria the night before. Maria told her she would check with his friends and let her know if she found out anything.

"What do you think?" she asked Carlito. "Angel's been out all night and is still not home."

"I think Angel's a frightened boy who knows much more than he's told us. I also think he will come to my office sometime today with Ricky's gun."

"He's got Ricky's gun?"

"If he doesn't have it himself, he knows who does. I warned him last night to get it to me."

But Angel did not show up at Carlito's office that day, nor did he return to his apartment. Angel was missing.

After breakfast of Carlito's special scrambled eggs—his secret was browning the butter at high heat just short of burning it, then pouring in the seasoned, beaten eggs at exactly the right moment—crispy crusted rolls, and strong Spanish coffee, Carlito and Maria scheduled their day. Maria was due at Lincoln Hospital on the four-to-midnight shift, so she would contact Luis and Pancho to learn what they had found in front of La Marimba and see if they had information about where Angel was. Carlito had appearances in Bronx Criminal and Queens Supreme Courts that morning, so he would be busy until after one o'clock. They decided to meet in Carlito's office at three. If Maria had found Angel by that time, she was to bring him along with her.

At two o'clock Maria changed into her nurse's uniform. She had recorded as much information as she could gather to hand over to Carlito. At the moment it didn't seem to have too much importance, but Carlito would know better. Carlito—what was she going to do about him?

From the moment she had met him she knew she

could easily get too involved with this man, and she had been fighting that involvement. She treasured her independence so much that any emotional commitment posed a threat. Until now she had held him off, seeing him infrequently—although after her first date with him she never went out with another man—denying him the opportunity to spend more than a few hours at a time with her, and using Eloida as her excuse for avoiding commitment. This morning, though, everything had turned topsy-turvy. She was annoyed with herself for her feelings, and annoyed with Carlito as well for stirring those feelings.

She decided that this afternoon when she went to his office she would cool things down, revert to old habits, avoid the commitment. She hoped.

At the stroke of three, Maria entered Carlito's office alone. She was wearing her uniform with the cap perched precariously between her coiled braids. She was all business this afternoon. "I hope Mr. Rivera can see me promptly," she told Lisa. "I'm due at work soon."

"He's got old Mrs. Arbenez who's being evicted again," Lisa sighed. "But he's expecting you. I'll buzz him."

Within a few moments Carlito opened his office door and led a short, birdlike old woman who was twittering away in Spanish while seeming to be waving each hand and every one of her ten fingers in different directions. "Si, mamita. Si. Yo sé, yo sé. Si. Grácias. Vaya con Dios," said Carlito as he ushered her through the outer office to the door.

Maria didn't blink an eye and marched right in. She sat stiffly at his desk and said in a tight voice, "I don't have much time and you know how I hate to be late, especially for work. So let me tell you what I have found out without any waste of time."

"Now look, Maria," he barked at her, "you can pretend all you want that last night was nothing special—that my sleeping over made no difference between us. But I know better, and if you're the honest woman you claim to be, you'll stop trying to fool yourself. Okay, now you can tell me what you found out."

Maria blinked, half rose from her seat, sank back again, pulled a notebook from her pocketbook, and read: "I met with Luis and Pancho at the grocery store of Pancho's uncle. They told me that after we had left, Angel suggested to them that they go to La Marimba right away, to see what they could find. They agreed, deciding that they could return in the morning if they were unsuccessful in locating any of the shells Mr. Rivera was looking for. They got off the bus at one-twenty A.M. and when they reached La Marimba the street was empty. They split up and started to search, Luis in front of the door, Pancho about a hundred feet away, and Angel in the alley. They were there for about fifteen minutes, finding nothing. They went into a bar across from La Marimba for a beer. The Puerto Rican barman told them he had been watching them and they were wasting their time. Whatever it was they were looking for must have been found by the big cop who was searching the area about two hours earlier. They finished their beers and as they left the bar

Angel Colon had an epileptic seizure. The witnesses did not tell me this, but from their description it could only be that," Maria interpolated. "The boys stayed with Angel until the ambulance came and took Angel away. A check of the hospitals in the area shows that Columbia-Presbyterian treated an Angel Colon for the residuals of an epileptic seizure. Injuries were bruises of the face and nose and a black eye—all consistent with the fall that occurred during the seizure. Patient was released at five A.M. Angel Colon has not returned home as of two P.M." As she finished her reading, she tore the paper out of her notebook and handed it to Carlito.

"That's an excellent report. Thank you," he said. "But since it's all written out and you're in a hurry to get to work, why did you bother to read it to me? You could have left it with Lisa."

Maria didn't answer. She got up stiffly and started toward the door. Carlito stepped quickly between the door and Maria, effectively barring her way without touching her and said in a steely but quiet tone: "Listen, Maria, and listen well. I am not a boy. I am thirty-five years old. I'm Puerto Rican. I'm a lawyer. I'm proud of my heritage and I'm proud of my profession. Don't trifle with me. Don't play games with me. Either we're lovers or we're not. But if we are to have a relationship—with me it's all or nothing. You decide."

Woody Fertig sat in front of his locker gazing at the slug he had found in front of La Marimba when he went there after leaving the courthouse. He was certain this was not a .38. He didn't need ballistics to tell him that. This confirmed Eloida's story. There must have been another gun. Then which gun had killed Alvarado? If it wasn't the .38, then the case against Betancourt had a serious flaw. But where did the .38 come from? He'd check that out next. He'd wait another few days before speaking to the A.D.A.

Carlito got home at about ten that night. It had been a long, hard day, and that session with Maria had made it worse. He decided to shower and go to bed early. He called his office to check the messages on the telephone answering machine, all of which had come in after he left the office at eight-thirty. The last message on the tape was recorded at nine-fifty and said in Spanish: "I'm sorry for the way I acted. You were right. If it's possible for you to pick me up at the hospital at twelve-fifteen I'd like to talk to you. And Carlito, bring your toothbrush."

T W E L V E

The funeral parlor stood bare and separated from the tenement slums on either side by the rubble of apartment buildings condemned and torn down. Across the street stood an old Catholic church, its forbidding granite front stained by the grime of the South Bronx ghetto. Maria parked the car, and Carlito carefully closed and locked both doors and set the burglar alarm in the left front fender. The rain poured down mercilessly, creating soggy flotsam in the garbage-strewn street.

As they entered, the sound of wailing reached them from the chapel closest to the door. The carpeting in the entryway was worn and ragged, and the dim bulbs cast muddy shadows over the peeling walls. The sign indicated that Alvarado was in Chapel Number Two.

Maria led a reluctant Carlito down the smoke-filled hallway. "I don't enjoy this at all, Maria. Let's try to get out of here as soon as we can," he whispered.

"I know," said Maria, "but it has to be done."

"Ever since my parents' funeral I can't even pass a funeral parlor without getting the shakes," Carlito said as he withdrew a sweating palm.

Chapel Number Two, at the end of the hall, was a long, narrow room; at the far end lay Alvarado in an open casket. A blond girl knelt in prayer in front of it.

"*Quien es?*" Maria asked of an elderly woman seated next to the door.

"*La esposa de Alvarado,*" she replied, pointing an arthritic finger at the blond.

Maria glanced at Carlito. "His wife? She doesn't look Spanish from here."

"*Es gringa—Americana,*" the old woman continued.

At that moment the blond stood and turned. Her tall, thin figure seemed incongruously large in the small chapel.

"No doubt about it," said Carlito, "blue eyes, fair skin."

The girl moved slowly down the center aisle sobbing, her nose and mouth pinched red with grief. No one came to assist her as she seated herself on a settee that stood against the chapel's far wall.

Carlito squared his shoulders. "Well, here we go. Let's see what we can find out. By the way, does she look familiar to you? I could swear I've seen her before."

"Not to me," replied Maria. "Maybe she was one of your clients."

The blond looked up as Maria and Carlito approached. Carlito extended his hand. "My deepest condolences, Mrs. Alvarado."

"Who are you?" she asked irritably. "One of his Mafia friends? I never saw you before."

"My name is Carlos Rivera, Mrs. Alvarado. I'm a lawyer, and this is my fiancée, Maria Fuentes."

"A lawyer, eh? Are you the guy that got Pablo two years in Elmira?"

"No, no, I never represented him. I represent the boy who is accused of shooting him."

Her blue eyes snapped alertly open, taking Carlito in from head to toe. "Betancourt's lawyer, eh. Well, maybe he did it, I don't know. I didn't think the kid had the balls."

"He tells us he didn't do it, Mrs. Alvarado, and we believe him," interjected Maria.

"What do I know, he could've done it. He had reasons. Hell, a lot of people had reasons."

"What reasons did Ricky have?" asked Carlito.

"Don't you know? Ricky worked for a numbers runner that was wiped out. That put Ricky out of business. Pablo was the runner that took over, as well as an enforcer."

"Did Pablo and Ricky ever run up against each other recently?"

Her eyes narrowed in thought. "Nah, there was others who hated Pablo more—for a lot better reasons."

"Like who?" Carlito pressed.

"I just told you, he was an enforcer. Do you think you make friends doing that?"

"But you said there were people who hated Alvarado. Tell me about them."

"Well, there's Jose, the Mafioso's bodyguard who thought Pablo was bucking for his job. Colon, who was crippled by a hit-and-run car, who always believed it was Pablo driving, on account they never bothered him for the money he owed the Mafia after it happened. Three different guys who know it was Pablo who broke their arms when they were slow in payments, and—" She caught her breath and then stopped talking.

"Who else, Mrs. Alvarado?" Carlito urged. "You were going to name someone else."

"No I wasn't, and you can stop calling me Mrs. Alvarado. I was never married to him. My name is Patty. Patty Powers."

Now Carlito knew why she looked so familiar; she was a female version of Patrolman Robert Powers. "Oh," he said, "then your brother is the policeman who arrested Betancourt?"

"Yeah, isn't that something." She looked away from

Carlito, picking at a thread on her dress.

Maria, looking stunned, had stepped back, and as if it were rehearsed, Carlito moved in, taking all the space in front of the blond. "How did your brother get along with Pablo?"

"How do you think? He hated him." She hesitated a moment. "But not enough to kill him. After all, Pablo helped him out when he was in trouble."

"Really?"

"Yeah, really. Got him a loan when he needed it—and waited plenty long to get it back."

"So Alvarado loaned your brother money."

"Are you kidding? He put my brother in touch with the right people is what he did—and went easy on him when he didn't pay back on time."

"Then your brother should have been grateful to Pablo."

"Well, my brother, he's funny. He don't like Puerto Ricans—you know what I mean?"

THIRTEEN

Three days had passed and Angel Colon was still missing. Carlito had interviewed three other Puerto Rican youths who had been at La Marimba on the night of the shooting, but two had left the disco before the fight, and the third was inside when the shots were fired. That one told Carlito that he definitely heard four shots.

Ricky had been transferred from Bellevue to Rikers

Island the day before, and Carlito decided now was the time for them to have a long talk.

As he approached the checkpoint at the mainland side of the only bridge to the island, he brought his car to a stop, left it, and presented his notice to the warden in the guardhouse. After the notice and his credentials were checked, he was issued a large cardboard rectangle with the word VISITOR spelled out in big letters. This he placed on the dashboard and drove over the bridge. He was stopped again at the island checkpoint of the bridge and then allowed to leave his car in the parking complex.

The administration building was a huge barnlike structure straddling the roadway, just inside the second checkpoint. Carlito presented his credentials again, was issued a visitor's tag to pin to his lapel, and then exited through the rear of the building, where numerous buses picked up passengers for different areas of the island.

The prison at Rikers Island consisted of approximately ten large brick dormitories, reachable only by buses that operated along winding roads that serpentined through the island. No one (including any employee) was permitted to walk from one building to another because of the risk of being gunned down by guards who kept constant vigil on the towers of each of the buildings. Ricky had been assigned to the youth detention building, which housed all inmates under twenty-one. The bus that ran the route left every half hour. Carlito had never visited that particular building, and asked the guard operating the bus to let him know when they arrived. The guard-driver, a blond, blue-eyed giant, cast a scornful look at Carlito and grunted as Carlito settled himself in the second seat behind him.

After the bus had made its fifth stop, Carlito approached the driver. "How many stops till we get to the youth detention building?"

The driver looked up from behind the wheel, sneered, and garbled something.

"I didn't understand what you said?"

The bus accelerated suddenly, throwing Carlito backward in the aisle. "You missed it, counselor. Have to go back to the ad building and get another bus."

Carlito moved forward, crowding against the driver. "What do you mean I missed it? You were supposed to let me know when we got there."

"Sorry, I thought I announced it. I guess I forgot. It was the first one we came to." The driver measured Carlito from head to toe, moved his right hand as if to push Carlito back, stopped in midair as Carlito braced to resist the push, and said in an ominous but quiet tone, "Move back, will you, counselor, I need more room to drive."

"No," answered Carlito, matching tone for tone. They remained that way while the driver completed the circuit. As the bus stopped back at the administration building, the driver announced, "Last stop, everyone off." The four other passengers, apparently unaware of what was happening, filed off. The driver leaned back, faced Carlito, put his hand on his gun, and added, "That means you, too, señor—off."

Carlito took one step back, braced his rear against the post at the door of the bus, dropped his briefcase on the nearest seat, and hunched his shoulders for instant action. "Listen, Mister," he hissed. "You were to take me to the youth detention dorm. We're not there yet. You and I are going to ride this bus till we get there."

The driver stood up, filling the space Carlito had vacated, and said menacingly: "You want me to arrest you? Is that what you want? It would be a pleasure, you know. Maybe you'll feel more at home inside with all your countrymen anyhow."

"I want you to try, Americano. Go ahead, try."

The driver looked nervously at Carlito. He hadn't expected to run into this buzz saw. The guy wasn't that big, but he looked dangerous enough, and the bastard wasn't going to back down. "Okay, señor, but see, this bus ain't goin' anywhere. This was my last run. I'm off now. So why don't you just step off and wait for the next bus?"

"I'm not getting off here. This is where I got on. I'm getting off at the youth detention dorm, and you're taking me there."

"Excuse me, sir—what's the problem?"

Carlito turned slightly and glanced over his right shoulder at the sound of the Spanish inflection. A tall Hispanic guard with lieutenant's bars on his shoulders was standing on the first step of the bus right behind him. "Ask him, Lieutenant!" Carlito snapped, looking back at the driver.

"He missed his stop. Says I didn't call it out, Lieutenant. Now he won't get off the bus. I told him I don't make this trip again, but he still wants me to take him to the youth dorm."

"I want to put this man on report, Lieutenant. I'm an attorney trying to visit my client, and I asked him to tell me when we reached the youth dorm. He drove the whole route without saying a word, and now I'm supposed to wait a half-hour for the next bus."

"But I'm off duty now, Lieutenant . . ."

"Shut up, Mankowski," the lieutenant interrupted. "Take the man where he wants to go." Turning to Carlito he continued: "I'm sorry for the inconvenience, counselor. I'm sure the driver will get you to the right place now." He winked at Carlito. "No need to put him on report when he cooperates—right, counselor?"

Carlito nodded grudgingly and turned to pick up his briefcase. He had now officially returned to his lawyer's image. He stood while the blond giant got back behind the wheel, bit his lip, and backed the bus out. The bus made a wide semicircular loop to a dorm facing the administration building and stopped. Carlito got out slowly, lingering on the bottom step. He realized that he was not more than one hundred yards in a straight line from the administration building. He turned to the driver, who was staring straight ahead, said "You're a shit," and left the bus.

They brought Ricky down about a half-hour later. Carlito was appalled. Someone had decided that Ricky should be given a preventive haircut—prison euphemism for a baldie. He had lost more weight from his already skinny frame and he was still bent stiffly forward from the knife wound. The only improvement apparent was his acne, which seemed to have paled along with the rest of his complexion.

"How is Eloida?" were the first words Ricky spoke.

"She's fine, no need to worry about her. How are you?"

"I'm okay, I guess. My gut still hurts, and I don't feel like eating much. What's happening with my case?"

"It's going the way I expected. We're supposed to have a felony hearing tomorrow, but the assistant D.A. will have an indictment ready, so we'll be denied that. Did they ever give you that paraffin test?"

"No, they never did nothing like you told me they would."

"Good. Now I want you to tell me the whole story. Start from telling how and when you got the gun." Carlito took out a cigarette, lit it, and passed it over to Ricky.

"Well, a couple weeks ago me and Angel and Luis and Pancho were talking about me getting married. And them guys said to me, 'We ought to have a big bash for you, for you getting married.' 'Yeah,' I said, 'like we see them guys in the movies, y'know?' What do they call them?"

"Bachelor parties," Carlito supplied.

"Yeah, that's right. But you know, we ain't got no dough or nothing to spend. So I got this idea. I told the guys let's go to a disco—but not just any disco, y'know? A disco where there's something doing— something different. So Angel pipes up, 'Yeah, let's go

61

to La Marimba where they got the dance contests all the time. You the best dancer in the Bronx, you probably win.' All the guys start popping Angel on the head and saying what a stupid idea, 'cause La Marimba is Dominican territory and we'd be taking a chance on getting beat up or something if we went there. But I liked the plan. First, we ain't never been there. Second, I been winning dance contests all over, why not at La Marimba, and third—we don't take our women there, we enter the contest with their women. If we win, dancing with their women—it makes them look bad in front of their own girls. Like rubbing their nose in it—y'know? Angel is all for it, like he is with anything I say, but Luis and Pancho, they say, 'You're crazy, man—you askin' for it! No way,' and shit like that. So Angel gets this great flash, y'know, and says, 'Hey, man, suppose we got us a rod and we pack it with us when we go. Ain't nobody gonna mess with us, we got a rod.' And I say, 'That's cool, man, but we ain't got us a rod!' I tell them let's pool our cash, let's see how much we got.

"Well, anyway, when we throw it in the middle, all we got between the four of us is ten dollars. I tell them that ain't enough. I don't feel like packing no gun that's maybe gonna blow up in my face insteada shooting. So Luis and Pancho say, 'Cool it, man, we get you more green,' and sure enough the next day they bring twenty-five George Washingtons, and they say, 'Here, Ricky, add this to the ten. If you have any left over, keep it. It's like our wedding present.' 'O.K.,' I say, 'but we keep it just for protection at the disco. After that we dump it. Ya dig?'

"The next day I went down to Thirty-fourth just like the numbers guy told me, long ago, and I caught this Rican pushing a dress truck. He gives me a twenty-two nickel-plated with a six-shot loader with the bullets in it for fifteen dollars. I went into Macy's and bought a disco shirt with the dough left over." Ricky paused. "Man, that sure was a nice shirt!" He smiled ruefully, shrugged, and went on: "The dance contest was Monday, so that's when we went—me and Angel and Luis and Pancho. I stuck the rod in my belt and dropped the shirt over it. It covered the rod until I danced. But, that's what I wanted. No sense packing a rod if them bozos don't know it.

"When they announce the dance contest, I go right over to where the Dominicans is sitting with their women, see, and I say to the honcho there, 'Man, you mind if I ask one of your women to dance in this here contest?' Now I know asking him in front of his gang and his women, no way he can say no. Like, he's got to lose face if he says no on account, one, it means he don't trust his women and two, he's scared of the competition. So he says, 'Yeah, O.K., go ahead.' I make sure I pick his girl. She can't say no 'cause her old man already said all right.

"I win the contest, and the prize is four free drinks. So I ask the man what he's drinking, 'cause whatever it is the next one's on me. Like I'm paying him back for borrowing his girl. Well, he don't like *that* much either, but again he ain't got no choice. Now all this time I'm being polite, see, but he knows I'm rubbing his nose in it and he can't do nothing. And I know I got to be careful not to give him an excuse to start a fight.

"Then Angel came up and ruined the whole scam. He starts saying how good this guy's woman looked dancing with me, like we was a natural together and other stupid things like that. The guy jumps up and lays one on Angel's nose. I got to help Angel, and so I push the guy back so he don't hit Angel again, and he trips, falls against the table, and spills the drink that I bought him on himself and his woman. That did it— the shit hit the fan, and we started to hustle out. When we got downstairs, there was a whole pack of them Dominicans waiting for us. I figured then that I was the one who was scammed. That Dominican bastard was going to find a way to start a fight no matter what, so he could get back at me. The guys was downstairs just waiting for a signal. I told Angel stay close and get your back to the building. I felt Angel's shoulder touching mine. I pulled out the gun. All I wanted was to get them guys off of us. And it worked, too, they were moving back, until someone behind me grabbed the rod outa my hand. As soon as that happened, it was like a signal. Those Dominicans closed in on me, I got stuck, went down, and they was all over me. I never heard no one shooting that gun."

Carlito peered at Ricky and asked: "What *was* the last thing you heard, Ricky?"

"The last thing I heard was Angel scream right behind me, 'They gonna kill us, Ricky—they gonna kill us!' "

Carlito looked at Ricky and knew that Ricky had been telling him the story exactly as he recalled it. But Carlito was taking no chances, and he went over the story again and again, interrupting, making Ricky start at different points in the story, asking for details, details, details. Each time Ricky was consistent. Finally Carlito was satisfied. He leaned back, took out two cigarettes, and handed one to Ricky.

"What do you think, Mr. Rivera—can we beat it?"

"I don't know, Ricky. The cops have a corpse on their hands. They've got to hang it on somebody. As far as they're concerned, you're it."

"I know. I wouldn't be the first guy to catch time for something he didn't do. But I'm telling you one thing—I ain't copping a plea. If they hang it on me, I go down, and that's it."

"Why?" Carlito asked. "If they reduce to manslaughter second it's only one and a third to four years. That wouldn't be bad."

"You don't understand, Mr. Rivera. I can't do no time, because Eloida needs me. I got to be out to be with her and take care of her."

Carlito was amused. He knew that Eloida had the capacity to make people protective over her, yet Ricky was talking as if Maria did not exist.

"You see, she's the only person in this world ever needed me. She needs me, and I ain't going to let her down."

FOURTEEN

Carlito sat at his desk sorting the papers in front of him. Just one week after the shooting, the D.A.'s office had brought down an indictment accusing Ricky of committing murder in the second degree, a crime punishable by a minimum sentence of seven years. He paid special attention to the voluntary disclosure statements provided by the D.A.'s office, along with a copy of the indictment. He noted that the police claimed to have four witnesses to the shooting, and they obviously would be the witnesses ready to testify at the line-up identification scheduled for the next day. He also noted that the gun was recovered by Police Officer Robert Powers in the jacket of the defendant, and that one spent shell and one slug had been recovered at the scene. Since Carlito already had four separate statements that specified the number of shots to be three to six, Carlito wondered where the other bullets were. He also made a notation to ask Ricky about the jacket, because Carlito's notes had no mention of any jacket. The damned case was getting muddier by the minute.

Patrolman Woody Fertig sat in front of his locker and gazed at the .38 Smith and Wesson in the plastic bag. Powers had checked it out from the property clerk's office for the purpose of testifying at the grand jury, but Woody had offered to return it for him and

Powers had seemed eager to let him do it. For Fertig, it was a perfect opportunity to examine the gun more closely. He took a small notepad from his breast pocket and copied down the serial number. After returning the gun, Fertig went down to the file room, took out a large ledger, sighed, and started to run his finger down the columns.

Maria sat in the nurses' lounge having a cup of coffee while she evaluated the change in her life since Carlito had moved in. The night she had left the message on his telephone recorder, he had brought more than just his toothbrush. Although they had made no formal agreement, Carlito had spent every night with her since then. Independence, she realized, could still be maintained with a man like Carlito. At least now it could, but later? *Quien sabe?*

A nurse's aide broke into her reveries. "There's a phone call for you, Fuentes." Maria gulped her coffee and went to her station to pick it up.

"Hello, Maria, this is Cruzita—Cruzita Colon, Angel's mother. You told me I could call you at work. I hope I am not disturbing you."

"Have you heard from Angel, Mrs. Colon?" Maria gasped.

"Yes, today—just now. Angel is in P.R., in Santurce, with a cousin. He's all right, but frightened. He will not tell me why he ran away, but he says he will not come home now. I'm so worried. He does not have his pills with him. He will be sick if he doesn't take them. I do not know what to do." The words came tumbling out on a wave of hysteria, and dissolved finally into a sobbing wail.

"Don't worry, Mrs. Colon. Angel will be all right. Please calm yourself." Maria had a sudden inspiration. "I will see to it that he gets his pills."

"But how—the mail to P.R. takes too long, and maybe they will spill or the bottle will break or they will be spoiled!"

"I will have someone take the pills to him—someone who is going to P.R."

"If you could find such a person I would pay their fare, I swear!"

"That isn't necessary, Mrs. Colon. Maybe I myself will go."

"Bless you—bless you. You are a saint, a sweet person, I always knew you were." Mrs. Colon continued to babble and Maria had to cut her off.

"I'm sorry, Mrs. Colon, a patient needs me. I must hang up. I will call you tomorrow to make arrangements." Maria pressed her finger down and cut Mrs. Colon off in mid sob. She waited just long enough to be sure she'd been disconnected, and then dialed Carlito.

Ricky Betancourt sat in his cell at Rikers and worried. He worried about Eloida, he worried about Angel, but most of all he worried about himself. He had just had his disco shoes taken from him because one of the bully boys decided he liked them. Maybe I'm lucky I'm too sick to fight. Probably wind up dead. Have to ask Eloida to bring my sneakers. If I ever get out of this mess there ain't ever gonna be a repeat performance. One thing I know about myself now: I ain't made for street life. I sure as hell failed the code. The guy who said "If you're man enough to carry a gun you got to be man enough to use it" was full of shit. It's no big deal to use a gun. I know now that no matter what happened that night, I would not have fired that gun.

FIFTEEN

Carlito and Maria argued halfway through the night about Maria's plan. Finally, because it was logical and there was no other practical way it could be done, Carlito agreed. Maria would use the week's leave she had previously arranged to orchestrate Ricky and Eloida's wedding to bring Angel back to New York from Puerto Rico. Carlito instructed Maria painstakingly on how she was to approach Angel and exactly how to give him the impression that she knew a lot more about Angel's motive for running away than she actually did. Maria, once she understood Carlito's legal concerns, felt adequate to handle Angel.

As Carlito was about to leave after breakfast, a rueful look spread over his face. "I just realized, *querida*, that you won't be here with me tonight. Shall I sleep here, or at my own place?"

"I want you here, Carlito. I don't want Eloida left alone."

"Won't your neighbors gossip?"

69

"Frankly, *amigo*, I don't give a damn. Besides, I'll feel safer in P.R. knowing that you're here when I get home." Maria shrugged. Another step toward total commitment.

Carlito cocked his head, took her in his arms, and kissed her longingly. "Good luck," he whispered and left.

At ten A.M. Carlito entered the side door to 100 Centre Street that led to the Manhattan D.A.'s office. After being checked in at the desk in the small lobby, he took the elevator to the ninth floor to meet with Ted Warren, the assistant in charge of Ricky's case.

Ted Warren was a midwesterner, a blond incarnation of Abe Lincoln. At six-foot-four he towered over Carlito by more than half a foot. As he ambled out of his small cubicle of an office to greet Carlito, he was all angles and pivots. His broad shoulders pitched first one way, then yawed another, his elbows jutted out at odd declinations, his large flat feet made a strange contrast to the bony knees that threatened to cut through the baggy trousers. At first sight, Ted Warren gave every appearance of a man who did not know where he was going. Any adversary who made that mistaken assumption was in for a rude awakening. Warren knew exactly where he was going, and how to get there. He had, during his eight years with the D.A.'s office, amassed a brilliant trial record, while earning a reputation for honesty and integrity. No one had ever accused Ted Warren of taking cheap shots or unfair advantage, but his homespun appearance, combined with his midwestern twang, had convinced many a juror that apparent weaknesses in the People's case were really strong points after Warren finished with them.

Carlito knew him by reputation only, and was prepared for a tough battle. Warren had never heard of Carlito at all before this case, but he had already made prudent inquiry of his brethren in the Bronx. Without ever having met, Honest Abe and The Gray Bantam had great respect for each other.

"You'll forgive me, Mr. Rivera, for not observing the social nicety of shaking hands with you, but I make it a practice never to shake hands with my adversary. It is not meant as any disrespect."

"I understand, Mr. Warren. No sense in giving the impression that you're being led down the garden path."

Warren looked sharply at Carlito as Carlito bowed slightly and smiled.

"Not likely, Mr. Rivera, not likely."

Warren led Carlito to a back elevator that took them to the second floor, where they wound their way through a labyrinth of hallways and offices until they reached the line-up rooms. There Carlito saw the five men who were to appear in the line-up with Ricky. Under Warren's direction, the police had selected carefully. All were Hispanic, all short and slender, one even had acne like Ricky. "Is the group satisfactory, Mr. Rivera?" Warren asked.

"I'm afraid not, Mr. Warren. This group is definitely unsuitable to put into a line-up identification with my client."

Warren scratched his ear, another obvious mid-western mannerism. "What's wrong?"

"Get my client in here with them, and you'll see for yourself."

Ricky, who had already been installed in a small cell just outside the line-up room, was brought in. "Well, I'll be durned, we surely do have a problem." Warren laughed more in embarrassment than glee. Ricky's scalp, it appeared, had not yet recovered from the shearing bestowed by the barbers at Rikers. Small black shoots, barely a quarter-inch long, stood like sentinels in a stockade all along his head. All the other men had long, luxuriant manes, one even sporting a huge afro. The police sergeant in charge said, "How about we put hats on all of them, Mr. Warren?"

Warren pondered for a moment. "Hats could do it, but they'd have to be the kind that cover the whole head."

Carlito now felt it was time to offer a suggestion. He had known from the moment he had seen Ricky at Rikers Island that with Ricky's hair cut off he would stick out like a sore thumb at any line-up. He had long ago decided how he could turn that seeming disadvantage around, and now made his pitch: "Excuse me, Mr. Warren, but I would suggest the only type of hat that would be fair to use is a knit stocking hat that could at the same time be pulled low enough on the forehead and down over the ears and neck."

"There surely wouldn't be much face sticking out of that contraption, would there," said Warren.

Carlito looked at Warren and shrugged. That's just

the point, my friend. That's just the point.

"Okay," said Warren, and he turned to the sergeant. "Get six stocking hats and let's have each of them wearing one."

Ricky was asked to choose a number from one to six as a place in the line-up while they were waiting for the stocking hats to be brought in. Ricky chose Number Five, as Carlito had instructed him on their last visit. Carlito's theory was that positions One and Six were undesirable because the witness's attention was more acutely focused on the first and the last. Positions Three and Four were less desirable because they were centrally located and were the obvious choice of someone trying to lose himself in a crowd. Position Number Five was better than Number Two because the witness would be exposed to four faces before seeing Ricky, and any uncertainty of the witness would be compounded by having to select and reject four faces before choosing Ricky.

Carlito watched carefully as the hats were donned and the number cards hung around the subjects' necks. By the time the hats had been adjusted to Carlito's satisfaction, their foreheads had been covered to within two inches of their eyebrows. All the temples and sideburns were covered, as well as the ears and nape of the neck. Even Eloida might have trouble picking Ricky out of that group.

The sergeant first photographed the entire group seated, then standing, then each one individually. The line-up men were then directed to be seated in their numbered order on a bench against one wall, while all the others left. Carlito accompanied the sergeant and Warren to the viewing room, where Warren had four witnesses assembled. At Carlito's insistence three of the witnesses were removed from the viewing room while one was permitted to remain. Warren agreed that each of the witnesses was to be removed from the area after he viewed the line-up and made his choice, so that there would be no contact between the witness who had made a selection and the next witness.

The first witness, Guanerge Quinones, was a cocky and aggressive Hispanic. Carlito had an idea that this was the Dominican boy whose girlfriend had danced with Ricky, but Ricky had known him only as Chico. As Carlito observed him, though, he seemed to fit the description supplied by Ricky. The room was darkened and the glass viewer swiveled into place. Guanerge stood up on a small platform and looked through what to him, Warren, and Carlito who flanked him on either side, was a two-foot-by-two-foot window opening into the viewing room where the six subjects were seated in numerical order. Carlito knew, however, that to Ricky and the others in the viewing room the window appeared to be a glass mirror. Carlito watched Guanerge carefully as his eyes swung from one end of the line to the other. He seemed confused and uncertain, and as he started to speak, Warren, who had been observing him as closely as Carlito, put his arm on the boy's shoulder and said, "Wait, don't say anything now. We're just getting started." The sergeant pressed a buzzer that rang in the viewing room, and upon hearing the signal the men in the viewing room stood up. Then, as they had been instructed, each walked straight up to the mirror and stopped about three inches from it. At that point the witness on the other side was about six inches from the man he was viewing. Each one then turned first to the right and stopped, then to the left and stopped, and then returned to his seat. Guanerge showed no reaction to the first four men who marched up and back. He didn't react to Ricky either until Ricky had turned to the right. At that moment, the puzzled frown was replaced by a wide smile. Warren saw the reaction at the same time Carlito did, but could do nothing to restrain the boy for fear of ruining the validity of the entire identification process.

"That's him, that's the bastard!" he called triumphantly. Guanerge had spotted the acne and remembered it.

Warren replied in a cold, steely voice: "Please wait, Mr. Quinones, there is still another man to look at."

"I don't gotta look at nobody no more—that's the guy—Number Five!"

"Look at Number Six anyhow," Warren snapped, and Guanerge finally got the message. After Number Six had gone through the routine, the identification of Ricky was duly noted and signed by Guanerge. Carlito wanted to make sure that this was the Chico Ricky had described. As the boy turned to leave, Carlito dropped his pen a few feet to his right, moved quickly to retrieve it, squatted down so that his voice was coming from a different direction, and called hoarsely, "Ai, Chico!"

Guanerge spun around and looked toward the voice.

Carlito stood up, smiled, and in his normal voice said, *"Muchas grácias."*

Warren looked at Carlito, then at Guanerge, and sighed. "Okay, get him out. Bring in the next witness."

Nereida Pagan was a small, thin, nervous young girl, no more than eighteen. Carlito immediately pegged her as Ricky's dancing partner at the disco. She seemed reluctant to participate in the whole procedure, and indeed dropped her eyes when Ricky stood staring unseeingly at her through the one-way window. When all six had gone through the routine, she stepped back off the platform and whispered in a barely audible voice, "I don't know. I don't recognize no one there."

"Are you sure?" countered Warren. "Do you want them to go over it again?"

"No, it's no use. I don't know none of those guys."

Warren shook his head. "Next witness."

Hector Cruz was next. "It's Number Five. I know the guy from before he came to the disco. That's Ricky Betancourt."

Edgardo Concepcion, the last witness, was, at twenty-eight, older than the rest. He sported a small mustache, two-tone shoes, and an alcoholic breath. He wavered between Numbers Three and Four, finally settling on Four. He signed the affidavit in a shaky scribble and left.

Carlito looked at Warren and asked, "Is that it, Mr. Warren?"

Warren looked slightly grim. "That's it for today, Mr. Rivera. Thank you for coming." As he reached the door, Warren angled his body toward Carlito. "Oh, Mr. Rivera. There'll be another line-up. After Betancourt's hair grows back, and without hats. I'll be in touch." And Ted Warren lurched down the hall back to his office.

That night as Carlito lay in Maria's bed he reviewed the events at the line-up once again. Two out of four had identified Ricky. Of the two, one had a bias against Ricky and may not have seen the shooting, the other had known Ricky before, so that didn't count. The girl would not get involved. That left Edgardo Concepcion, he of the alcoholic breath, who might be able to identify Ricky next time. He'd have to investigate Mr. Concepcion. Maria could do that.

Maria! My God, she's gone one night and I ache for her already. I wonder if she misses me. Maria, I need you!

S I X T E E N

Within a half hour after Carlito had left her for the line-up identification, Maria had completed a series of phone calls implementng her plan to go to P.R. In rapid succession she reserved a seat on the nine o'clock night flight, arranged to reinstate the week's leave from Lincoln Hospital, broke the news of her trip to Mrs. Colon, and made arrangements (over a deluge of blessings) to pick up Angel's medicine. She reserved for last the phone call to her mother-in-law in San Juan.

Maria had explained to Carlito that any visit to P.R., no matter how short, without stopping over to see her dead husband's mother would constitute a mortal insult to the old lady. Besides, Doña Esperanza Fuentes was one of the pluses derived from her marriage. She loved the old lady who held sway over a small neighborhood fiefdom in the Old San Juan section of the city. Although Francisco had been her only natural child, Señora Fuentes was the complete earth mother. Stray and orphan children found their way to her door and were taken in—for a week, for a month, for years. As many people in her barrio referred to her as Titi or Mami or Mamita as called her Doña. Her store, where she sold religious items and curative herbs, was always filled with people, more of whom were there to seek and get advice from her than to buy anything. And since Doña Esperanza's largesse extended to dogs and cats as well as children, they were also to be found there in abundance. Through it all, Doña Esperanza moved her large round body calmly and easily, her scolding and nagging alternating with kissing and hugging; a bravura woman giving a bravura performance.

"Hello, Mamita, it is Maria."

"Of course it is you. I recognize your voice always."

"I'm coming to P.R. tonight."

"Fine. I hope you can stay longer than last time. Will you bring Eloida?"

"No, Mamita, I'm coming alone."

"I see. Eloida's fiancé is in trouble."

"How did you know that?"

78

"I felt it in my heart, and trips made on short notice mean trouble. I can tell it is not your trouble, and if it were trouble with Eloida you would bring her or not come at all. So it must be with her man."

"You are right, Mami. I'll explain when I see you."

"Good. What time will your plane arrive? Raul will meet you." And thus it was arranged.

The nine o'clock flight was crowded with Puerto Rican families, and only a few tourists. The atmosphere at takeoff was loud and carnivallike, but after a couple of hours the humming throb of the jet engines had quieted all but an occasional infant and Maria was able to nap for awhile. She was awakened by the flight attendant's announcement to fasten seat belts in preparation for landing. Within moments the lights of the Isla Verde airport came rushing toward her in a kaleidoscopic barrage, and then a bump, and the plane had landed.

Raul was waiting for her just outside the baggage pickup area. He was one of many cousins who formed the official retinue of Doña Esperanza.

Tall, thin, and saturnine, he projected a villainous appearance. In reality he was the most good-natured of men, ready to perform any service for Doña Esperanza or any of her family. He smiled broadly, flashing at least three gold-capped teeth as he took Maria's bag and steered her to his car. The night air clung to Maria like a wet sheet. Though it was not particularly cool, the intense humidity chilled her, making her shiver. As they arrived at Doña Esperanza's, the dogs started barking. Maria gasped. "My God, they'll wake the whole neighborhood, and it's after two in the morning!"

"No need to worry, Señora Fuentes, the whole neighborhood knows of your arrival, and anyhow they are used to Titi's dogs barking."

"*Basta, callate!*" the voice of Doña Esperanza commanded and received silence from the dogs.

Maria rushed into the arms of Doña Esperanza and was quickly enfolded in a fierce hug. Maria sighed. How wonderful to feel like a little girl for awhile, safe and warm in Doña Esperanza's embrace.

"You look well, *nena*, even with your troubles." Doña Esperanza was the only one who ever called Maria "child" and Maria loved it.

"I'm feeling fine, Mamita, though I'm tired from the flight."

"Come, I will put you to bed, and we'll talk in the morning. Your room is ready." Doña Esperanza, still holding Maria around the waist, led her to a small room behind the kitchen, helped her undress, and tucked a wrinkled but clean sheet around Maria's chin. "*Buenas noches, hija,*" she murmured and kissed her cheeks, forehead, and nose. One kiss was never enough for Doña Esperanza.

"Good night, Mami." Maria closed her eyes, drugged by the honeyed words and aura of love enveloping her. As the familiar peeps of the coquils faded slowly from her consciousness, she fell asleep.

She was awakened by a slanting ray of sunshine that warmed her face and blinded her as she opened her eyes. When she sat up she noticed a clean towel and new bar of soap stacked neatly on the windowsill beside her. Maria remembered that the shower stall was outside the house, and the water in it unheated, but already at nine A.M. the sun was warm enough to make the cold shower not only bearable but comfortable.

Back in her room she put on denim shorts, sandals, and a sleeveless blouse and entered the busy kitchen. Three young children were already seated at the table, eating farina and a fourth was washing dishes. Doña Esperanza turned from the stove and waved a wooden ladle at an empty chair. Maria spent the next hour eating, catching up with the progress of events and people in the barrio, and recounting the reason for her visit.

"Now I know why you look so well, *nena*. This Carlito, he is a good man, eh!"

Maria blushed. "Well, Mami, he is a friend, that is all, but he is a wonderful lawyer."

"That may be, but there is more between you than just the law. You will marry him soon?"

"Oh, no, Mami, I'm not ready to get married again—not yet, anyhow."

"Don't be a fool, Maria. Marry him soon, while you can still have babies."

Maria was saved the necessity of further protest by the arrival of Raul. "Maria needs to go to Santurce, Raul," Doña Esperanza told him.

"I would be honored if you will permit me to drive you there, Señora Fuentes. That is, if it is all right with you, Titi." Raul looked at Doña Esperanza for approval.

"Of course she will let you drive her there, Raul. Are you not my favorite nephew? How could she refuse?"

Maria marveled at the charade. Everyone knew that Raul was extending the favor, but Doña Esperanza's rule of etiquette required that it be made to appear that the favor was Maria's. Maria played the game. "Of course, I could not refuse you, Raul, but only if you permit me to buy gasoline for the car." Maria knew that this was a necessity, since Raul could not afford the trip otherwise, even though Santurce was not more than a half-hour ride from Doña Esperanza's. Maria, always conscious of how desperately poor these people were, insisted on having the gas tank filled to the top. Raul's old Chevrolet was not even his but had been purchased by the pooling of money of at least six cousins.

Angel was staying with his uncle, Elizondo Pabon, a huge, muscled man with a handlebar mustache. He greeted Maria with courtly formality and ushered her into a large kitchen. "Angel has not arisen, I will go wake him. I am glad you have brought his medicine. Since he has been in my house he has had three attacks."

Maria sat while Pabon knocked and entered one of the many doors that opened onto a long hallway behind the kitchen. A moment later Pabon rushed back into the kitchen. "Señora, you are a nurse, no?" Maria stood and nodded. "Please come to see Angel, something is bad with him." The big man was trembling.

Maria rushed past him into the room he had just left and saw Angel lying face down on the small cot, his body cold to her touch. She turned him around and gasped at the blue, cyanotic face. Angel Colon was dead.

SEVENTEEN

Maria looked closely at Angel. He had obviously suffocated. She surmised that he had suffered an epileptic seizure while sleeping and had choked in his own spittle, the seizure having forced his head into the pillow he was sleeping on.

The doctor, who arrived within a few minutes, confirmed her diagnosis. In the meantime, complete chaos had gripped the Pabon household. The large, strong Elizondo was completely consumed with guilt—how would he explain to his sister in New York the death of her son in his household? Señora Pabon and her six daughters were equally incapable of understanding or coping with the tragedy, and Maria had to take over. Since the Pabons had no telephone, she sent Raul, who had been waiting for her outside, to contact the local priest. Maria knew that he would be able to bring order to the household and make the necessary plans for burial. In the meanwhile she assigned household chores to Señora Pabon and her daughters to keep them busy for awhile. There was nothing she could do with Elizondo Pabon, and she left him sobbing and muttering in the kitchen.

The priest arrived as Maria was placing Angel in the proper position of repose on the bed. He nodded curtly to her and began immediately to administer the last rites.

Maria watched the young, blue-eyed Father Placido McGuire go through the ritual quickly and efficiently. Father McGuire was the son of a Puerto Rican mother and an American soldier who abandoned his Kentucky farm to live in San Juan. McGuire Senior had used his separation pay from the service to purchase and set up a small store selling local artifacts and curiosities to the tourist trade. The store had prospered enough to permit him to send his youngest son to college and then to the seminary. When he finished his prayers, McGuire turned to Maria and said in perfect English: "Are you here from New York?"

A startled Maria looked up at him. "Why yes, Father, how did you know?"

"Angel was expecting that someone would soon be looking for him. Are you a policewoman?"

"No, Father, I'm not. Is that what Angel was expecting?"

"Yes, he was sure he would be arrested soon. He told me the whole story."

"Father, I came here to get help from Angel for his best friend who is accused of murder in New York, and now Angel is dead. If there is something he told you about what happened in New York, please, please tell me."

"I will see. First I must comfort the family and make

arrangements for his burial. Meet me at the rectory in an hour. I will talk to you then."

Maria paced back and forth in front of the rectory, counting the minutes and glancing at her watch constantly. Finally, she saw the tall, spare figure of Father McGuire striding toward her. He ushered her into a small room, obviously used as his office. He motioned her to a chair while he sat down at his desk. "Angel was very disturbed when he came to see me. He told me many things. Tell me, what is your connection with the matter?"

Maria explained her purpose in coming to P.R. while the priest sat silently with his hands tented in front of him, nodding at appropriate intervals. He was indeed a man well-versed in listening. When she had finished, he placed his palms down on his desk, pushed his chair back, and stood up. "I have been considering the matter since I first saw you, and I believe you have a right to know all that Angel told me. May God forgive him." With that, he walked over to an oversized combination safe in the corner of the room, extracted a large paper bag from it, and placed it on his desk. "I believe this is the gun that was used in the shooting. Angel gave it to me yesterday." He opened the bag, reached in, pulled out a nickel-plated .22 caliber pistol, and handed it to her. "I will give this to you if you promise me to deliver it to the police in New York."

Maria caught her breath as she took the gun from the priest. "I don't know, Father. How will I explain how I got it?"

"Let me tell you Angel's story and then you will know."

When Father McGuire had finished, Maria sat in stunned silence. For the first time since she had started her trip she felt incompetent to handle the situation. "I don't know what to tell you. I don't understand the legal implications. I must call my—I mean the boy's lawyer."

"Of course, Señora Fuentes. I, too, am ignorant of the legal consequences, and how this information can help your daughter's fiancé."

"Father, if you will permit me, I would like to call New York right now. Of course, I will place the call collect."

The priest smiled. "I am sorry, Señora, that I didn't offer you the use of my phone right away, but the bishop frowns on bills for overseas telephone calls." He handed her the phone from his desk and said, "Go right ahead."

Maria murmured a short prayer that Carlito would be in his office to accept her call.

As soon as she heard Carlito's voice, Maria launched into a recital of the events of the past two hours. However, she was not at that moment her cool, professional self, and it took numerous interruptions and questions by Carlito to get the story accurately and cohesively. Finally Carlito said, "Let me speak to Father McGuire please." His voice was cool and distant and seemed to reflect his disappointment over her inadequate performance. Maria handed the phone to Father McGuire, stumbled to a chair, and promptly threw up her breakfast. Father McGuire made hasty arrangements with Carlito to call back, hung up, and turned his attention to Maria. He led her to another small room behind his office, assisted her onto a cot, placed a cool washcloth on her forehead, and left her. When he returned about ten minutes later, Maria had recovered and was sitting on an old caned rocker. Father McGuire smiled, handed her the paper bag, and said, "It is all arranged. The lawyer and I have reached an understanding. Take the gun, and *vaya con Dios.*"

Maria held the bag close to her as Raul drove her back to Doña Esperanza. Perhaps her mother-in-law would know how in the world she would get this damned gun past the security checks at the airport. Maria had not the faintest notion of how to accomplish that, but she was determined not to call Carlito again.

When Doña Esperanza saw the gun she called Raul aside, handed over the paper bag with the gun, and sent him out. "Don't worry, *nena,* you will not have any trouble to take the gun back. I am taking care of everything. You look weak. Come and eat something."

Maria realized that she was indeed hungry and certainly ready to have Doña Esperanza take over her care and custody.

Once again, the efficient ministrations of Doña Esperanza made her feel secure and protected, and she sighed contentedly. Doña Esperanza smoothed back the hair from her forehead. "You see, Maria, it is not that you need a man. You need a loving person to share your troubles with and give you comfort. Too long you have been alone. Remember what I say."

Maria looked at her as the realization struck her: she had been alone too damned long!

An hour later Raul returned. Instead of a paper bag, the gun was now encased in a very ornate wooden box covered by a heavy lucite lid. Raul handed her the box, together with an official-looking document duly notarized and embossed with an official-looking seal. The document, signed by a licensed gun antiquarian, stated that the gun was an antique model S.N.S. .22 calibre and that the bearer had duly acquired this rare "pistola" as a gift from the Church of Santa Esperanza as an acknowledgment of past services performed.

"Will this work?" Maria asked, staring incredulously.

"Of course it will!" replied Doña Esperanza. "The document is official, is it not?"

EIGHTEEN

Maria glowed at Carlito's obvious satisfaction with the way things had turned out in P.R. "I can't tell you how upset I was when you asked to talk to Father McGuire. I was sure I had done everything wrong."

"*Perdone, mi amor*, that was only my lawyer's business voice." He leaned over the candlelit table of the small French restaurant he had extravagantly insisted on to celebrate her return and kissed her cheek. "You've been absolutely magnificent. And getting the gun past security back into the U.S.—pure genius!"

"I had nothing to do with that. You can thank Doña

Esperanza—and her friend the antique dealer."

The waiter interrupted their conversation by serving their entrée. "Frog's legs for the gentleman—oui? And coq au vin for the lady?"

Carlito nodded, and as the waiter moved away he said, "Have I told you how much I missed you?"

"Only five times so far, but I'm not complaining. The fact is, my charming prince, I missed you, too." Maria reached across the table and took his hand.

He raised it to his lips and kissed her fingers gently. "Marry me," he murmured.

"We'll see. Now let's eat before our dinner gets cold. Really, Carlito, I don't see how you can eat frog's legs, they remind me so much of our little Puerto Rican coquils." She smiled tenderly and withdrew her hand.

Carlito sighed. "They are my only passion besides you. Are you jealous?"

"Yes, I think so. But I also think they're aphrodisiac, so I'll bear it as long as it replenishes your machismo."

"Have no fear, constancy is my middle name."

After coffee, Carlito leaned back and extracted an envelope from his breast pocket. "Here's some more good news." He placed it on the table in front of her.

Maria picked it up and spread out the contents. "It's the coroner's report! Give me a moment to look it over." Suddenly her eyes widened. "Did you notice who assisted at the autopsy?"

"Of course I did—" Carlito was smiling— "your good friend Charlie Han."

"Will he be testifying in court?"

"I hope not. Usually it's the medical examiner who

performs the autopsy that testifies, not the assistant. I was hoping you could arrange a meeting with Charlie so I could pick his brains."

"I think I can. Carlito, what do you want to find out from him?"

"Look at the report. You'll see that the M.E. states there are two bullet wounds in the chest. One bullet entered the chest two inches to the right of the sternum and sixteen inches from the top of the head at the fifth rib. See, here it is on the diagram. That bullet traveled in an upward path, passing through the right auricle of the heart and then through the aorta. Notice that the M.E. describes heavy tampanade from each of those areas, which I needn't remind you means profuse bleeding. The entry hole is small with no powder burns, indicating that the shot was fired from a distance of no less than five feet. The slug exited the body under the left clavicle, and no remnants are found in the body."

He pointed to the diagram again. "The other wound is located one inch to the left of the sternum, also sixteen inches from the top of the head at the fifth rib. This bullet traveled an almost straight path from chest to back, passing through the right ventricle and out the back at the lower extremity of the shoulder blade. No tampanade is described, the entry hole is larger, no remnant of this bullet remains in the body, and there are powder burns around the entry hole. What does that suggest to you?"

Maria studied the report. "First, it appears that the bullets were fired from different distances. Second, the bullets were fired at different angles. Third, the bullets were of unequal size."

"Perfect, that's it!" cried Carlito. "And there's one other peculiarity."

"I see what you mean—the difference in the bleeding from the two wounds." Maria looked puzzled. "But frankly, I'm not sure how to account for that."

"That's why I want to talk to Charlie Han. Ricky is accused of killing Alvarado with a .38 revolver. But what if, my dear Maria—what if Alvarado was already dead before he was shot with the .38?"

"You mean. . . ?"

"Exactly. If I'm right, Ricky was framed."

N I N E T E E N

Woody Fertig stood in front of the desk sergeant for the last time. He had already cleared out his locker, and now he handed over his badge and his gun. Thirty years ago he had stood in front of a different desk sergeant in another precinct reporting for duty for the first time to receive his first assignment, and now it was all over. He sighed, and thought: I don't feel a thing except relief. Of course this last tour of duty with Powers had done much to harden his resolve to retire, and his conscience was clear. He had delivered his information, had been sworn to silence, and the responsibility was lifted from his shoulders. He was a civilian again.

He squared his shoulders as he left the precinct,

strode jauntily down the steps to his old Ford coupe parked in front, and sped off. He never looked back. The past six months since the murder of the young Puerto Rican at La Marimba disco had been the most difficult time in his life. From the moment he had carried Eloida from the courtroom he had become more and more enmeshed in the web of perjury, deceit, and criminality involved in this case, and he was just about rid of it. Of course he would still have to testify at the trial, but that no longer concerned him. There was still one more thing he had to do, and he was on his way to tie up this last loose end.

He parked his car on a side street near 149th Street and Third Avenue, carefully noting that he was not violating the alternate side of the street parking restrictions. After all, he was no longer entitled to use his police business placard to prop in the windshield, and he couldn't afford a fifteen-dollar ticket. He looked at his watch, noted that he still had a half-hour, and decided to spend it shopping for a new tie. He walked into Alexander's department store at 152nd Street and Third Avenue, worked his way to the rear of the main floor, and began his search. After ten minutes he found one that suited him and paid the cashier for it. As he left the store, he glanced at his watch. Still fifteen minutes to wait. He bought a container of coffee and a doughnut at the shop next door and stationed himself at the employees' entrance to Alexander's.

Eloida never noticed him as she left the store, busily chattering to her two friends who worked with her in the dress department. Woody smiled when he saw

Eloida, warmed by the youthful glow that emanated from her as she bobbed along the street. He was in no hurry to follow her, knowing that she would walk to Melrose Avenue and get in the long line for the bus that took her home. The first time he had followed her after work, he had told himself he was just checking up on where she was working and what her schedule was in case he had to contact her. But after awhile, he admitted to himself that the reason he waited for her to leave work and followed her to the bus stop was to be sure she was not molested or mugged. Later, he began to worry about what might happen to her after she got off the bus, so he would drive to her street and wait in his car until he saw her safely enter her apartment building. Woody realized that he was not acting rationally; that such behavior might be called psychotic; but he couldn't help it. He loved the girl—not in the way most people might think—but loved her as if she were his daughter. "Dammit," he had told himself a hundred times, "you have no daughter!" "Never mind," he answered himself, "if I had a daughter, this is what she would be like, and she has no father. She needs me."

This time Woody didn't wait for her to get in the bus, but approached her as she got in line.

"Why hello, Miss Fuentes—er, Eloida, what a pleasant surprise."

Eloida turned to him with a smile, which froze into a grimace when she recognized Fertig. "What do you want from me, Officer—what did I do?"

"Why, nothing." Fertig was appalled at her reaction

to him. "I just came from shopping at Alexander's," and he shoved his Alexander's bag with his tie inside at her face, "and I noticed you on the line here."

"That's not true, Officer," she retorted, "you've been following me for months. I've seen you at the store, and in front of my house, too. Why?"

The boarding line began to move as people started piling on the bus. Eloida turned away and moved with the line.

"Wait, please, Eloida. I'm not a cop anymore. But I have to talk to you—about Ricky—his case—please?" Desperately he put his hand on her arm.

Eloida stopped, turned to him, and looked straight up into his eyes. "I'm not afraid of you, you know." Woody smiled. Dumb kid, he thought, you ought to be—a wacko like me! She smiled back. "Okay, but you're talking to me, not me to you. Last time I got into a lot of trouble talking to you."

Woody led her out of the line. "Come have a cup of coffee, we can sit and talk awhile, then I'll drive you home. My car is parked nearby."

"I'll bet it is, but I'm not buying no ride from you. I'm not that dumb. Anyhow, I guess a cup of coffee can't hurt no one."

They crossed to the Burger King across the street and Woody said, "You want a Whopper too, maybe? Some apple pie?"

"Sure, why not? Mami's not home tonight, so I'd only have to cook for myself."

"Swell, go sit down and I'll fix us up."

They made a strange-looking couple seated at the

plastic table; he with his big earnest face creasing with wrinkles and later smiles, her large dark eyes opening wide in astonishment as he talked.

A half hour later, as they left Burger King, Woody took her arm and led her to his car. Except for the fact that they bore no physical resemblance to each other, any passerby would swear father and daughter were on their way home.

TWENTY

Carlito glanced once again at the amended indictment, as he had perhaps a hundred times before during the past week of jury selection. Despite the fact that Carlito was more confident of winning his case than ever before, he knew it would be fatal to underestimate Warren's ability, and fought the A.D.A. at every step.

Warren had apparently noted and reacted to the M.E.'s report, and had brought in an amended indictment that accused Ricky of murder by the use of a .38 Smith and Wesson, and/or a small caliber handgun, the exact description of which the People could not provide. Of course, Warren had had no choice, and it was evident that he had lost confidence in his case to the extent that he had offered to let Ricky cop a plea as the jury selection started.

The plea offer was a good one considering the circumstances—a sentence of one to three years on a plea of possession of a gun as a felony. Ricky had almost accepted. Six months at Rikers had taken its toll on him. Two fights with hoods who had decided he was fair game for pillage after he didn't fight to keep his disco shoes, and an attempted gang rape, had left him with a tic in his left eye and the need to turn his head from side to side constantly, as if to see where the next blow would come from.

It was Eloida, finally, who turned the tide. She had drawn on some inner strength not previously evident, and actually compelled Ricky to stand fast. Neither Maria nor Carlito knew how she did it, but one day, after watching Ricky dodge, cringe, and vacillate in court, she demanded to be permitted to visit Ricky in the holding pen during the lunch break. Since the judge and Warren were hopeful that such a visit might quicken a decision by Ricky to plead guilty, the judge gave his permission. Carlito tried to dissuade Eloida.

"Listen, Eloida," Carlito had warned, "Ricky is on the edge of jumping off the roof. If you say the wrong thing to him, he'll go."

"Please, Mr. Rivera, don't talk to me like a child. Ricky's my man, and I know what to say to him and how to say it, and you better believe that I'm not gonna let him plead guilty."

"But what are you going to say to him?"

"That, Mr. Rivera, is none of your business!" And Eloida, her head high and back arched, strode quickly to the door of the holding pens.

At two P.M. the court officer delivered a message to the judge that the prisoner had a statement to make. The judge cleared the jury panel from the courtroom, and Ricky was ushered in. For the first time since his arrest he looked like the Ricky they had all known.

"I wish to state in front of everybody, including my lawyer, that I ain't guilty of any of those charges against me, and I ain't gonna plead to nothin'. And I also want to say that I don't want to hear no more talk about my copping out." With that he turned to Eloida, sitting in the front row. Carlito wasn't sure whether Ricky cast an involuntary tic or a genuine wink at her, but the die had been cast.

Carlito looked up to appraise the next prospective juror. He realized that he had lost the last one by asking one question too many, but he had to take the risk. That juror, a young, pretty Oriental woman of twenty-five, had seemed ideal. She worked as a computer programmer at IBM but lived in Greenwich Village. Carlito had asked her if she realized that there was antagonism between different groups of Hispanics in the city, such as between Puerto Ricans and Dominicans, and she had replied, "Oh, yes, I know very well. My boyfriend is Puerto Rican." That had sealed her doom as a juror on the case. Warren challenged her, and off she went.

The judge had just finished asking the tenth prospective juror whether he or any of his family had ever been a victim of a crime. The juror, a large, blond, bony man in a tweedy sport jacket, said, "Well, yes. But could I tell you about it in private?"

Judge Corliss Breeden motioned the man to the bench. Breeden, a former commissioner appointed during the Lindsay administration, was a handsome if pedestrian jurist. Always aware of his good looks, he seemed constantly posing and displaying his profile to the public.

"Two years ago, your honor, my daughter was raped in Puerto Rico, on a visit there when she was fifteen."

Warren quickly asked, "Would that make you feel some prejudice against this defendant, merely because he's Puerto Rican?"

"No, no. Not at all. But the judge asked, and I thought I ought to let you know."

"If Your Honor pleases," Carlito interjected, "may I ask the gentleman some questions in connection with the crime?"

"Unless Mr. Warren has some further questions?" Breeden looked at Ted Warren.

"Not at the moment, Your Honor."

"Then you may proceed, Counselor."

Carlito turned so that the juror had to face him and turn his back completely to the other jurors in the box, a precaution Carlito was expert in accomplishing. "What was the occasion for your daughter's visit to Puerto Rico?"

"A vacation I promised her for getting good grades. She went with her older sister and they shared a hotel room in San Juan."

"Did the crime occur at the hotel?"

"Yes, she went back to her room alone after dinner and was followed from the dining room."

"Was your daughter assaulted in any other manner during the rape?"

"No, he threatened her with a knife, and she was afraid to resist."

"Did she become pregnant or contract a venereal disease as a result of the rape?"

"No."

"Did she require extended medical or psychiatric treatment afterwards?"

"Well, yes. She was in therapy for a year. And she's fully recovered."

"Is she now leading a normal school and social schedule?"

"Yes."

"In that case, Your Honor," Carlito concluded, "I have no challenge for cause."

Breeden nodded and returned the juror to his seat. Carlito hoped that Warren would not use a peremptory challenge to remove the man, since, in Carlito's view, the man was an ideal juror.

This juror, Mr. Martin, was a blue-eyed giant who worked as an administrator of a city social agency. Carlito believed that such a man would have positive feelings toward the social class that Ricky represented, and the fact that his daughters had chosen Puerto Rico for a vacation indicated at least some family interest in the culture. His disclosure of the rape of his daughter would, Carlito hoped, result in the man bending over backward to be fair to Ricky.

Warren, in his evaluation of the merits of keeping this juror, was impressed by Martin's Protestant background and his devotion to his church, his employment as an administrator by the city, which meant he was committed to the establishment, and by the fact that when push came to shove, the man could empathize more with Warren than with Rivera. As a result, Martin became Juror Number Ten.

By five P.M. the selection of twelve jurors and two alternates had been completed. It was, Carlito decided, a good representative Manhattan jury. As he had always done, Carlito had classified them under several different categories, such as: man/woman; white/nonwhite; over fifty/under fifty; professional/blue-collar/government employee; Jewish/Catholic/Protestant— and found each group adequately represented, except that there were no Hispanics on the jury. In large measure, Warren had maneuvered successfully to reject all but one who would have been Juror Number Twelve. Carlito, however, had used his nineteenth peremptory challege to remove him, basing his action on the theory that one lone Hispanic would have been intimidated by his own solitary presence on the jury, unless he had a very strong personality. The man was a cutter for a dress manufacturer, and not adequate to the pressures he would have had to withstand on this jury, Carlito decided.

Ricky was handcuffed and led away as Eloida, who was sitting in the front spectator row behind Ricky, blew him a kiss. Carlito stored his file in his attaché case and turned to Eloida. She ran to him, pecked him lightly on the cheek, and murmured, "Don't worry, Mr. Rivera, I know you'll win this one. Please don't worry!"

Carlito looked up sharply from the contemplation of

his shoe tips. How the hell does she know how worried I am? He twisted his mouth into what passed for a smile and said, "C'mon, Eloida, let's go home."

TWENTY-ONE

Maria had never seen Carlito in this mood before. He looked lost in thought, answered questions tentatively, picked at his dinner, and squirmed nervously. After they had cleared the dishes, she took his hand and sat him on the sofa beside her. "What's wrong, Carlito?"

"I'm scared—frightened to death—that's what's wrong."

"Why not? You're certainly not a fool, and only a fool wouldn't be scared."

"You don't understand, Maria, it's this way every time I finish picking a jury. The picadors have readied the bull for the kill, and I'm the matador whose one slight error may spell disaster. And I'm scared. Especially with this case. A lot of things could go wrong, you know."

He stood up and crossed the room, looked at Maria and shrugged. It seemed to Carlito that his whole life had led to this one case, and his future with Maria hung on the outcome. Carlito had been orphaned at the age of twelve by a hurricane that had raged through Puerto Rico one September, ripping the small house he and his parents lived in from its roots. A sister and a brother had been trapped in the house of

101

death with his parents, but Carlito was across the street playing with his friend. He had been sent to live with his mother's spinster sister in New York, and grew up mostly alone, while his aunt worked to eke out a living. He had learned to survive by being faster, stronger, and smarter than his would-be oppressors in his new neighborhood. Once he had graduated from high school his aunt issued an ultimatum: work or get out. He did both. He drove a gypsy cab at night and went to City College during the day. After college graduation, he shifted the schedule around. He drove a beer distributing truck during the day on a route he could complete by two o'clock in the afternoon, and attended law school at night. He was the only gray-haired twenty-seven-year-old Fordham Law School had ever graduated.

Despite the fact that he had graduated in the upper third of his class, the only job he could land was with the Bronx Legal Aid Society. There his enthusiasm, ability, and interest in his clients set him apart from the majority of his colleagues. He joined the local Democratic club and was slotted as a district leader in an all-Hispanic election district. When an opening arose in the Bronx D.A.'s office, and it was made known that the D.A. would welcome the opportunity to add a Hispanic to the staff, Carlito was recommended by the chairman of the Democratic club.

After two years as a defense lawyer, Carlito stepped over the line and became a prosecutor. He felt like a spy in the enemy camp. Never in his long-range plans for his career had he considered working as a prosecut-

102

ing attorney. He stuck it out for a year, saved money for the first time, and opened a storefront office in the Hunt's Point section of the South Bronx. It had all worked out very well, and within two years he moved his office to the 149th Street and Third Avenue area, historically the hub of the Bronx. As a matter of fact, it was and remained the only place where there was a cluster of office buildings in all of the Bronx.

He had met Maria when he went to visit his old aunt who was dying of a worn-out heart at Lincoln Hospital. Maria was the floor nurse in charge of the ward section that Carlito's aunt had been assigned to and was extremely helpful when the old lady died. Her cool poise balanced marvelously with her warm sympathy, and Carlito was entranced. Carlito had allocated two weeks for mourning the well-meaning but distant woman he had called Titi Anna, and then phoned Maria for a date.

Maria went to him now, thrust her hips sensuously against him, and said, "I don't care how scared you are. To me you are the bravest, smartest, and most expert torero in the world." She threw one arm around his neck and drew him toward her while she rested her other hand on his lap.

Carlito smiled, kissed her quietly at first, and then more passionately as his manhood rose to meet the warmth of her body. "With you I feel more than a match for anybody." He lifted Maria as easily as though she were a small child and carried her into the bedroom.

103

TWENTY-TWO

"Oyez, Oyez, this is the Supreme Court New York County, Trial Term Part 27, the Honorable Justice Corliss Breeden presiding. Draw near and ye shall be heard."

Judge Breeden stepped into the courtroom, stood solemnly in front of his chair, displayed his profile to the jury, and sat down.

The court clerk intoned, "Be seated, please," and looked toward the judge.

"Call the case," said Breeden, and the clerk continued: "The case of the People of the State of New York against Ricardo Betancourt. Are the People ready?"

"Yes—ready."

"Is the Defendant ready?"

"Defendant is ready."

"Mr. Warren, call your first witness."

Warren stood and called: "Patrolman Robert Powers."

Carlito watched carefully as Powers took the stand and swore the oath. Powers was not the sneering, loutish bully Carlito had last seen at Ricky's arraignment. Today he seemed somehow to have withered and shrunk. When he sat in the witness chair he slumped down as if to ward off any blows that were forthcoming.

Warren took Powers skillfully through a recital of his discovery of the body of Pablo Alvarado in the alley, the discovery of the .38 in Ricky's jacket, and Ricky's arrest. Now it was Carlito's turn.

Carlito, under the guise of looking through his notes and papers, let Powers simmer for awhile. When finally he rose to begin cross-examination, he remained well behind the counsel table—about as far from Powers as he could get. His first questions to Powers were delivered almost sotto voce, so that Powers had to lean forward to hear. The result was that Powers was now slumped forward so far it would appear a slight push would topple him right onto his face.

Q: *As I understand from your testimony, you and Patrolman Woodrow Fertig shared patrol on the night of the killing.*

A: *Yes, sir.*

Q: *And you were driving.*

A: *Yes, sir.*

Q: *When you arrived on the scene, describe exactly what you did, starting from the time you brought your car to a stop.*

A: *As I told Mr. Warren, Woody got out first and ran over to the defendant. I was about ten feet behind him when he called to me, "This kid's been stuck, knifed in the belly." Well, no one else was around, so I ran to scout the area.*

Q: *How long did you scout the area before you entered the alley?*

A: *Not long, the alley was a natural hiding place—maybe two minutes, maybe more.*

Carlito took two steps toward Powers and continued:

Q: *How long were you in the alley before you found Alvarado?*

Powers hesitated, then said:

A: *Hell, I don't know, maybe a minute, maybe more.*

Carlito advanced another step closer.

Q: *Didn't you just testify that you found Alvarado lying just inside the alley no more than three feet from the sidewalk?*
A: *Well . . . yeah, I guess so.*
Q: *Then you found him immediately.*
A: *Yeah, I suppose.*
Q: *Did you find him before the shot was fired at you as you have testified, or after?*
A: *Jeez, what the hell difference does that make?*

Carlito waited a full ten seconds, looked up at Judge Breeden, and said: "Your Honor, I move that the witness's last answer be stricken as not responsive to the question, and I ask that Your Honor direct the witness to give a proper answer."

Breeden turned his profile to the jury and said, "Yes, Counselor, your motion is granted. The jury is directed to disregard the last answer, and the witness is admonished to answer properly."

Carlito took another step forward. He had by this time covered half the original distance between them. "Answer the question, please," he said.

Powers had also noticed that suddenly Carlito was much closer, and leaned back slightly. "I don't remember the question."

"Will the court reporter please read the question again?" Carlito exulted as the reporter thumbed back to the question. It was going just as he had hoped. The jury would remember this question and answer later on.

When the reporter had repeated Carlito's question, Powers said, "Yeah, I remember, the shot was fired just after I entered the alley, before I found the victim."

Carlito continued:

Q: *What did you do when the shot was fired?*

A: *I ran down to the end of the alley. There was a fence, and I decided to get more help before I hopped it. So I went back to see what shape the victim was in. He was dead.*

Q: *Did you call for help at any time?*

A: *Yeah, I ran out and told Fertig to call for backup.*

Q: *Did you go back into the alley after coming out and calling to Fertig?*

A: *No, while Fertig was calling I ran to the defendant and searched him and found the gun—the .38.*

Carlito walked up close to Powers now and Powers pulled back, slumping against the back of the witness chair.

Q: *Tell me again, Officer: what part of the defendant's clothing did you find the .38 in?*

A: *Like I told Mr. Warren, in his blue jacket.*

Q: *Was the defendant wearing that jacket?*

A: *Sure he was wearing it.*

Q: *How was he wearing it, Officer Powers?*

A: *Like anybody wears a jacket, how do you think?*

Q: *I don't know. But I'd like you just to identify that jacket. Is that it—marked "People's Exhibit #1"? Is this the jacket?*

A: *Sure it is, I already identified it.*

Q: *Patrolman Powers, will you demonstrate to the jury the manner in which the defendant was wearing the jacket?*

A: *How can I do that?*

Carlito stepped back, motioned to Ricky, and said: "Mr. Betancourt, will you step forward. Now, Mr. Powers, will you put the jacket on the defendant to show exactly how he was wearing it the night of the murder?"

Powers stood up; Ricky placed first one arm, then the other, into the sleeves and Powers pulled it over Ricky's shoulders and stepped back. Ricky turned to face the jury. The jacket was four sizes too big for Ricky. The sleeves dangled ludicrously over his fingertips.

"Is this the defendant's jacket, Mr. Powers, that you found the murder weapon in?" Carlito now snarled into Powers's face.

Powers blanched, then flushed. "I don't know," he hesitated, and then again, "I don't know."

TWENTY-THREE

Woody Fertig sat in the crowded kosher deli restaurant, his hot pastrami sandwich in hand, gazing out the window onto 161st Street. This deli was the southernmost one of its kind in the Bronx, one of the last vestiges of what had once been a thriving Jewish middle-class neighborhood. With the Concourse Plaza hotel, billed as the home of the New York Yankees while at home, as its eastern crown, and the Yankee Stadium its western boundary, the three blocks between had once supported two kosher delicatessens and the Jerome cafeteria, a huge emporium offering Jewish-style cooking, good restaurants, four banks, three men's haberdasheries, and a movie theater. Now there were pizza shops, fast-food places, fruit and vegetable stores, and cheap bars, and the once splendid Concourse Plaza hotel was closed, its opulent ballrooms and reception halls in the process of being converted to a senior citizen housing site. Only the Court Delicatessen restaurant remained, surviving by virtue of its proximity to the Bronx County Courthouse across the street, and crowded during the lunch hour with judges, lawyers, court personnel, litigants, and witnesses in the cases on trial there. Fertig saw Carlito, Eloida, and Maria pass in front of the restaurant window and enter. He waved and smiled at Eloida as she entered first but was relieved when Carlito steered her and her mother away to a far corner. Despite the fact that he was now a civilian, he didn't think he ought to be seen publicly with the defendant's family and lawyer, especially since he was scheduled to testify this afternoon. He returned his attention to his sandwich, confident and determined that the role he would play in this afternoon's drama was more courageous than anything he had done in his career as a police officer.

Eloida frowned at the menu, completely uninterested in eating, and allowed Carlito to order for her. As soon as the waiter had left, she fixed blazing eyes on Carlito. "I can't understand why you didn't use the information I gave you in your cross-examination!"

"Easy, Eloida, have patience," Carlito remonstrated. "Everything in good time. I'll use it when it's most effective and will have the greatest impact. Don't you have confidence in me?" Carlito was surprised by her fiery response.

"I do trust you, but it seems to me that now was the time to use it."

Maria frowned and interrupted. "Please, Eloida. Let Carlito handle it his way." Maria looked at Eloida as if she were a stranger. Where had the passive, naïve baby disappeared to? This Eloida was a different person.

"I'm sorry," Eloida relented, "but you know how concerned I am. It's our future, you know."

Ricky munched listlessly on a dried out ham and cheese sandwich in the holding pen behind the courtroom. I hope this trial is over soon, one way or another. I can't keep on much longer. Ricky was indeed on the edge of breaking down. Judge Breeden, a hard worker, had insisted that court sessions begin promptly at nine-thirty and continue until five. Each morning then, since jury selection had begun ten days ago, Ricky had been awakened at Rikers at six A.M. and hustled through the lengthy process required to get him onto the early bus to Manhattan scheduled to leave at eight o'clock. Because of this, he missed breakfast. When the lunch recess was declared in court, and the meager sandwich brought in by the guards, Ricky's stomach was so churned up by the events of the morning he had no appetite. When the case was adjourned for the day at five o'clock he had already missed the early bus back to Rikers and was not removed from the holding pen until eight. By the time he was reprocessed through security at Rikers it was after ten o'clock, and he had missed the dinner meal. Getting to sleep was impossible, and he was lucky to grab two or three hours before being roused to start all over again. As a consequence, he had already lost ten pounds, which he could ill afford. His only succor was Eloida. It was her resolve and her strength that he relied on now. Each day when he stepped into the courtroom, her face was the first thing he saw. Her eyes bored into him, sending him messages of hope, her smile was soft and reassuring, her body seemed to float to him from that seat in the first spectator row, straightening his back and raising his chin. I been telling myself that she needs me, and maybe she does, but I sure as hell couldn't make it without her.

111

*   *   *

Ted Warren sipped coffee from a cardboard container as he finished his disappointing interview with Nereida Pagan, the girl who had failed to identify Betancourt at the original line-up. Although she had subsequently identified him in a line-up Warren had run after Ricky's hair grew back as the boy she had danced with in the contest, she had steadfastly refused to identify him as the man who had fired the gun. Her boyfriend, the gang leader of the Dominicans, was too positive. He obviously hated Ricky and made no bones about it. Warren felt that the jury wouldn't believe a word he said after Rivera finished cross-examination. That left Warren with Edgardo Concepcion as his only eyewitness. Obviously Concepcion was a man long habituated in the consumption of alcohol, if not already an alcoholic. Warren thanked God that the man had no prior criminal record, but wondered if he would stand up under cross-examination.

Warren tugged at his earlobe while studying his file. If Rivera could discredit these two witnesses, the case would crumble like a sand castle. Warren slowly shook his head. This case had started deteriorating from the moment he had received the M.E.'s report. Right now it was beginning to smell like stale fish, but Warren was stuck with it. He glanced at his watch, picked up the file, and stood up. It was time to get back to the battle, and Warren thought he knew how General Custer had felt.

TWENTY-FOUR

Woody Fertig finished reciting the oath to "tell the truth, the whole truth, and nothing but the truth" and sat down in the witness chair. Warren led him through his story with experienced smoothness, and Carlito approached to start cross-examination. Fertig clasped his hands and thought, Well, here we go.

Q: *Officer Fertig, you have testified that when you first approached the defendant he was lying on the ground; is that so?*

A: *Yes, sir.*

Q: *Will you describe to this jury the exact position in which you found the defendant?*

A: *He was unconscious, lying on his back against the building just to the left of the entrance to the La Marimba disco.*

Q: *Will you tell us, Officer, exactly what you saw in every detail that you can remember of the defendant's condition?*

A: *The defendant was bleeding from a stomach wound. His white embroidered shirt was ripped where the wound had been inflicted, also it was ripped on his chest. The blood was oozing from the stomach wound down onto a pair of blue pants.*

Q: *At that time did you see any blood on his jacket?*

A: *I don't remember seeing a jacket on the defendant when I first approached.*

Q: *Are you telling us that when you first approached this defendant he was not wearing a jacket?*

A: *No, sir, I am telling you that I cannot recollect seeing a jacket on the defendant when I first approached him.*

Q: *Officer Fertig, I show you People's Exhibit #1, a blue jacket, and ask you whether you can recall whether this jacket was ever worn by the defendant on the night of the murder.*

A: *Yes, sir, it was.*

Q: *When and under what circumstances did you see this defendant wearing the blue jacket?*

A: *As I said when the D.A. was questioning me, when Officer Powers ran out of the alley after the shot, I ran back to the car to radio for help. When I returned from the car Officer Powers was squatting next to the defendant. At that time I noticed that Powers was searching the jacket pockets. That was when I first noticed the jacket. It was covering only his right arm and shoulder, the other end had been pulled off. That's when Powers took the .38 Smith and Wesson out of the pocket.*

Carlito sat down at the counsel table and looked straight down as if studying some note in his file, not moving a muscle for at least a minute. He wanted the jury to have time to digest that tidbit. Finally, he took a sip of water, stood up, and started again.

Q: *When you went to call for backup, did you still have the defendant in your view?*

A: *No, sir, the way we were situated I was about fifty feet*

*from the defendant with my back turned to him when I
made my call. He was out of my line of sight for at
least two or three minutes.*

Q: *Did anyone move or touch that jacket before or after
Powers discovered the gun?*

A: *Yes, sir, I did. After Powers found the gun, and I saw
the jacket was half off anyway, I slipped it off his right
arm and shoulder and covered his chest and stomach
with it. That was where it was when the ambulance
took him. I thought it would be better for him to be
covered that way.*

Q: *Did you or Officer Powers or any other representative
of the police department conduct or arrange to conduct
a test of the defendant's hands to determine whether he
had fired a gun that evening?*

A: *You mean the paraffin-silver nitrate test? No, I didn't.
You see, it was Powers's nab—I mean arrest. He
wanted it, and I said okay. When we got the kid to the
hospital, I told Powers he ought to call the guys in
from forensics, but Powers said, "What the hell, we
got the kid dead to rights anyhow. We don't need
them." So I just shut up.*

Q: *Officer Fertig, why did you later gain sufficient interest in this case to go back to the scene and look for the
bullets you have already testified you found almost
twenty-four hours after the incident had occurred?*

A: *At the defendant's arraignment I had a conversation
with a relative of the defendant that indicated there
might have been a different gun used other than the
.38 we found.*

Q: *So you went back on your own and after searching the*

115

Q: area you found five .22 caliber slugs, four on Broadway and one in the alley—is that right?

A: Yes sir, that's right.

Q: But you found no .38 slugs other than the one Powers had recovered in the alley the night before.

A: Yes sir.

Q: Tell me, Officer Fertig, what did you think after making that discovery?

Woody Fertig took a deep breath, turned to look directly at the jury, and began.

A: My first thought was how could this defendant have killed the deceased in the alley, when he was lying unconscious about fifty feet from the alley. I also thought if there were two guns involved, two different guys must have been using them because it wasn't logical that the defendant would have two guns, and finally I decided that maybe the deceased owned that .38.

Q: Just a moment, Officer Fertig, didn't you just testify that you saw Officer Powers remove the .38 from the defendant's jacket?

A: Well, that's what bothered me. I just couldn't remember the defendant wearing that jacket when I first saw him.

Carlito walked slowly toward Fertig until he was standing next to him, carefully placing himself so that he did not obstruct the jury's view of Fertig. He asked the next question in a hushed but intense tone, slowly enunciating every word.

116

Q: Are you suggesting that Powers planted the .38 in the defendant's jacket?

"Objection!" Ted Warren's loud cry rang through the courtroom like an alarm bell. Warren was standing at full height, his face red with anger, his hands trembling. "That question is improper and irrelevant. It calls for a conclusory statement from the witness. The implications raised by it demand a mistrial and I so move."

Judge Breeden held up his hands placatingly. "Just a moment, gentlemen. Neither of you is to say another word. Bailiff, remove the jury from the box and, gentlemen, you will both approach the bench. The witness is to stay right where he is."

Judge Breeden stood up and watched while the jury filed out. When the bailiff reported back that the jury had been safely sequestered out of earshot he turned to Carlito and thundered: "What the hell are you trying to pull, Mr. Rivera?"

"I'm not trying to pull anything, Your Honor, but the import of the witness's testimony makes that a fair question."

"Like hell it does!" Warren interjected, still trembling with rage.

Judge Breeden turned to Fertig. "Mr. Fertig, are you intending to accuse your brother officer of framing this defendant?"

Fertig looked the coolest of all of them. "Your Honor, the fact is I already have. I am no longer a member of the Police Department, and Powers would

117

never be a brother of mine, so he's no brother officer."

"What in heaven's name are you talking about?" snapped Warren.

"Oh, not to you, Mr. Warren, to Internal Security, and they particularly forbade me from telling you as well as anyone else. But if I'm asked questions about it under oath, I'll have to answer, won't I?" Fertig sat back and crossed his arms across his chest.

Judge Breeden sat down, put his hand to his brow, and glared at Fertig. "You are telling us that you will testify under oath that Powers framed the defendant. Okay. I'll let your testimony continue, but I give you this warning. If your testimony turns out to be mere speculation or rumor, and you present no hard evidence, not only will I declare a mistrial, but I will hold you in contempt of court and punish you to the full extent of the law. And if I find that you have violated any police regulations in connection with this matter, I will recommend forfeiture of your pension." Judge Breeden stood up. "Are you ready to proceed, Mr. Fertig?"

"Yes, Your Honor." Fertig was unhesitating.

When the jury had been reassembled in the courtroom, Judge Breeden turned and said: "The last question was improper. The objection by the prosecution is sustained, and the jury is directed to disregard it. You may proceed, Mr. Rivera."

Carlito frowned and mumbled, "Note my exception." He returned to Fertig and placed himself in exactly the same position he had taken when he had asked the last question, as if to point out to the jury that he was not abandoning his line of questioning.

Q: *Tell me, Mr. Fertig, did you conduct any further investigation into this case on your own, and if so, what exactly did you do?*

A: *Yes, sir, I did. About a week later, I was given the .38 by Powers, who had testified about its recovery to the grand jury. I offered to return it to the police property clerk's office for him, and I did. I also made a notation of the serial number on the gun. It's right here. The number is Y4638701al. I then checked the serial number against the warrant book in the property clerk's office. It took me three weeks of my own time, but I found the following notation: On January 6, 1980, seven months before the shooting at La Marimba disco, a .38 caliber Smith and Wesson bearing serial number Y4638701al was recovered from a perpetrator of an armed robbery of a grocery store at Broadway and 180th Street. The arresting officer was Robert Powers.*

Eloida leaped from her seat and ran to the bench. "I knew he was framed, I knew it! Let him go now, will you? For God's sake, let him go!" Woody Fertig sprang forward and caught Eloida as she fell in a faint, reaching her just before she hit the floor.

119

TWENTY-FIVE

John Trent, bureau chief of the district attorney's Homicide Division, peered out over his Ben Franklins at Captain Roscoe Lorimer, seated on the edge of the chair across from Trent's desk. Lorimer, chief of internal security of the New York City Police Department, was not giving ground.

"I tell you, John, we felt we had no duty to notify you or anybody else—" at this point Lorimer moved his pointing finger from Trent to Ted Warren seated next to him— "until we completed our investigation. Anyhow, you ought to be able to get a conviction without the .38 evidence."

Warren pushed his hair off his forehead, uncrossed his legs, and leaned forward. "We might, Captain, we might. But that isn't the point. As a prosecutor my job is to convict criminals, but at the moment I ain't so sure the criminal in this case isn't running around in a blue uniform wearing a New York City Police badge." Although Warren's voice had remained calm and even, the stinging implication of his words had the desired effect on Lorimer, who jumped up on short legs, pressing his beer belly against Trent's desk.

"I know what your job is, and I don't need nobody to tell me what mine is—leastways you!"

Trent held up one large manicured hand, stroked his gray waxed mustache with the other. "Hold on, men,

120

no fighting without a referee. Anyway, we're all on the same side, I hope. Now sit down, Roscoe, and tell us exactly what you do have."

Lorimer picked up a file folder from Trent's desk and strutted to the far end of Trent's office, then turned to face them. "Okay," he said, and then continued in the rattling staccato inimical to bureaucrats. "Seven months before the incident at La Marimba, Officer Robert Powers made an arrest of one Anthony De Tiere during an armed robbery in progress. He recovered a .38 Smith and Wesson bearing serial number Y4638701al. It was vouchered into the property clerk's office on January 7, 1980, vouchered out to Powers on January 20, 1980 for presentment to the grand jury, and received back in the property clerk's office on January 21, 1980."

Trent arched an inquisitive eyebrow at Lorimer, but Lorimer held up his hand and continued: "There is no record of the gun ever being vouchered out again, nor any proof that it was not in the property clerk's office until the night of this incident. However, the name of the officer issuing the receipt of the gun from Powers on January 21, 1980 is fictitious. That name, Joseph Provisio, does not appear on any record of police department employees, either uniformed or civilian." Lorimer stopped reading.

Trent looked at him quizzically. "Is that it? It's not enough, Roscoe. You couldn't prove enough against Powers for even a reprimand."

"That's what I've been telling you, John, and up until last week that was all we had." Lorimer looked at

Warren. "Would that information have helped you present your case any differently than you had? Tell me."

"No, it wouldn't," Warren said, scowling, "but I would surely like to find out more about Mr. Powers."

"So did we," replied Lorimer, "but for months we came up dry. Then last week, on a fluke, we got a break. A detective James O'Brien of the Robbery Squad in the Thirty-fourth Precinct is going over some old A.P.B.s while investigating that Chemical Bank job on Hudson Street, and he comes across this." Lorimer pulled out an 8 × 10 glossy photograph and held it up.

"That's him—that's Powers!" exclaimed Warren in surprise, his voice showing emotion for the first time.

"Very good, Mr. District Attorney, very good." Lorimer made little effort to hide the contempt in his voice. "This picture shows Powers out of uniform holding a gun. It is one of a series of pictures taken by a hidden camera in a Somerville, New York, bank during a robbery there on March 23, 1980."

Trent let air out of his mouth as though struck in the solar plexus. "I'll be damned!"

Lorimer looked quickly from the photograph to Trent. "Not finished yet, John. There's more." He picked another document out of the file and continued: "O'Brien recognized Powers—used to work with him in the Seventeenth years ago. Came right to us with the picture. Gave us an affidavit. Also told us that the guard at the bank was shot in the left arm by the gunman as he attempted to chase him leaving the scene of

122

the robbery. The bullet was a .38. Ballistics is still checking for a matchup."

Warren stood up, shaking his creased pants legs down off his knees. "What a durned mess."

Trent also rose to his full six-foot-two height, smoothed his vest over the slight bulge peeking out from an otherwise trim, athletic figure, and toyed with his mustache again. "If Ballistics matches the bullet in the bank robbery with our gun you've got him dead to rights."

"Where does that leave me and my case?" Warren lamented.

"Wait a minute, Ted," Trent said, as he slowly paced across the room, "this may be a blessing in disguise." Warren looked at him. "The way I see it," Trent continued, "the big problem for your case has already been created by Fertig's testimony. The jury already believes that the kid was framed by Powers, and they probably think the D.A.'s office was in on it. But you have the M.E. to testify that it wasn't the .38 that caused his death."

"Do I?" Warren interjected. "So far all the M.E. is saying is that it's possible that the small caliber bullet caused the death but that the .38 finished him off. Anyhow, I don't have the .22 that inflicted the wound, and my witnesses have already given me sworn affidavits that the .38 is what they saw the kid using."

"Talk to your witnesses again. Maybe in the light of what I just gave you, they'll change their testimony," Lorimer offered.

Warren stared. "Like hell I will, Captain. I don't operate that way." He turned to Trent. "If there's going to be any shenanigans, I'm off this case."

"Hold it, Ted. All I'm suggesting is that you talk to the M.E. again, no one else."

"O.K., Mr. Trent, and suppose the M.E. does say that the .22 was the sole cause of death, what next?"

Trent went back to his desk, sat down, and began doodling on a pad while talking. "The way I see it, we get Powers back on the stand, ask him only enough questions to open up the whole issue of his possession of the .38, and let Rivera at him for cross-examination. What do you think will happen?"

Warren smiled. "Rivera's a sharp lawyer, give him that kind of an opening and he'll eat Powers alive."

"Exactly, and on redirect you'll pin Powers to the wall with our information about the bank robbery."

"Just a minute!" shouted an irate Lorimer. "Powers is our baby, we'll take care of him—keep away from the bank job."

"Don't be a fool, Roscoe," said Trent, displaying open hostility to Lorimer for the first time. "Here's what will happen. First it will dissociate the prosecutor from the frame-up and give us at least a crack at convicting him on the .22 slugs. Second, it will give us Powers's testimony under oath before he knows he's imperiling himself with regard to the .38. As long as he's testifying in a criminal case in which he made an arrest, he can't later claim entrapment. Don't you see, Roscoe, when he's finished testifying he'll be wrapped in such a neat package you won't have any more work to do. Just think of all the little tricks you'll be denying

124

the P.B.A. lawyer Powers is sure to hire the moment you accuse him."

"And," added Warren, "the D.A.'s office will regain respectability with the jury for going after a rogue cop. Not bad, not bad at all." Warren stopped suddenly, lifted his hand to his earlobe. "Except," he murmured, "what does Rivera have up his sleeve?"

"What do you mean?" demanded Lorimer. "It looks great to me."

"I told you Rivera is a sharp lawyer, and I meant it. I don't underestimate him for one moment." Warren, ignoring Lorimer, was directing himself to his bureau chief, as if Lorimer were no longer in the room. "He's had the M.E.'s report since we have, he knows the quality of our witnesses—more than that he understands their psychology better than we do; he obviously had been tipped by someone about the direction of Fertig's testimony—and he's refused to let the kid cop a plea. That means he's got something more than merely having his client deny the murder on the witness stand."

Trent, frowning and doodling, nodded in agreement. "So—what do you think he has, Ted?"

Warren smiled ruefully at his boss. "Maybe—just maybe he has the real murderer."

TWENTY-SIX

Carlito peered across the table of the coffee shop at Woody Fertig. "Thanks, Fertig. That was a courageous act you just performed. But I'm perplexed. As a lawyer, I'm always seeking motivation. Why, Fertig—why did you do it?"

Fertig took another sip of coffee and carefully placed his cup back in the saucer. "I'm in love."

Carlito gasped. "Not with Eloida!"

"Yes, in a way with Eloida, but it's not like you think. Look, I was an only child of parents who were the only members of their family to escape the Holocaust. I was nine years old when they came here in 1934. My father had been a magistrate in Germany and when they removed him only because he was a Jew, he saw the handwriting on the wall. He couldn't convince any of the others to go. Know what he did here? He was a cutter in the garment industry. That was the only job he could get and that was because a cousin owned the factory. Anyhow, he died when I was sixteen. Heart attack is what they called it. It doesn't really matter, but by that time he found out his whole family had been wiped out. I went to work, all kinds of jobs—none of them any good. I once tried out for the New York Giants in the Polo Grounds—you know, I was a helluva hitter. Too slow they said, but they wanted to sign me up and send me to their Auburn farm team. I didn't take it, even though Auburn was

Class A minors. I couldn't leave Mama alone. So I stayed, and got into the Police Department. Mama didn't mind my hours, so long as I came home after every tour. Day or night made no difference to Mama. She lived to be eighty, God bless her, and by then it was kind of late for me to get married. So you see, I never had a family. No wife, no kids. Now Eloida, she is a sweet kid; kind of like a little doe with those big eyes. Vulnerable, you know what I mean? And then she tells me her fiancé carried a .22 on the night of the murder. What the hell was I supposed to do with that? If I tell the D.A., the Betancourt kid is in up to his eyeballs. So I decided to nose around and see if I could find out more. Well, once I got into it, I couldn't stop—one thing led to another—and here I am. Trying to act like a father to a kid who probably won't even spit at me after the case is finished."

"That's not so," Carlito interrupted. "Eloida is kind and sensitive. And she likes you, Fertig, she really does."

"Yeah, I think so. I sure wish she'd let me keep in touch when this thing is over." The big man looked down at his coffee cup, his eyes brimming. "So, Counselor, what's your next step?" he asked, trying to hide his emotion.

Carlito seized the opportunity to change the subject. "Warren's just been thrown for a loss, but he still has the ball," Carlito murmured, staring up at the ceiling. "I think he's going to throw Powers to the wolves and dissociate the D.A.'s office from the frame-up. He still has the witnesses who identified Ricky at the second

127

line-up, and he has the M.E.'s testimony, which will now be geared to proving that it was the .22 that killed Alvarado. He could still get a conviction."

"And you," Fertig asked, "who do you have, Counselor, on your side?"

Carlito grinned. "God is on my side, Fertig. God and Father McGuire."

TWENTY-SEVEN

Carlito smiled at the irony. Warren, in a desperate attempt to salvage the case against Ricky, was now leading Forsythe Carrington, the medical examiner, onto the very path where Carlito had hoped to steer him on cross-examination.

Warren: And so, Dr. Carrington, after reconsidering the objective results of the autopsy, can you state with any degree of reasonable medical certainty whether Pablo Alvarado was dead at the time he received the .38 caliber wound you have described?

Carrington: Well, uh, Counselor—uh, Mr. Warren—I will say this: I have studied the autopsy results more, uh, carefully—that is to say, uh, in greater detail since I wrote the report. Yes, I can now state—uh, that is, I can definitely state that it was the small, uh—that is, the .22 caliber bullet that, uh, caused the death, and, uh, that the victim—that is to say the deceased, uh, was dead when the .38 caliber bullet entered his body.

Warren sighed with relief, turned to Carlito and said, "No further questions."

Judge Breeden nodded to Carlito. "You may cross-examine, Counselor."

Carlito stood and smiled warmly at the witness. "No questions, Your Honor. Thank you, Dr. Carrington, thank you very much."

Warren pulled furiously at his earlobe as Forsythe Carrington tried to saunter casually from the witness chair, stumbled, caught himself on the jury rail, and waddled thickly down the aisle to the door at the rear of the courtroom.

"Next witness," intoned the judge.

Warren, thrown off balance by Carlito's declination to cross-examine, was hastily rehashing the M.E.'s testimony in his mind, trying to find the mistake or omission he must have made on direct examination. Breeden stared impatiently at Warren and repeated sharply: "Call your next witness, Mr. District Attorney." Warren looked up distractedly and said, "Yes, oh yes. I'm sorry, Your Honor. The People call Sergeant Arthur Strong."

Sergeant Strong was a ballistics expert who patiently explained that the paraffin-silver nitrate test was no longer used in forensics because the presence of traces of urine, nicotine, and other common contaminants on the hands often gave positive findings. Therefore, a positive finding no longer established conclusively that the person tested had fired a gun. Carlito was prepared, and wasted no time.

Q: *Sergeant Strong, you have testified that the paraffin-silver nitrate test is of no probative value, is that correct?*

A: *Yes, sir, that's correct.*

Q: *No value at all?*

A: *No, sir.*

Q: *Well, Sergeant, what if the test is negative—does that prove anything?*

A: *I don't understand what you mean.*

Q: *If a person was suspected of firing a gun, and that person was subjected to a paraffin-silver nitrate test; and if that test—despite everything that could create a positive reaction—were negative, what would it prove?*

A: *Why, it would prove the person tested could not have fired a gun within the past twenty-four hours.*

Q: *So that if this defendant had been subjected to such a test within twenty-four hours of the time he is alleged to have shot someone, and the test were negative, that would prove this defendant innocent?*

A: *Yes, sir.*

"So much for ballistics," muttered Carlito, and then in a loud voice: "No further questions."

Judge Breeden declared a ten-minute recess and the jurors were ushered out. The court officers handcuffed Ricky and led him to the wooden railing separating the witnesses from the spectators where he sat down and whispered earnestly to Eloida over the rail. This had become a routine for them at each break in the court proceedings, Eloida having charmed the court officers into this slight breach of protocol. Carlito motioned to Maria, and they left the courtroom so that Carlito could smoke.

"You were great with the forensics guy!" Maria squeezed his arm possessively and treated him to one of her dazzling smiles. "I was watching the jury, and their reaction to Sergeant Strong was just what you had hoped for. Some of them were actually shaking their heads by the time you finished."

Carlito put his arm over her shoulder and pulled her close to him as they walked down the corridor. "If all goes well with the next three, we'll be home free," he said.

"You mean the Dominicans?" she asked.

"Yes, the eyewitnesses. We'll find out what they really saw."

Warren called Nereida Pagan as his first witness when court resumed. She steadfastly refused to identify Ricky shooting or even holding a gun at any time that night.

Carlito sensed her antagonistic attitude to Warren and decided to risk asking her about the dance contest. When he did, he hit the jackpot. The entire story, just as Ricky had related it on Carlito's first trip to Rikers, came tumbling out almost faster than Carlito could pose the questions.

Q: Did this defendant do or say anything to you during the dance to insult you?

131

A: No.

Q: Did this defendant do or say anything to you after the dance to insult you?

A: No, he was just a nice guy—you know, a great dancer, but not fresh—not fresh at all. I would say he was real gentle.

Carlito knew full well that Nereida Pagan really meant that Ricky was a gentleman, but the way she expressed it sounded better for Ricky, and he let it pass. He would repeat those words to the jury during summation.

Q: And then when you went back to the table where your fiancé was seated, did this defendant go with you?

A: Well, he ain't my fiancé no more, but yes, Ricardo said he wanted to see how proud Chico would be of me 'cause we won the dance contest.

Q: And did Ricardo say anything to Chico to insult him when he came back to the table with you?

A: Hell no, the wine we won in the contest, he shared it with Chico and the rest. Like I said before, he was real gentle, and all that it got him was Chico got mad, 'cause he was jealous. Chico, he can't dance for nothin'.

Carlito felt jubilant. The way Nereida Pagan rolled the name Ricardo off her lips and the way she glanced at Ricky when she mentioned his name made it obvious she had been smitten. Ricky had gained an ally that he hadn't even realized he had. Carlito hesitated for a moment, then his instincts overcame his lawyer's prudence about asking questions on cross-examination to which he didn't know the answers.

Q: *You said Guanerge is not your fiancé anymore. Is it because of this case?*

Warren jumped up as if someone had shoved a hot poker into his rear. "Objection, Your Honor, the question is irrelevant! The witness's relationship with Guanerge Quinones has no bearing on any issue in this case."

Breeden looked worriedly at Carlito, obviously not quite sure how to rule.

If Your Honor please," Carlito began, "this is cross-examination. If the relationship were such that Quinones exerted undue pressure on this witness to testify in a certain way, I should be entitled to inquire."

Breeden nodded. "Yes, Counselor, I see your point. Objection overruled. You may proceed."

Carlito continued.

Q: *Did Chico tell you what to say on the witness stand?*
A: *He tried to, but I didn't say nothin' that wasn't true.*
Q: *What did Chico want you to say?*

"Objection, Your Honor!" Ted Warren had regained his composure. "The witness has just testified that her testimony was not influenced by Mr. Quinones, therefore it is irrelevant what he wanted her to say."

Warren smiled as Breeden sustained the objection. Carlito, undaunted, plunged doggedly on.

> Q: *Did anybody threaten you harm if you did not testify against the defendant?*
> A: *No.*
> Q: *Well, is your testimony here what caused you and Chico to break your engagement?*
> A: *No.*

Carlito tried one last desperate question.

> Q: *Miss Pagan, you have testified that your engagement was broken because of this case. Can you tell us in what way this case caused that breakup?*
> A: *Because Ricardo got stabbed.*

Carlito was stunned. He couldn't believe what he was hearing.

> Q: *Are you telling us that Chico stabbed Ricardo?*
> A: *No, Abogado, I never said that, and I ain't sayin' it.*
> Q: *Do you know who stabbed Ricardo?*
> A: *I ain't sayin'. I take the Fifth.*

And with that Nereida Pagan stood up, walked off the witness stand, down the courtroom aisle, and out the door before anyone thought to stop her.

Carlito was the first to recover, and hurriedly murmured: "No further questions."

Breeden, realizing the witness had not been excused, dispatched a court officer to get her back into the courtroom and declared a ten-minute recess.

Carlito smiled. Nereida Pagan had just destroyed the effectiveness of any testimony Chico might offer against Ricky. "I wonder," he mused, "was it accidental, or had she planned it that way?"

TWENTY-EIGHT

Ted Warren shook his head somberly as he peered across the desk at his chief, John Trent. "I tell you, John, this case stinks to high heaven. From the git-go I had two strong witnesses. One was the cop—Powers—and we find out he planted the .38 on the kid. The other only reliable eyewitness turns out to be the guy who knifed the kid. Rivera will tear him apart."

Trent leaned back, swiveled his chair halfway, and hooded his eyes. "What about the other eyewitness?"

Warren slapped his knee in disgust. "Unreliable, a drunkard who was loaded to the gills on the night of the murder. Anyhow, John, I don't like it. We're supposed to be public prosecutors, not hangmen. Right now, I have a gut feeling the kid didn't do it. How in tarnation am I supposed to convince a jury that he did!"

"It's no use, Ted, the district attorney won't touch a nonsuit with a ten-foot pole. What with the public's concern for law and order, an election coming up, the D.A. feuding with the judges in the media, and the mayor screaming for the blood of every criminal, there is no way that we can move for dismissal. On top of that, we sold Roscoe Lorimer on pinning Powers to the mat with his testimony, and we're committed to that."

Warren angled out of his chair, brushed his hair out of his eyes, and shrugged. "One thing you won't ever have to worry about me, John, is that I ain't ever gonna be pushin' for your job."

Trent swiveled his chair back to face Warren. "How's that?"

"I knew you when you were a tough, hard-working prosecutor who wouldn't walk through the same door as a politician. I liked you better then."

Trent threw his glasses down on the desk, rose halfway out of his seat, then sat down again with a sigh. "Go to hell, Ted, go straight to fucking hell."

Tiny beads of perspiration popped out on Edgardo Concepcion's forehead and upper lip as Carlito approached him, menacingly brandishing a fistful of photographs.

Q: *Mr. Concepcion, I show this photograph marked "Defendant's Exhibit A-1" for identification and ask you if you can tell me what it shows.*

Concepcion peered at a picture of a dark street with all the street lamps out, illuminated only by a neon sign on the second floor of a building halfway down the street bearing the legend LA MARIMBA DISCO.

A: *Yeah, that's the street the disco is on.*

Q: *And would you say, Mr. Concepcion, that this photograph is a fair and accurate representation of the way the street looked on the night of the murder?*

A: *Yeah, I guess so.*

Carlito retrieved the photograph from Concepcion, walked over to Ted Warren, and dropped it on the desk in front of him as he said: "I offer this photograph in evidence and ask that it be marked 'Defendant's Exhibit 1-A in evidence.'"

Warren sighed as he studied the photograph. He had to give Rivera credit. The police had taken, and Warren had offered into evidence, photographs of the street in daylight. There had been no way to tell from those pictures that the street lights were not working. Rivera had hired a photographer to take pictures at night with extremely fast film, and had come up with a street that looked entirely different. It was dark as pitch in the spot where it was alleged Ricky had stood when he fired the pistol.

Warren thought fleetingly, Why bother to object? But his long training and his natural competitive attitude took over. "Objection, Your Honor; may I have a voir dire on the bona fides of these photographs?"

"Granted," mumbled Judge Breeden. Carlito's photographer was called to the stand, and for the next fifteen minutes Warren cross-examined him on every aspect of the photos: when they were taken, how they were taken, where the photographer stood when they were taken, as well as the make and date of manufacture of the camera and film used. It was all to no avail. Concepcion having identified the photo as being a fair and accurate representation of the scene in front of La Marimba, Judge Breeden allowed it into evidence.

Warren knew he was fighting a losing battle, hoping that the time he spent on the objection would give Concepcion an opportunity to think about the significance of the photo, and perhaps reconsider. But Concepcion adamantly continued to verify its authenticity and others taken the same night. Carlito then proceeded to destroy Concepcion's credibility by having Concepcion mark in the photos Ricky's position on the street, the positions of others on the street surrounding Ricky, and Concepcion's own position almost 100 feet away. When Carlito had finished, no one could possibly believe Concepcion's story, even if Concepcion had been sober on the night of the killing.

Warren sighed as Concepcion left the witness stand, stood up and announced, "Recall Patrolman Robert Powers."

Carlito was apprehensive as Powers walked to the stand and was informed by the court clerk that he was still under oath. Was Warren now going to sacrifice Powers to save his case—or did Warren have something new to offer? He didn't have to wait long to find out. Warren casually took Powers back to the discovery of the gun in the jacket and went on from there.

Q: Did you ever see that gun prior to the night of the murder?

A: I seen a lot of .38 Smith and Wessons in my time.

138

Q: *But what about this particular .38?*

A: *I don't know.*

Q: *I show you this document and ask you if you recognize what it is.*

A: *Sure, it's a property clerk voucher for a .38 Smith and Wesson.*

Q: *I ask that this document be marked "People's Exhibit H" for identification. Now, Officer, please read this document and tell me whether it refreshes your recollection as to whether you ever saw this particular gun prior to the night of the murder.*

Powers gave his full and careful attention to the voucher. When he looked up, his face was flushed.

A: *Yeah, it looks as if I vouchered it into the property clerk's office a couple of years ago after nabbing a guy pulling an armed robbery. Ain't that something?*

Q: *Now I show you these additional vouchers marked "People's Exhibit H-1 and H-2" for identification and ask you if your recollection is refreshed as to your connection with this particular gun.*

Powers wrinkled his forehead in apparent concentration.

A: *Well, I turned it into the property clerk's office, then picked it up to testify at the grand jury, then turned it back in.*

Q: *And are those the only times you had the gun in your possession?*

139

A: Yeah, sure, that's right. The only times.

Warren walked back to the counsel table and Powers leaned forward. When Warren spun around and announced, "No further questions," Powers started to leave his seat. Carlito waited until he had taken three steps, stood up, and held up his hand. "Just a moment, Officer," he said quietly, "I have just a few questions."

Powers stopped short as if he had walked into a brick wall, and backed into the witness chair as Carlito approached. Carlito waited a full minute after Powers sank back in his chair. His mind was racing furiously: Warren must have more than this on Powers. Right now it looked as if Warren was merely controverting Fertig's testimony. But that can't be! The jury, if it has to choose between Fertig and Powers, will believe Fertig. Well, here it goes: all or nothing.

Q: Isn't it a fact that the .38 Smith and Wesson you claim to have found in the defendant's jacket was in your possession when you arrived at the scene of the murder?

A: No—that's not true.

Q: Didn't you find Pablo Alvarado dead in the alley and shoot him with that .38?

A: No—no. Why would I do that?

Q: Didn't you then retrieve the shell and plant the gun on this defendant?

A: That's a damned lie!

140

Carlito stepped back and picked up the property clerk's vouchers, which Warren had placed on the counsel table. He waved them at Powers.

Q: *And you insist that you did not have possession of this gun except when it was vouchered to you?*
A: *That's right, and you can see that I returned it and had it vouchered in.*
Q: *And it was an Officer Provisio who vouchered it back in. Is that right?*
A: *Yeah.*
Q: *Do you know Officer Provisio? Is he a friend of yours?*
A: *No, he ain't no friend, but I know him.*

Carlito turned quickly to Warren and said, "I ask the district attorney to produce Officer Joseph Provisio from the property clerk's office."

Warren stood up slowly, untangling his arms and legs. "I can't, Counselor. There is no Joseph Provisio working for the property clerk's office, either as a uniformed officer or a civilian." Warren angled back to his seat and added: "And there never was."

Carlito finally realized the strategy. Ted Warren had permitted him to gun down Powers. The record looked better that way. Powers was staring at Warren with a fearful and baffled expression. Carlito turned his back on Powers and spat contemptuously: "I'm finished with this witness."

"But I'm not!" shot back Warren. "If Your Honor pleases, may I inquire of the witness as to the new

141

matter brought out on cross-examination?"

Judge Breeden, shocked and puzzled, threw up his arms. "Go ahead, Mr. Warren."

Warren plunged his hand into his file and brought out a fistful of papers. He stood at his place and asked quietly:

Q: *Officer Powers, you have testified that you never had the gun after you vouchered it back to the property clerk. Is that right?*

A: *Yeah, yeah, that's right.*

Q: *Then you could not have had the gun on March 30, 1980?*

A: *No, I never had the gun.*

Warren shoved an 8 × 10 glossy at him and said:

Q: *So that the gun you are holding in this photograph is not the .38 Smith and Wesson recovered on the night of the murder?*

Powers looked at the photograph showing him pointing the gun at a frightened bank teller, dropped it to the floor, and slumped down with his head over his knees. Carlito thought the man was passing out. But an instant later Powers had not only straightened up, but jumped out of the witness chair, his complexion flushed to an angry red.

"You guys are trying to railroad me! You and that spic lawyer! Well, I ain't waiting around for the hanging." As he moved toward the spectator section,

Judge Breeden banged his gavel and shouted, "Officer Powers!"

Powers turned toward the judge, and Eloida, who had been in her usual seat in the front row, stood up behind him and swung an umbrella at the back of his head. The umbrella glanced off his head, and he swung menacingly toward her. Carlito was the first to reach him. He caught him from behind. His arms circled Powers's rib cage, and a powerful downward thrust cracked Powers's ribs. Carlito slipped his arms down a few inches; placed his fist against Powers's diaphragm, and heaved upward. The air went out of Powers in a terrifying *whoosh,* and he collapsed like a rag doll over Carlito's straining forearms. When Carlito dropped him to the floor, he was already unconscious.

TWENTY-NINE

Judge Breeden regarded Carlito from deep within his richly upholstered recliner chair in chambers and favored him with one of his dazzling public appearance smiles.

"Well, Counselor, that was one hell of a performance yesterday. The question is, what do we do for an encore?"

Carlito, recognizing a rhetorical question when he heard one, merely returned the dazzler with a small grin of his own and remained silent. Ted Warren, seated next to Carlito across the large modern oak desk from Breeden, opened his file and waited also.

"Despite the fact that I was forced to declare a mistrial yesterday, I have kept the case in this part, in the hope that we can make some disposition here. I want to avoid sending it back for reassignment for a new trial." Breeden continued without missing a beat. "Mr. District Attorney, what is your pleasure?"

Warren looked up from his open file. "There's no pleasure in this case for me, Your Honor. The stench has penetrated this courthouse like the stinkbag of a trapped skunk. Nevertheless, I am obliged to remind this court that there is still some proof that the defendant shot Pablo Alvarado with a .22 caliber gun, even if the gun has not been recovered. The People will prosecute a new trial." Warren turned to Carlito with a pained look.

Carlito nodded agreement. "Yes, I can see that the People have every obligation to continue this prosecution. Powers's bullet certainly did not kill Alvarado, and, given all the circumstances, a new trial might result in a conviction. But let me ask you, Mr. Warren, what would be the People's position if I could produce incontrovertible proof that my client did not kill Alvarado?"

Warren cocked an eyebrow. "Incontrovertible? Incontrovertible to whom—you—me—Judge Breeden?"

"All of us," snapped Carlito, "and I'm prepared to produce that proof right now."

Warren pulled at his ear furiously. "We-ell, I'd say we'd be ready to accept a plea of attempted assault as a felony with a sentence of one to four."

"No dice, Mr. D.A.," Carlito snarled. "I want a dismissal or retry your case." Carlito turned to Judge Breeden. "In the meantime, Your Honor, I want my client released from jail on his own recognizance or minimum bail. This will serve to lessen damages after acquittal when we sue the District Attorney for malicious prosecution."

"Just a minute, gentlemen, this party's getting rough." Judge Breeden pointed a finger at Carlito. "On what basis could you possibly sue for malicious prosecution? Let's stop these ridiculous threats."

"Not ridiculous at all, Your Honor," Carlito countered. "Consider this: the People indicted the defendant on a charge of having murdered a man with either a .38 Smith and Wesson or a .22 caliber gun. They also charged him with possession of a .38 Smith and Wesson as a felony. I happen to know that the Internal Investigations Unit of the Police Department knew as long as four months before trial that the .38 Smith and Wesson did not cause the death of Alvarado and could not possibly have been in the possession of the defendant on the night of the murder. Since I have incontrovertible proof that the defendant did not shoot Alvarado, the People must answer the question: Why didn't they drop the original charges? Who covered up and why? I think we might have a pretty good case."

Breeden glared at Warren. "Is this true, Mr. Warren? Did the People know about Powers and the .38 as long as four months before the trial?"

Warren drummed his fingers slowly on his open file.

145

"In a sense it is. Although I will tell you that I personally didn't know anything until after the trial had started." Warren sighed.

Breeden turned back to Carlito. "Okay, Counselor, you seem to have some winning cards. Make a proposal that both the D.A. and I can live with. You know as well as anyone we can't give you a dismissal."

Carlito nodded with satisfaction. "I believe you gentlemen are as truly interested in seeing that justice is served as I am, so what I will do is present my evidence first, and after you've had a chance to evaluate it I'll make my offer."

Judge Breeden and Warren exchanged glances. Warren turned to Carlito. "No promises, Mr. Rivera. You know I have superiors to answer to. But give me something I can present to my boss and I'll do my darndest."

Breeden nodded. "Go ahead, Counselor."

Carlito sat studying his file for a few moments. He knew the next few minutes would seal Ricky's fate, and the risk he was taking was not without peril. *"Vamanos, compadre!"* he muttered under his breath, then stood up abruptly and left Breeden and Warren with puzzled looks as he strode purposely to the door.

THIRTY

Father Placido McGuire, in full priestly garb, entered Judge Breeden's chambers behind Carlito. Slung under his left arm was a large box wrapped in brown paper. Carlito ushered him to the empty chair that he had just vacated. "Your Honor, Mr. Warren, this is Father Placido McGuire, priest of Our Lady of Hope Roman Catholic Church in the Santurce parish of Puerto Rico."

Judge Breeden half rose from his seat as if to extend a greeting, thought better of it, and asked, "Do we need a Spanish interpreter?"

"Not at all, Your Honor," replied Father McGuire. "As you can hear, my English is perfectly understandable."

Breeden flushed and sank into his chair. "I, er, ah, see. Well, shall we proceed?"

Carlito positioned himself standing halfway between Breeden and Warren against the far wall of Breeden's chambers. "Do you want him sworn, Your Honor?"

"No, no, that won't be necessary." Breeden was obviously ill at ease. "After all, this is not an official hearing, and no record is being made. Why don't you just get started."

Carlito smiled in quiet satisfaction. He had certainly gotten Breeden's attention, and surveying Warren as he worked at his earlobe, he knew Warren was ready to listen also. "Father McGuire, please tell these gentlemen your story."

Father McGuire adjusted the brown parcel in his lap and leaned back in his chair. "As Mr. Rivera told you, I am, and have been, the priest at Our Lady of Hope Church in Santurce for the past ten years. I take confession on Friday nights between six and eight o'clock. Six months ago on just such a Friday I had completed hearing confessions at about eight and was about to leave the confessional when a stranger slipped in. It was a voice I had never heard before.

"'Father,' it said, 'I have sinned.'

"'Tell me, my son, how have you sinned?'

"'Father, I have run away from my home in New York.'

"'Yes?'

"'Father, I have lied.'

"'Yes, my son, and how else have you sinned?'

"'Father, I killed a man,' the voice sobbed and then broke into uncontrollable crying. I waited for the crying to stop, knowing that it is best to let contrition run its course. However, in the midst of a great sob, the crying ceased and there was a thud as of someone falling. I opened the curtain to the confessional and saw a young boy lying on the floor. He was now gagging and frothing at the mouth, and I recognized it at once as an epileptic seizure. I relieved the gagging immediately by prying his mouth open, shoving the edge of my missal between his teeth and pulling his tongue out. When the spasms had passed I noticed that he had cut the back of his scalp in falling, and I assisted him to my office. I applied some gauze to his cut and studied him while he recovered from the attack. 'I think, my son, that you are a very sick boy. Are you taking medication for your epilepsy?' "'That's just it, Father. When I left New York I didn't take no pills with me. That's why I came to confess. These attacks are getting worse. I'm going to die one of these times.' The boy was thin and pale. He had some bruises on his face and his eye from what I assumed to be a fall during a recent seizure. 'You must go to a hospital immediately.' 'No, Father, I can't. They'll be looking for me in the hospitals, and I don't wanna go back. I'm afraid and ashamed. Yeah—really ashamed.' 'If you've killed a man, you must go back. Sooner or later, they will find you and take you back.' 'The thing is, Father, they ain't looking for me for killing a man. Nobody knows that yet—except you.' 'Listen, my son, you are not in the confessional anymore. Whatever you told me in there is sealed in my heart forever. What you tell me now may not be.' 'But, Father,' he interrupted, 'I need to tell you so you can tell me what to do. I don't care if you don't keep it a secret. I want to help Ricky, and I'm afraid I'm going to die.'"

During this recital Father McGuire had closed his eyes. Now he opened them and looked around the room. "The conversation between us for the next ten minutes dealt with the relationship of man to God and good and evil. I have a feeling that such a dialogue would bore you. It is sufficient for you to know that the boy decided to tell me the whole story without restricting me to secrecy." Father McGuire leaned back once again, and closed his eyes. Ted Warren swore softly. "Son of a gun, a witness with total recall. He's giving it to us verbatim!"

Father McGuire continued to relate the boy's story.

"'My name is Angel—Angel Colon, and I come from the Bronx. My best friend is Ricky Betancourt. He's a real cool cat. He's little, but he don't take nothing from no one. He knows how to do things, ya know. He's the best dancer in the crowd—he's got the prettiest girl, still he's cool—ya know what I mean? He don't take advantage. He don't treat me like shit 'cause I'm sick, ya dig? The others, they do all the time.

"'Anyway, we went to this Dominican disco, and Ricky, he takes the head man's girl, and he wins this here dance contest. Cool, ya see? I'm so excited, I say some stupid things—and those Dominicans, they start a fight. Ricky, he's real sore at me for opening my trap, but he's still cool. He tells me you stay with me, Angel, 'cause I got this rod and they ain't gonna mess with us. I'm scared, Father. I'm so scared I figure I'm gonna have an attack right there. But Ricky he says "Don't worry, Angel, you stick with me." So we go downstairs. As soon as we get out the door there's about a dozen Dominicans waiting, and they surround us. Ricky says to me, "Get behind me, Angel," and I do. Ricky pulls the gun and yells, "Get away, you motherfuckers. This gun's got a bullet for any mother gets too close." These guys start backing away—real slow, ya know. And then the Dominican whose girl Ricky danced with comes out the door of the disco be-

150

hind us. Ricky don't see him, but I do. He's got a shiv in his hand, and he don't care if Ricky's got a gun. He's comin' at us fast. I grab Ricky's gun and start shooting straight up in the air. I don't know what made me do it—maybe 'cause I know deep down Ricky ain't gonna use that gun and here comes that guy with the knife. Anyhow, shootin' or not, this guy runs right past me and shoves the knife into Ricky. I started to run, and the last thing I saw was a bunch of them Dominicans pounding on Ricky in front of the disco. There's an alley nearby, and I run in there. The truth, Father, I can't run no more. I'm shakin' all over and can't stand up. Well, I'm sittin' there, still shakin', when this dude Alvarado comes slidin' into the alley. He looks at me and says, "Oh, here you are, shithead faggot." Now, Father, you got to know that Alvarado wasn't no stranger to me. He's an enforcer for the rackets, and he's mean as shit. I don't say nothin' 'cause I know if I do I'm in trouble. He says, "Okay, give me that rod—a faggot like you, it's a waste." "It ain't mine, it's Ricky's," I tell him. "Don't make no never mind," he says. "On account of you, Ricky's dead, knifed in the belly. Now give me that gun, mother." And he starts walkin' at me. Well, Father, I don't know what happened to me. I ain't never shot no one before, but when he tole me my best friend was dead on account of me, I knew he was right, and it made me mad at myself, and Ricky, and Alvarado— the whole fuckin' world. I pick up the gun and point it right at his belly. "Screw you, you bastard. If Ricky's dead, this here's mine, and you ain't gettin' it." He smiles but kinda with only half his face, the other half is sayin' You're dead, mother, and he says "Give it to me, Angel, or I mash you like a potato." He keeps comin' at me. I don't know, Father, whether I really pulled the trigger 'cause I meant to or 'cause I was shakin' so, but that gun pointed at his belly goes off, and he's not more than six feet from me.'"

Father McGuire opened his eyes and straightened in his chair. He opened the brown parcel in his lap and gave it to Judge Breeden. It contained the .22 Gerstenhaber pistol still in the elaborate box that Maria had transported from Puerto Rico.

Carlito stepped forward. "Do you have any questions, Your Honor?"

"No, I don't think so."

"And you, Mr. Warren?"

"No, Mr. Rivera."

"In that case," said Carlito, "may I ask you to step outside, Father, and thank you."

As soon as the priest had left the room, Carlito continued. "Gentlemen, I think that testimony is admissible under the exceptions to the hearsay rules, which allow such statements made under extremis or in the imminent contemplation of death. Of course, Colon's death has removed any strictures of the confidentiality of the confessional that might have bothered Father McGuire. Do you agree?"

Breeden looked up from his chair. "You do have a flair for the dramatic, Mr. Rivera. That encore performance was a gem."

Carlito laughed. "Well, I don't think it beat yesterday's antic, but it does come close. At any rate, are you now prepared to hear my suggestion as to how to wind this case up?"

Breeden cocked his head and shot a glance at Warren. "Go ahead, Counselor."

Carlito took a deep breath. "I want a dismissal of the murder charge and a reduction of the felonious possession of a gun charge to a misdemeanor. Betancourt will plead guilty to the misdemeanor, and the sentence on that plea will be time already served. Tomorrow, Ricky Betancourt walks out of Rikers Island a free man." The only sound punctuating the heavy silence of the room was the tick of Judge Breeden's antique wall clock.

Finally, Warren looked up from his file. "What about your suit for malicious prosecution?"

Carlito was prepared, knowing that without the abandonment of the civil suit, Warren could never get the deal approved. "Betancourt signs any and all waivers required to release the district attorney, the City of New York, and the Police Department from any claim for civil damages."

Judge Breeden stood up and offered Carlito his hand. "Congratulations, Mr. Rivera, your encore does beat yesterday's performance." He reached down to his desk, picked up the phone, and said: "Send in a court reporter, we've got a disposition to put on the record."

THIRTY-ONE

Woody Fertig fidgeted uncomfortably in his tuxedo. If Mama could see me now in a Catholic church she'd turn over in her grave.

From his position at the rear of the church just outside the door to the chapel he could see Father McGuire at the pulpit. Carlito had told him the priest had been hard to persuade. He had wanted them to come down to Our Lady of Hope in Santurce for the ceremony, but Carlito had explained that the economics of the situation prevented that. Of course, Carlito had to do some hard selling to convince the priest here to permit Father McGuire to officiate. Well, it had all worked out. There was Doña Esperanza, up from P.R. also. He couldn't understand a word she said, but her effusive embrace and obvious good humor made him feel warm all over. Seated next to her was Angel Colon's mother, a kind of sad day for her in a way, but she seemed to be holding up. The other faces in the crowded church were unfamiliar to him, and Woody marveled at the number of people who were there, not related but just friends. The sound of footsteps behind him distracted his attention from the chapel. Carlito approached, dressed elegantly in a morning coat and striped pants.

"Are you nervous, Woody?" Carlito asked as he put one arm over Woody's shoulder.

"I sure am, Mr. Rivera—how about you?"

"I'd rather be summing up to the jury," he

chuckled. "By the way, everyone calls me Carlito, so you better practice."

Woody smiled. "Even if I accept your offer?"

"Particularly so. We'll be two professionals working together. As my investigator you'll have to share the blame for any case I lose, but I'll get the glory for a win. In an unfair situation like that at least you should be able to curse me on a first-name basis."

Woody's big hand enveloped Carlito's. "I'm taking it, you know. I'll be damned glad to be working again. I never realized how much I enjoyed being a cop until I stopped being one. Anyhow, you want an investigator—you've got one."

"You know it will have to be on a case by case basis at the beginning. I can't afford to take you on full time right now." Carlito adjusted his tie and glanced around nervously.

"That's fine with me," said Woody. "With my pension, I don't really need full time. I have no family, you know."

Carlito stopped pacing and faced him. "Sure you do, Woody. We're your family now."

At that moment the front door of the church opened and Ricky hurried in, dressed in a morning coat that fit not quite as well as Carlito's. "Am I late? Jeez, Eloida will kill me!"

Carlito smiled and reassured him: "You're not late, but mighty close. What kept you?"

"Couldn't figure out how to clip the bow-tie on."

Ricky winked at Carlito. "Finally glued it. I hope it lasts till after the ceremony."

"How's the job going?" Fertig asked.

"Not bad. I never thought I'd like working for the enemy, but that part-time job at the D.A.'s office sure helps pay the bills. I guess that guy Warren ain't so bad after all."

"It's guilt, Ricky, pure guilt." Carlito chuckled. "Warren is expiating his sins by getting you that clerical job."

"And you, Mr. Rivera—what's your excuse for all this? Paying for the wedding, and these monkey suits, and the party?"

Carlito smiled. "I'm not really paying for it. A lot of this money came from your future mother-in-law when she gave it to me to defend you. I just put it away and added to it whatever was necessary. After all, it's my wedding too."

At that moment, Father McGuire signaled and the first chords of the church's organ reverberated through the chapel. Woody watched as the two bridegrooms marched slowly down the aisle. "Thank God I'm last," he muttered as he stepped aside for the ushers and bridesmaids. Behind him stood the two brides, each beautiful in her own special way. Woody's eyes smarted with tears of pride as he extended an arm to each.

Maria gave Woody an exaggerated once-over and said, "Not bad, Woody, not bad at all."

Eloida took his arm and gave it a special little squeeze as she whispered, "Thank you, Poppy."

Woody Fertig, Jewish cop, was escorting both brides to the altar. Midway down the aisle he stopped and looked up. It's okay, Mama. I've got a family now.